Offic

Google Professional
Cloud Architect

Study Guide

Official
Google Professional Cloud Architect
Study Guide

Dan Sullivan

SYBEX®
A Wiley Brand

to Katherine

About the Author

 **Dan Sullivan** is a principal engineer and software architect at New Relic. He specializes in streaming analytics, machine learning, and cloud computing. Dan is the author of the *Official Google Cloud Certified Associate Cloud Engineer Study Guide* (Sybex, 2019), *NoSQL for Mere Mortals* (Addison-Wesley Professional, 2015), and several LinkedIn Learning courses on databases, data science, and machine learning. Dan has certifications from Google and AWS along with a PhD in genetics and computational biology from Virginia Tech.

About the Technical Editor

Valerie Parham-Thompson has experience with a variety of open source data storage technologies, including MySQL, MongoDB, and Cassandra, as well as a foundation in web development in software-as-a-service environments. Her work in both development and operations in startups and traditional enterprises has led to solid expertise in web-scale data storage and data delivery.

Valerie has spoken at technical conferences on topics such as database security, performance tuning, and container management. She also often speaks at local meetups and volunteer events.

Valerie holds a bachelor's degree from the Kenan Flagler Business School at UNC-Chapel Hill, has certifications in MySQL and MongoDB, and is a Google Certified Professional Cloud Architect. She currently works in the Open Source Database Cluster at Pythian, headquartered in Ottawa, Ontario.

Follow Valerie's contributions to technical blogs on Twitter at @dataindataout.

Acknowledgments

I have been fortunate to work again with professionals from Waterside Productions, Wiley, and Google to create this study guide.

Carole Jelen, vice president of Waterside Productions, and Jim Minatel, associate publisher at John Wiley & Sons, led the effort to continue to create Google Cloud certification guides. It was a pleasure to work with Gary Schwartz, project editor, who managed the process that got us from an outline to a finished manuscript. Thanks to Katie Wisor, production manager, for making the last stages of book development go as smoothly as they did.

I am especially grateful for Valerie Parham-Thompson's expertise in Google Cloud. In addition to catching my subtle and not-so-subtle errors, I learned some nuances of GCP that I was not aware of.

I appreciate the close reading by the technical reviewer, Stacy Veronneau, who agreed to continue working with our team after having been a reviewer of the *Official Google Cloud Certified Associate Cloud Engineer Study Guide.*

Thank you to Google Cloud subject-matter experts Jasen Baker, Marco Ferarri, Rich Rose, Grace Mollison, Samar Bhat, Josh Koh, Kuntal Mitra, Michael Arciola, Lisa Guinn, Eoin Carrol, Tony DiLerto, Volker Eyrich, and Teresa Hardy, who reviewed and contributed to the material in this book.

My sons James and Nicholas, both technology writers themselves, were my first readers and helped me get the manuscript across the finish line. Katherine, my wife and partner in so many ventures, supported this work while fostering her increasingly impactful projects in literary publishing.

—Dan Sullivan

Contents at a Glance

Contents at a Glance

Contents

Introduction

The Google Cloud Platform is a diverse and growing set of services. To pass the Google Cloud Professional Architect exam, you will need to understand how to reason about both business requirements and technical requirements. This is not a test of knowledge about how to do specific tasks in GCP, such as attaching a persistent disk to a VM instance. That type of question is more likely to be on the Google Cloud Certified Associate Cloud Engineer exam. The Google Cloud Certified Professional Architect exam tests your ability to perform high-level design and architecture tasks related to the following:

- Designing applications
- Planning migrations
- Ensuring feasibility of proposed designs
- Optimizing infrastructure
- Building and deploying code
- Managing data lifecycles

You will be tested on your ability to design solutions using a mix of compute, storage, networking, and specialized services. The design must satisfy both business and technical requirements. If you find a question that seems to have two correct technical answers, look closely at the business requirements. There is likely a business consideration that will make one of the options a better choice than the other. For example, you might have a question about implementing a stream processing system, and the options include a solution based on Apache Flink running in Compute Engine and a solution using Cloud Dataflow. If the business requirements indicate a preference for managed services, then the Cloud Dataflow option is a better choice.

You will be tested on how to plan the execution of work required to implement a cloud solution. Migrations to the cloud are often done in stages. Consider the advantages of starting with low-risk migration tasks, such as setting up a test environment in the cloud before moving production workloads to GCP.

The business and technical requirements may leave you open to proposing two or more different solutions. In these cases, consider the feasibility of the implementation. Will it be scalable and reliable? Even if GCP services have high SLOs, your system may depend on a third-party service that may go down. If that happens, what is the impact on your workflow? Should you plan to buffer work in a Cloud Pub/Sub queue rather than sending it directly to the third-party service? Also consider costs and optimizations, but only after you have a technically viable solution that meets business requirements. As computer science pioneer Donald Knuth realized, "The real problem is that programmers have spent far too much time worrying about efficiency in the wrong places and at the wrong times; premature optimization is the root of all evil (or at least most of it) in programming."[1] The same can be said for architecture as well—meet business and technical requirements before trying to optimize.

[1] *The Art of Computer Programming, Third Edition.* Addison Wesley Longman Publishing Co., Inc. Redwood City, CA, USA.

The exam guide states that architects should be familiar with the software development lifecycle and agile practices. These will be important to know when answering questions about developing and releasing code, especially how to release code into production environments without shutting down the service. It is important to understand topics such as Blue/Green deployments, canary deployments, and continuous integration/continuous deployments.

In this context, managing is largely about security and monitoring. Architects will need to understand authentication and authorization in GCP. The IAM service is used across GCP, and it should be well understood before attempting the exam. Stackdriver is the key service for monitoring, logging, tracing, and debugging.

How Is the Google Cloud Professional Architect Exam Different from the Google Cloud Associate Engineer exam?

There is some overlap between the Google Cloud Professional Architect and Google Cloud Associate Cloud Engineer exams. Both exams test for an understanding of technical requirements and the ability to build, deploy, and manage cloud resources. In addition, the Google Cloud Professional Architect exam tests the ability to work with business requirements to design, plan, and optimize cloud solutions.

The questions on the architect exam are based on the kinds of work cloud architects do on a day-to-day basis. This includes deciding which of several storage options is best, designing a network to meet industry regulations, or understanding the implications of horizontally scaling a database.

The questions on the Cloud Engineer exam are based on the tasks that cloud engineers perform, such as creating instance groups, assigning roles to identities, or monitoring a set of VMs. The engineering exam is more likely to have detailed questions about gcloud, gsutil, and bq commands. Architects need to be familiar with these commands and their function, but a detailed knowledge of command options and syntax is not necessary.

This book is designed to help you pass the Google Cloud Professional Architect certification exam. If you'd like additional preparation, review the *Official Google Cloud Certified Associate Cloud Engineer Study Guide* (Sybex, 2019).

What Does This Book Cover?

This book covers the topics outlined in the Google Professional Cloud Architect exam guide available here:

https://cloud.google.com/certification/guides/professional-cloud-architect/

Chapter 1: Introduction to the Google Professional Cloud Architect Exam   This chapter outlines the exam objectives, scope of the exam, and three case studies used in the exam. One of the most challenging parts of the exam for many architects is mapping business requirements to technical requirements. This chapter discusses strategies for culling technical requirements and constraints from statements about nontechnical business requirements. The chapter also discusses the need to understand functional requirements around computing, storage, and networking as well as nonfunctional characteristics of services, such as availability and scalability.

Chapter 2: Designing for Business Requirements   This chapter reviews several key areas where business requirements are important to understand, including business use cases and product strategies, application design and cost considerations, systems integration and data management, compliance and regulations, security, and success measures.

Chapter 3: Designing for Technical Requirements   This chapter discusses ways to ensure high availability in compute, storage, and applications. It also reviews ways to ensure scalability in compute, storage, and network resources. The chapter also introduces reliability engineering.

Chapter 4: Designing Compute Systems   This chapter discusses Compute Engine, App Engine, Kubernetes Engine, and Cloud Functions. Topics in this chapter include use cases, configuration, management, and design. Other topics include managing state in distributed systems, data flows and pipelines, and data integrity. Monitoring and alerting are also discussed.

Chapter 5: Designing Storage Systems   This chapter focuses on storage and database systems. Storage systems include object storage, network-attached storage, and caching. Several databases are reviewed, including Cloud SQL, Cloud Spanner, BigQuery, Cloud Datastore, Cloud Firestore, and Bigtable. It is important to know how to choose among storage and database options when making architectural choices. Other topics include provisioning, data retention and lifecycle management, and network latency.

Chapter 6: Designing Networks   This chapter reviews VPCs, including subnets and IP addressing, hybrid cloud networking, VPNs, peering, and direct connections. This chapter also includes a discussion of regional and global load balancing. Hybrid cloud computing and networking topics are important concepts for the exam.

Chapter 7: Designing for Security and Legal Compliance   This chapter discusses IAM, data security including encryption at rest and encryption in transit, key management, security evaluation, penetration testing, auditing, and security design principles. Major regulations and ITIL are reviewed.

Chapter 8: Designing for Reliability   This chapter begins with a discussion of Stackdriver for monitoring, logging, and alerting. Next, the chapter reviews continuous deployment and continuous integration. Systems reliability engineering is discussed, including over-loads, cascading failures, and testing for reliability. Incident management and post-mortem analysis are also described.

Chapter 9: Analyzing and Defining Technical Processes   This chapter focuses on software development lifecycle planning. This includes troubleshooting, testing and validation, business continuity, and disaster recovery.

Chapter 10: Analyzing and Defining Business Processes   This chapter includes several business-oriented skills including stakeholder management, change management, team skill management, customer success management, and cost management.

Chapter 11: Development and Operations   This chapter reviews application development methodologies, API best practices, and testing frameworks, including load, unit, and integration testing. The chapter also discusses data and systems migration tooling. The chapter concludes with a brief review of using Cloud SDK.

Chapter 12: Migration Planning   This chapter describes how to plan for a cloud migration. Steps include integrating with existing systems, migrating systems and data, license mapping, network management and planning, as well as testing and developing proof-of-concept systems.

Interactive Online Learning Environment and Test Bank

Studying the material in the *Official Google Certified Professional Cloud Architect Study Guide* is an important part of preparing for the Professional Cloud Architect certification exam, but we also provide additional tools to help you prepare. The online Test Bank will help you understand the types of questions that will appear on the certification exam.

The sample tests in the Test Bank include all of the questions in each chapter as well as the questions from the assessment test. In addition, there are two practice exams with 50 questions each. You can use these tests to evaluate your understanding and identify areas that may require additional study.

The flashcard in the Test Bank will push the limits of what you should know for the certification exam. There are more than 100 questions that are provided in digital format. Each flashcard has one question and one correct answer.

The online glossary is a searchable list of key terms introduced in this exam guide that you should know for the Professional Cloud Architect certification exam.

To start using these to study for the Google Certified Professional Cloud Architect exam, go to www.wiley.com/go/sybextestprep, and register your book to receive your unique PIN; then once you have the PIN, return to www.wiley.com/go/sybextestprep, find your book, and click Register or Login to register a new account or add this book to an existing account.

Additional Resources

People learn in different ways. For some, a book is an ideal way to study, while auditory learners may find video and audio resources a more efficient way to study. A combination of resources may be the best option for many of us. In addition to this study guide, here are some other resources that can help you prepare for the Google Cloud Professional Architect exam.

The Professional Cloud Architect Certification Exam Guide:
https://cloud.google.com/certification/guides/
professional-cloud-architect/

Exam FAQs:
https://cloud.google.com/certification/faqs/#0

Google's Assessment Exam:
https://cloud.google.com/certification/practice-exam/cloud-architect

Google Cloud Platform documentation:
https://cloud.google.com/docs/

Cousera's on demand courses in the "Architecting with Google Cloud Platform Specialization":
https://www.coursera.org/specializations/gcp-architecture

QwikLabs Hands-on Labs:
https://google.qwiklabs.com/quests/47

Google's instructor-led courses:
https://cloud.google.com/training/courses/core-fundamentals

A Cloud Guru's Google Certified Professional Cloud Architect video course:
https://acloud.guru/learn/gcp-certified-professional-cloud-architect

The best way to prepare for the exam is to perform the tasks of an architect and work with the Google Cloud Platform.

Exam objectives are subject to change at any time without prior notice and at Google's sole discretion. Please visit the Google Professional Cloud Architect website (https://cloud.google.com/certification/cloud-architect) for the most current listing of exam objectives.

Objective Map

Objective	Chapter
Section 1: Designing and planning a cloud solutions architecture	
1.1 Designing a solutions infrastructure that meets business requirements	2
1.2 Designing a solutions infrastructure that meets technical requirements	3
1.3 Designing network, storage, and compute resources	4
1.4 Creating a migration plan (i.e., documents and architectural diagrams)	12
1.5 Envisioning future solutions improvements	2
Section 2: Managing and provisioning solutions Infrastructure	
2.1 Configuring network topologies	6
2.2 Configuring individual storage systems	5
2.3 Configuring compute systems	4
Section 3: Designing for security and compliance	
3.1 Designing for security	7
3.2 Designing for legal compliance	7
Section 4: Analyzing and optimizing technical and business processes	
4.1 Analyzing and defining technical processes	9
4.2 Analyzing and defining business processes	10
4.3 Developing procedures to test resilience of solutions in production (e.g., DiRT and Simian Army)	8
Section 5: Managing implementation	
5.1 Advising development/operation team(s) to ensure successful deployment of the solutions	11
5.2 Interacting with Google Cloud using GCP SDK (gcloud, gsutil, and bq)	11

Assessment Test

1. Building for Builders LLC manufactures equipment used in residential and commercial building. Each of its 500,000 pieces of equipment in use around the globe has IoT devices collecting data about the state of equipment. The IoT data is streamed from each device every 10 seconds. On average, 10 KB of data is sent in each message. The data will be used for predictive maintenance and product development. The company would like to use a managed database in Google Cloud. What would you recommend?

   A. Apache Cassandra

   B. Cloud Bigtable

   C. BigQuery

   D. CloudSQL

2. You have developed a web application that is becoming widely used. The frontend runs in Google App Engine and scales automatically. The backend runs on Compute Engine in a managed instance group. You have set the maximum number of instances in the backend managed instance group to five. You do not want to increase the maximum size of the managed instance group or change the VM instance type, but there are times the frontend sends more data than the backend can keep up with and data is lost. What can you do to prevent the loss of data?

   A. Use an unmanaged instance group

   B. Store ingested data in Cloud Storage

   C. Have the frontend write data to a Cloud Pub/Sub topic, and have the backend read from that topic

   D. Store ingested data in BigQuery

3. You are setting up a cloud project and want to assign members of your team different permissions. What GCP service would you use to do that?

   A. Cloud Identity

   B. Identity and Access Management (IAM)

   C. Cloud Authorizations

   D. LDAP

4. You would like to run a custom container in a managed Google Cloud Service. What are your two options?

   A. App Engine Standard and Kubernetes Engine

   B. App Engine Flexible and Kubernetes Engine

   C. Compute Engine and Kubernetes Engine

   D. Cloud Functions and App Engine Flexible

5. PhotosForYouToday prints photographs and ships them to customers. The frontend application uploads photos to Cloud Storage. Currently, the backend runs a cron job that checks Cloud Storage buckets every 10 minutes for new photos. The product manager would like to process the photos as soon as they are uploaded. What would you use to cause processing to start when a photo file is saved to Cloud Storage?

   A. A Cloud Function

   B. An App Engine Flexible application

   C. A Kubernetes pod

   D. A cron job that checks the bucket more frequently

6. The chief financial officer of your company believes that you are spending too much money to run an on-premises data warehouse and wants to migrate to a managed cloud solution. What GCP service would you recommend for implementing a new data warehouse in GCP?

   A. Compute Engine

   B. BigQuery

   C. Cloud Dataproc

   D. Cloud Bigtable

7. A government regulation requires you to keep certain financial data for seven years. You are not likely to ever retrieve the data, and you are only keeping it to be in compliance. There are approximately 500 GB of financial data for each year that you are required to save. What is the most cost-effective way to store this data?

   A. Cloud Storage multiregional storage

   B. Cloud Storage Nearline storage

   C. Cloud Storage Coldline storage

   D. Cloud Storage persistent disk storage

8. Global Games Enterprises Inc. is expanding from North America to Europe. Some of the games offered by the company collect personal information. With what additional regulation will the company need to comply when it expands into the European market?

   A. HIPAA

   B. PCI-DS

   C. GDPR

   D. SOX

9. Your team is developing a Tier 1 application for your company. The application will depend on a PostgreSQL database. Team members do not have much experience with PostgreSQL and want to implement the database in a way that minimizes their administrative responsibilities for the database. What managed service would you recommend?

   A. Cloud SQL

   B. Cloud Dataproc

   C. Cloud Bigtable

   D. Cloud PostgreSQL

10. What is a service-level indicator?

   A. A metric collected to indicate how well a service-level objective is being met

   B. A type of log

   C. A type of notification sent to a sysadmin when an alert is triggered

   D. A visualization displayed when a VM instance is down

11. Developers at MakeYouFashionable have adopted agile development methodologies. Which tool might they use to support CI/CD?

   A. Google Docs

   B. Jenkins

   C. Apache Cassandra

   D. Clojure

12. You have a backlog of audio files that need to be processed using a custom application. The files are stored in Cloud Storage. If the files were processed continuously on three n1-standard-4 instances, the job could complete in two days. You have 30 days to deliver the processed files, after which they will be sent to a client and deleted from your systems. You would like to minimize the cost of processing. What might you do to help keep costs down?

   A. Store the files in coldline storage

   B. Store the processed files in multiregional storage

   C. Store the processed files in Cloud CDN

   D. Use preemptible VMs

13. You have joined a startup selling supplies to visual artists. One element of the company's strategy is to foster a social network of artists and art buyers. The company will provide e-commerce services for artists and earn revenue by charging a fee for each transaction. You have been asked to collect more detailed business requirements. What might you expect as an additional business requirement?

   A. The ability to ingest streaming data

   B. A recommendation system to match buyers to artists

   C. Compliance with SOX regulations

   D. Natural language processing of large volumes of text

14. You work for a manufacturer of specialty die cast parts for the aerospace industry. The company has built a reputation as the leader in high-quality, specialty die cast parts, but recently the number of parts returned for poor quality is increasing. Detailed data about the manufacturing process is collected throughout every stage of manufacturing. To date, the data has been collected and stored but not analyzed. There are a total of 20 TB of data. The company has a team of analysts familiar with spreadsheets and SQL. What service might you recommend for conducting preliminary analysis of the data?

   A. Compute Engine

   B. Kubernetes Engine

   C. BigQuery

   D. Cloud Functions

15. A client of yours wants to run an application in a highly secure environment. They want to use instances that will only run boot components verified by digital signatures. What would you recommend they use in Google Cloud?

   A. Preemptible VMs

   B. Managed instance groups

   C. Cloud Functions

   D. Shielded VMs

16. You have installed the Google Cloud SDK. You would now like to work on transferring files to Cloud Storage. What command-line utility would you use?

   A. bq

   B. gsutil

   C. cbt

   D. gcloud

17. Kubernetes pods sometimes need access to persistent storage. Pods are ephemeral—they may shut down for reasons not in control of the application running in the pod. What mechanism does Kubernetes use to decouple pods from persistent storage?

   A. PersistentVolumes

   B. Deployments

   C. ReplicaSets

   D. Ingress

18. An application that you support has been missing service-level objectives, especially around database query response times. You have reviewed monitoring data and determined that a large number of database read operations is putting unexpected load on the system. The database uses MySQL, and it is running in Compute Engine. You have tuned SQL queries, and the performance is still not meeting objectives. Of the following options, which would you try next?

   A. Migrate to a NoSQL database.

   B. Move the database to Cloud SQL.

   C. Use Cloud Memorystore to cache data read from the database to reduce the number of reads on the database.

   D. Move some of the data out of the database to Cloud Storage.

19. You are running a complicated stream processing operation using Apache Beam. You want to start using a managed service. What GCP service would you use?

   A. Cloud Dataprep

   B. Cloud Dataproc

   C. Cloud Dataflow

   D. Cloud Identity

20. Your team has had a number of incidents in which Tier 1 and Tier 2 services were down for more than 1 hour. After conducting a few retrospective analyses of the incidents, you have determined that you could identify the causes of incidents faster if you had a centralized log repository. What GCP service could you use for this?

    A. Stackdriver Logging

    B. Cloud Logging

    C. Cloud SQL

    D. Cloud Bigtable

21. A Global 2000 company has hired you as a consultant to help architect a new logistics system. The system will track the location of parts as they are shipped between company facilities in Europe, Africa, South America, and Australia. Anytime a user queries the database, they must receive accurate and up-to-date information; specifically, the database must support strong consistency. Users from any facility may query the database using SQL. What GCP service would you recommend?

    A. Cloud SQL

    B. BigQuery

    C. Cloud Spanner

    D. Cloud Dataflow

22. A database architect for a game developer has determined that a NoSQL document database is the best option for storing players' possessions. What GCP service would you recommend?

    A. Cloud Datastore

    B. Cloud Storage

    C. Cloud Dataproc

    D. Cloud Bigtable

23. A major news agency is seeing increasing readership across the globe. The CTO is concerned that long page-load times will decrease readership. What might the news agency try to reduce the page-load time of readers around the globe?

    A. Regional Cloud Storage

    B. Cloud CDN

    C. Fewer firewall rules

    D. Virtual private network

24. What networking mechanism allows different VPC networks to communicate using private IP address space, as defined in RFC 1918?

    A. ReplicaSets

    B. Custom subnets

    C. VPC network peering

    D. Firewall rules

25. You have been tasked with setting up disaster recovery infrastructure in the cloud that will be used if the on-premises data center is not available. What network topology would you use for a disaster recovery environment?

   A. Meshed topology

   B. Mirrored topology

   C. Gated egress topology

   D. Gated ingress topology

Answers to Assessment Test

1. B. Option B is correct. Bigtable is the best option for streaming IoT data, since it supports low-latency writes and is designed to scale to support petabytes of data. Option A is incorrect because Apache Cassandra is not a managed database in GCP. Option C is incorrect because BigQuery is an analytics database. While it is a good option for analyzing the data, Bigtable is a better option for ingesting the data. Option D is incorrect. CloudSQL is a managed relational database. The use case does not require a relational database, and Bigtable's scalability is a better fit with the requirements.

2. C. The correct answer is C. A Cloud Pub/Sub topic would decouple the frontend and backend, provide a managed and scalable message queue, and store ingested data until the backend can process it. Option A is incorrect. Switching to an unmanaged instance group will mean that the instance group cannot autoscale. Option B is incorrect. You could store ingested data in Cloud Storage, but it would not be as performant as the Cloud Pub/Sub solution. Option D is incorrect because BigQuery is an analytics database and not designed for this use case.

3. B. The correct answer is B. IAM is used to manage roles and permissions. Option A is incorrect. Cloud Identity is a service for creating and managing identities. Option C is incorrect. There is no GCP service with that name at this time. Option D is incorrect. LDAP is not a GCP service.

4. B. The correct answer is B. You can run custom containers in App Engine Flexible and Kubernetes Engine. Option A is incorrect because App Engine Standard does not support custom containers. Option C is incorrect because Compute Engine is not a managed service. Option D is incorrect because Cloud Functions does not support custom containers.

5. A. The correct answer is A. A Cloud Function can respond to a create file event in Cloud Storage and start processing when the file is created. Option B is incorrect because an App Engine Flexible application cannot respond to a Cloud Storage write event. Option C is incorrect. Kubernetes pods are the smallest compute unit in Kubernetes and are not designed to respond to Cloud Storage events. Option D is incorrect because it does not guarantee that photos will be processed as soon as they are created.

6. B. The correct answer is B. BigQuery is a managed analytics database designed to support data warehouses and similar use cases. Option A is incorrect. Compute Engine is not a managed service. Option C is incorrect. Cloud Dataproc is a managed Hadoop and Spark service. Option D is incorrect. Bigtable is a NoSQL database well suited for large-volume, low-latency writes and limited ranges of queries. It is not suitable for the kind of ad hoc querying commonly done with data warehouses.

7. C. The correct answer is C. Cloud Storage Coldline is the lowest-cost option, and it is designed for data that is accessed less than once per year. Option A and Option B are incorrect because they cost more than Coldline storage. Option D is incorrect because there is no such service.

8. C. The correct answer is C. The GDPR is a European Union directive protecting the personal information of EU citizens. Option A is incorrect. HIPAA is a U.S. healthcare regulation. Option B is incorrect. PCI-DS is a payment card data security regulation; if Global Games Enterprises Inc. is accepting payment cards in North America, it is already subject to that regulation. Option D is a U.S. regulation on some publicly traded companies; the company may be subject to that regulation already, and expanding to Europe will not change its status.

9. A. The correct answer is A. Cloud SQL is a managed database service that supports PostgreSQL. Option B is incorrect. Cloud Dataproc is a managed Hadoop and Spark service. Option C is incorrect. Cloud Bigtable is a NoSQL database. Option D is incorrect. There is no service called Cloud PostgreSQL in GCP at this time.

10. A. The correct answer is A. A service-level indicator is a metric used to measure how well a service is meeting its objectives. Options B and C are incorrect. It is not a type of log or a type of notification. Option D is incorrect. A service-level indicator is not a visualization, although the same metrics may be used to drive the display of a visualization.

11. B. The correct answer is B. Jenkins is a popular CI/CD tool. Option A is incorrect. Google Docs is a collaboration tool for creating and sharing documents. Option C is incorrect. Cassandra is a NoSQL database. Option D is incorrect. Clojure is a Lisp-like programming language that runs on the Java virtual machine (JVM).

12. D. The correct answer is D. Use preemptible VMs, which cost significantly less than standard VMs. Option A is incorrect. Coldline storage is not appropriate for files that are actively used. Option B is incorrect. Storing files in multiregional storage will cost more than regional storage, and there is no indication from the requirements that they should be stored multiregionally. Option C is incorrect. There is no indication that the processed files need to be distributed to a global user base.

13. B. The correct answer is B. This is an e-commerce site matching sellers and buyers, so a system that recommends artists to buyers can help increase sales. Option A is incorrect. There is no indication of any need for streaming data. Option C is incorrect. This is a startup, and it is not likely subject to SOX regulations. Option D is incorrect. There is no indication of a need to process large volumes of text.

14. C. The correct answer is C. BigQuery is an analytics database that supports SQL. Options A and B are incorrect because, although they could be used to run analytics applications, such as Apache Hadoop or Apache Spark, it would require more administrative overhead. Also, the team members working on this are analysts, but there is no indication that they have the skills or desire to manage analytics platforms. Option D is incorrect. Cloud Functions is for running short programs in response to events in GCP.

15. B. The correct answer is D. Shielded VMs include secure boot, which only runs digitally verified boot components. Option A is incorrect. Preemptible VMs are interruptible instances, but they cost less than standard VMs. Option B is incorrect. Managed instance groups are sets of identical VMs that are managed as a single entity. Option C is incorrect. Cloud Functions is a PaaS for running programs in response to events in GCP.

16. B. The correct answer is B. `gsutil` is the command-line utility for working with Cloud Storage. Option A is incorrect. `bq` is the command-line utility for working with BigQuery. Option C is incorrect. `cbt` is the command-line utility for working with Cloud Bigtable. Option D is incorrect. `gcloud` is used to work with most GCP services but not Cloud Storage.

17. A. The correct answer is A. PersistentVolumes is Kubernetes' way of representing storage allocated or provisioned for use by a pod. Option B is incorrect. Deployments are a type of controller consisting of pods running the same version of an application. Option C is incorrect. A ReplicaSet is a controller that manages the number of pods running in a deployment. Option D is incorrect. An Ingress is an object that controls external access to services running in a Kubernetes cluster.

18. C. The correct answer is C. Use Cloud Memorystore to reduce the number of reads against the database. Option A is incorrect. The application is designed to work with a relational database, and there is no indication that a NoSQL database is a better option overall. Option B is incorrect. Simply moving the database to a managed service will not change the number of read operations, which is the cause of the poor performance. Option D is incorrect. Moving data to Cloud Storage will not reduce the number of reads.

19. C. The correct answer is C. Cloud Dataflow is an implementation of the Apache Beam stream processing framework. Cloud Dataflow is a fully managed service. Option A is incorrect. Cloud Dataprep is used to prepare data for analysis. Option B is incorrect. Cloud Dataproc is a managed Hadoop and Spark service. Option D is incorrect. Cloud Identity is an authentication service.

20. A. The correct answer is A. Stackdriver Logging is a centralized logging service. Option B is incorrect. There is no such service at this time. Option C and Option D are incorrect because those are databases and not specifically designed to support the logging of the use case described.

21. C. The correct answer is C. Cloud Spanner is a globally scalable, strongly consistent relational database that can be queried using SQL. Option A is incorrect because it will not scale to the global scale as Cloud Spanner will. Option B is incorrect. The requirements describe an application that will likely have frequent updates and transactions. BigQuery is designed for analytics and data warehousing. Option D is incorrect. Cloud Dataflow is a stream and batch processing service.

22. A. The correct answer is A. Cloud Datastore is a managed document NoSQL database in GCP. Option B is incorrect. Cloud Storage is an object storage system, not a document NoSQL database. Option C is incorrect. Cloud Dataproc is a managed Hadoop and Spark service. Option D is incorrect. Cloud Bigtable is a wide-column NoSQL database, not a document database.

23. B. The correct answer is B. Cloud CDN is GCP's content delivery network, which distributes static content globally. Option A is incorrect. Reading from regional storage can still have long latencies for readers outside of the region. Option C is incorrect. Firewall rules do not impact latency in any discernible way. Option D is incorrect. VPNs are used to link on-premises networks to Google Cloud.

24. C. The correct answer is C. VPC peering allows different VPCs to communicate using private networks. Option A is incorrect. ReplicaSets are used in Kubernetes; they are not related to VPCs. Option B is incorrect. Custom subnets define network address ranges for regions. Option D is incorrect. Firewall rules control the flow of network traffic.

25. B. The correct answer is B. With a mirrored topology, the public cloud and private on-premise environments mirror each other. Option A is incorrect. In a mesh topology, all systems in the cloud and private networks can communicate with each other. Option C is incorrect. In a gated egress topology, on-premises service APIs are made available to applications running in the cloud without exposing them to the public Internet. Option D is incorrect. In a gated ingress topology, cloud service APIs are made available to applications running on-premises without exposing them to the public Internet.

Chapter

1

Introduction to the Google Professional Cloud Architect Exam

PROFESSIONAL CLOUD ARCHITECT CERTIFICATION EXAM OBJECTIVES COVERED IN THIS CHAPTER INCLUDE THE FOLLOWING:

Section 1: Designing and planning a cloud solution architecture

✓ **1.1 Designing a solution infrastructure that meets business requirements. Considerations include:**

- Business use cases and product strategy
- Cost optimization
- Supporting the application design
- Integration
- Movement of data
- Tradeoffs
- Build, buy or modify
- Success measurements (e.g., Key Performance Indicators (KPI), Return on Investment (ROI), metrics)
- Compliance and observability

This Study Guide is designed to help you acquire the technical knowledge and analytical skills that you will need to pass the Google Cloud Professional Architect certification exam. This exam is designed to evaluate your skills for assessing business requirements, identifying technical requirements, and mapping those requirements to solutions using Google Cloud products, as well as monitoring and maintaining those solutions. This breadth of topics alone is enough to make this a challenging exam. Add to that the need for "soft" skills, such as working with colleagues in order to understand their business requirements, and you have an exam that is difficult to pass.

The Google Cloud Professional Architect exam is not a body of knowledge exam. You can know Google Cloud product documentation in detail, memorize most of what you read in this guide, and view multiple online courses, but that will not guarantee that you pass the exam. Rather, you will be required to exercise judgment. You will have to understand how business requirements constrain your options for choosing a technical solution. You will be asked the kinds of questions a business sponsor might ask about implementing their project.

This chapter will review the following:

- Exam objectives

- Scope of the exam

- Case studies written by Google and used as the basis for some exam questions

- Additional resources to help in your exam preparation

Exam Objectives

The Google Cloud Professional Cloud Architect exam will test your architect skills, including the following:

- Planning a cloud solution

- Managing a cloud solution

- Securing systems and processes

- Complying with government and industry regulations

- Understanding technical requirements and business considerations

- Maintaining solutions deployed to production, including monitoring

It is clear from the exam objectives that the full lifecycle of solution development is covered from inception and planning through monitoring and maintenance.

Analyzing Business Requirements

An architect starts the planning phase by collecting information, starting with business requirements. You might be tempted to start with technical details about the current solution. You might want to ask technical questions so that you can start eliminating options. You may even think that you've solved this kind of problem before and you just have to pick the right architecture pattern. Resist those inclinations if you have them. All architecture design decisions are made in the context of business requirements.

Business requirements define the operational landscape in which you will develop a solution. Example business requirements are as follows:

- The need to reduce *capital expenditures*
- Accelerating the pace of software development
- Reporting on *service-level objectives*
- Reducing time to recover from an incident
- Improving compliance with industry regulations

Business requirements may be about costs, customer experience, or operational improvements. A common trait of business requirements is that they are rarely satisfied by a single technical decision.

Reducing Operational Expenses

Reducing operational expenses may be satisfied by a combination of managed services, preemptible virtual machines, and the use of *autoscalers*.

Managed services reduce the workload on systems administrators and DevOps engineers because they eliminate some of the work required when managing your own implementation of a platform. A database administrator, for example, would not have to spend time performing backups or patching operating systems if they used Cloud SQL instead of running a database on Compute Engine instances or in their own data center.

Preemptible VMs are low-cost instances that can run up to 24 hours before being preempted, or shut down. They are a good option for batch processing and other tasks that are easily recovered and restarted.

Autoscaling enables engineers to deploy an adequate number of instances needed to meet the load on a system. When demand is high, instances are increased, and when demand is low, the number of instances is reduced. With autoscaling, organizations can stop purchasing infrastructure adequate to meet peak capacity and can instead adjust their infrastructure to meet the immediate need.

Accelerating the Pace of Development

Successful businesses are constantly innovating. Agile software development practices are designed to support rapid development, testing, deployment, and feedback.

A business that wants to accelerate the pace of development may turn to managed services to reduce the operational workload on their operations teams. Managed services also allow engineers to implement services, such as image processing and natural language processing, which they could not do on their own if they did not have domain expertise on the team.

Continuous integration and *continuous deployment* are additional practices within software development. The idea is that it's best to integrate small amounts of new code frequently so that it can be tested and deployed rather than trying to release a large number of changes at one time. Small releases are easier to review and debug. They also allow developers to get feedback from colleagues and customers about features, performance, and other factors.

As an architect, you may have to work with monolithic applications that are difficult to update in small increments. In that case, there may be an implied business requirement to consider decomposing the monolithic application into a *microservice architecture*. If there is an interest in migrating to a microservices architecture, then you will need to decide if you should migrate the existing application into the cloud as is, known as *lift and shift*, or you should begin transforming the application during the cloud migration.

There is no way to make a decision about this without considering business requirements. If the business needs to move to the cloud as fast as possible to avoid a large capital expenditure on new equipment or to avoid committing to a long-term lease in a co-location data center or if the organization wants to minimize change during the migration, then lift and shift is the better choice. Most important, you have to assess if the application can run in the cloud with minimal modification. Otherwise, you cannot perform a lift-and-shift migration.

If the monolithic application is dependent on deprecated components and written in a language that is no longer supported in your company, then rewriting the application or using a third-party application is a reasonable choice.

Reporting on Service-Level Objectives

The operational groups of a modern business depend on IT applications. A finance department needs access to accounting systems. A logistics analyst needs access to data about how well the fleet of delivery vehicles is performing. The sales team constantly queries and updates the customer management system. Different business units will have different business requirements around the availability of applications and services.

A finance department may only need access to accounting systems during business hours. In that case, upgrades and other maintenance can happen during off-hours and would not require the accounting system to be available during that time. The customer management system, however, is typically used 24 hours a day, every day. The sales team expects the application to be available all the time. This means that support engineers need to find ways to update and patch the customer management system while minimizing downtime.

Requirements about availability are formalized in *service-level objectives (SLOs)*. SLOs can be defined in terms of availability, such as being available 99.9 percent of the time. A database system may have SLOs around durability or the ability to retrieve data. For example, the human resources department may have to store personnel data reliably for seven years, and the storage system must guarantee that there is a less than 1 in 10 billion chance of an object being lost. Interactive systems have performance-related SLOs. A web application SLO may require a page loading average response time of 2 seconds with a 95th percentile of 4 seconds.

Logging and monitoring data is used to demonstrate compliance with SLOs. *Stackdriver logging* is used for collecting information about significant events, such as a disk running out of space. Monitoring services collect metrics from infrastructure, such as average CPU utilization during a particular period of time or the number of bytes written to a network in a defined time span. Developers can create reports and dashboards using logging details and metrics to monitor compliance with SLOs. These metrics are known as *service-level indicators (SLIs)*.

Reducing Time to Recover from an Incident

Incidents, in the context of IT services, are a disruption that causes a service to be degraded or unavailable. An incident can be caused by single factors, such as an incorrect configuration. Often, there is no single root cause of an incident. Instead, a series of failures and errors contributes to a service failure.

For example, consider an engineer on call who receives a notification that customer data is not being processed correctly by an application. In this case, a database is failing to complete a transaction because a disk is out of space, which causes the application writing to the database to block while the application repeatedly retries the transaction in rapid succession. The application stops reading from a message queue, which causes messages to accumulate until the maximum size of the queue is reached, at which point the message queue starts to drop data.

Once an incident begins, systems engineers and system administrators need information about the state of components and services. To reduce the time to recover, it is best to collect metrics and log events and then make them available to engineers at any time, especially during an incident response.

The incident might have been avoided if database administrators created alerts on free disk space or if the application developer chose to handle retries using *exponential backoff* instead of simply retrying as fast as possible until it succeeds. Alerting on the size of the message queue could have notified the operations team of a potential problem in time to make adjustments before data was dropped.

Improving Compliance with Industry Regulations

Many businesses are subject to government and industry regulations. Regulations range from protecting the privacy of customer data to ensuring the integrity of business transactions and financial reporting. Major regulations include the following:

- *Health Insurance Portability and Accountability Act (HIPAA)*, a healthcare regulation
- *Children's Online Privacy Protection Act (COPPA)*, a privacy regulation
- *Sarbanes-Oxley Act (SOX)*, a financial reporting regulation
- *Payment Card Industry Data Standard (PCI)*, a data protection regulation for credit card processing
- *General Data Protection Regulation (GDPR)*, a European Union privacy protection regulation

Complying with privacy regulations usually requires controls on who can access and change protected data. As an architect, you will have to develop schemes for controls that meet regulations. Fine-grained access controls may be used to control further who can update data. When granting access, follow security best practices, such as granting only the permissions needed to perform one's job and separating high-risk duties across multiple roles.

Business requirements define the context in which architects make design decisions. On the Google Cloud Professional Architect exam, you must understand business requirements and how they constrain technical options and specify characteristics required in a technical solution.

Business Terms to Know

Brick and Mortar   A term to describe businesses with physical presence, especially retail stores.

Capital Expenditure (Capex)   Funds spent to acquire assets, such as computer equipment, vehicles, and land. Capital expenditures are used to purchase assets that will have a useful life of at least a few years. The other major type of expenditure is *operational expenditures*.

Compliance   Implementing controls and practices to meet the requirements of regulations.

Digital Transformation   Major changes in businesses as they adopt information technologies to develop new products, improve customer service, optimize operations, and make other major improvements enabled by technology. Brick-and-mortar retailers using mobile technologies to promote products and engage with customers is an example of digital transformation.

Governance   Procedures and practices used to ensure that policies and principles of organizational operations are followed. Governance is the responsibility of directors and executives within an organization.

Key Performance Indicator (KPI)   A measure that provides information about how well a business or organization is achieving an important or key objective. For example, an online gaming company may have KPIs related to the number of new players acquired per week, total number of player hours, and operational costs per player.

Line of Business   The parts of a business that deliver a particular class of products and services. For example, a bank may have consumer banking and business banking lines, while an equipment manufacturer may have industrial as well as agricultural lines of business. Different lines of business within a company will have some business and technical requirements in common as well as their own distinct needs.

Operational Expenditures (Opex)   An expense paid for from the operating budget, not the capital budget.

Operating Budget   A budget allocating funds to meet the costs of labor, supplies, and other expenses related to performing the day-to-day operations of a business. Contrast this to capital expenditure budgets, which are used for longer-term investments.

Service-Level Agreement (SLA)   An agreement between a provider of a service and a customer using the service. SLAs define responsibilities for delivering a service and consequences when responsibilities are not met.

Service-Level Indicator (SLI)   A metric that reflects how well a service-level objective is being met. Examples include latency, throughput, and error rate.

Service-Level Objective (SLO)   An agreed-upon target for a measurable attribute of a service that is specified in a service-level agreement.

Analyzing Technical Requirements

Technical requirements specify features of a system that relate to functional and nonfunctional performance. Functional features include providing ACID transactions in a database, which guarantees that transactions are atomic, consistent, isolated, and durable; ensuring *at least once* delivery in a messaging system; and encrypting data at rest. Nonfunctional features are the general features of a system, including scalability, reliability, and maintainability.

Functional Requirements

The exam will require you to understand functional requirements related to computing, storage, and networking. The following are some examples of the kinds of issues you will be asked about on the exam.

Understanding Compute Requirements

Google Cloud has a variety of computing services, including *Compute Engine*, *App Engine*, and *Kubernetes Engine*. As an architect, you should be able to determine when each of these platforms is the best option for a use case. For example, if there is a technical requirement to use a virtual machine running a particular hardened version of Linux, then Compute Engine is the best option. Sometimes, though, the choice is not so obvious.

If you want to run containers in the Google Cloud Platform (GCP), you could choose either App Engine Flexible or Kubernetes Engine for a managed service. If you already have application code running in App Engine and you intend to run a small number of containers, then *App Engine Flexible* is a good option. If you plan to deploy and manage a large number of containers and want to use a service mesh like *Istio* to secure and monitor microservices, *Kubernetes Engine* is a better option.

Understanding Storage Requirements

There are even more options when it comes to storage. There are a number of factors to consider when choosing a storage option, including how the data is structured, how it will be accessed and updated, and for how long it will be stored.

Let's look at how you might decide which data storage service to use given a set of requirements. Structured data fits well with both relational and *NoSQL* databases. If SQL is required, then your choices are Cloud SQL, Spanner, BigQuery, or running a relational database yourself in Compute Engine. If you require a global, strongly consistent transactional data store, then Spanner is the best choice, while Cloud SQL is a good choice for regional-scale databases. If the application using the database requires a flexible schema, then you should consider NoSQL options. Cloud Datastore is a good option when a document store is needed, while Bigtable is well suited for ingesting large volumes of data at low latency.

Of course, you could run a NoSQL database in Compute Engine. If a service needs to ingest time-series data at low latency and one of the business requirements is to maximize the use of managed services, then Bigtable should be used. If there is no requirement to use managed services, you might consider deploying Cassandra to a cluster in Compute Engine. This would be a better choice, for example, if you are planning a lift-and-shift migration to the cloud and are currently running Cassandra in an on-premises data center.

When long-term archival storage is required, then Cloud Storage is probably the best option. Since Cloud Storage has four types of storage, you will have to consider access patterns and reliability requirements. If the data is frequently accessed, then regional or multiregional class storage is appropriate. If high availability of access to the data is a concern or if data will be accessed from different areas of the world, you should consider multiregional storage. If data will be infrequently accessed, then Nearline or Coldline storage is a good choice. Nearline storage is designed for data that won't be accessed more than once a month. Coldline storage is well suited for data that will be accessed not more than once a year.

Understanding Network Requirements

Networking topics that require an architect tend to fall into two categories: structuring virtual private clouds and supporting hybrid cloud computing.

Virtual private clouds (VPCs) isolate a Google Cloud Platform customer's resources. Architects should know how to configure VPCs to meet requirements about who can access specific resources, the kinds of traffic allowed in or out of the network, and communications between VPCs. To develop solutions to these high-level requirements, architects need to understand basic networking components such as the following:

- Firewalls and firewall rules
- Domain name services (DNS)
- *CIDR* blocks and IP addressing
- Autogenerated and custom subnets
- *VPC peering*

Many companies and organizations adopting cloud computing also have their own data centers. Architects need to understand options for networking between on-premises data centers and the Google Cloud Platform network. Options include using a virtual private network, dedicated interconnect, and partner interconnects. Virtual private networks are a good choice when bandwidth demands are not high and data is allowed to traverse the public Internet. Partner interconnects provide a minimum of 50 Mbps bandwidth, and data is transmitted through the partner's network, not the public Internet. Dedicated interconnects are used when bandwidth requirements are 10 Gbps or greater.

Nonfunctional Requirements

Nonfunctional requirements often follow from business requirements. They include the following:

- Availability
- Reliability
- Scalability
- Durability

Availability is a measure of the time that services are functioning correctly and accessible to users. Availability requirements are typically stated in terms of percent of time a service should be up and running, such as 99.99 percent. Fully supported Google Cloud services have SLAs for availability so that you can use them to help guide your architectural decisions. Note, alpha and beta products typically do not have SLAs.

Reliability is a closely related concept to availability. *Reliability* is a measure of the probability that a service will continue to function under some load for a period of time. The level of reliability that a service can achieve is highly dependent on the availability of systems upon which it depends.

Scalability is the ability of a service to adapt its infrastructure to the load on the system. When load decreases, some resources may be shut down. When load increases, resources can be added. Autoscalers and instance groups are often used to ensure scalability when using Compute Engine. One of the advantages of services like Cloud Storage and App Engine is that scalability is managed by GCP, which reduces the operational overhead on DevOps teams.

Durability is used to measure the likelihood that a stored object will be retrievable in the future. Cloud Storage has 99.999999999 percent (eleven 9s) durability guarantees, which means it is extremely unlikely that you will lose an object stored in Cloud Storage. Because of the math, as the number of objects increases, the likelihood that one of them is lost will increase.

The Google Cloud Professional Cloud Architect exam tests your ability to understand both business requirements and technical requirements, which is reasonable since those skills are required to function as a cloud architect.

Exam Case Studies

 Exam case studies are reprinted with permission from Google LLC. They are subject to change as are the exams themselves. Please visit the Google website to check for the latest Google Cloud Professional Architect exam case studies.

The Google Cloud Professional Cloud Architect Certification exam uses three case studies as the basis for some questions on the exam. Become familiar with the case studies before the exam in order to save time while taking the test.

Each case study includes a company overview, solution concept, technical requirements, business requirements, and an executive statement. As you read each case study, be sure that you understand the driving business considerations and the solution concept. These provide constraints on the possible solutions.

When existing infrastructure is described, think of what GCP services could be used as a replacement if needed. For example, Cloud SQL can be used to replace an on-premise MySQL server, Cloud Dataproc can replace self-managed Spark and Hadoop clusters, and Cloud Pub/Sub can be used instead of RabbitMQ.

Read for the technical implications of the business statements—they may not be stated explicitly. For example, in the Dress4Win case study, the statement "Improve business agility and speed of innovation through rapid provisioning of new resources" could mean that you should plan to use infrastructure-as-code deployments and enable autoscaling when possible. There is also the statement: "Our traffic patterns are highest in the mornings and weekend evenings; during other times, 80% of our capacity is sitting idle," which describes an opportunity to use autoscaling to optimize resource usage. Both examples show business statements that imply additional requirements that the architect needs to identify without being told that there is a requirement explicitly stated.

The three case studies are available online here:

Dress4Win
```
https://cloud.google.com/certification/guides/cloud-architect/
casestudy-dress4win-rev2
```

Mountkirk Games
```
https://cloud.google.com/certification/guides/cloud-architect/
casestudy-mountkirkgames-rev2
```

TerramEarth
```
https://cloud.google.com/certification/guides/cloud-architect/
casestudy-terramearth-rev2
```

 Real World Scenario

Dress4Win

Company Overview

Dress4Win is a web-based company that helps their users organize and manage their personal wardrobe using a web app and mobile application. The company also cultivates an active social network that connects their users with designers and retailers. They monetize their services through advertising, e-commerce, referrals, and a freemium app model. The application has grown from a few servers in the founder's garage to several hundred servers and appliances in a collocated data center. However, the capacity of their infrastructure is now insufficient for the application's rapid growth. Because of this growth and the company's desire to innovate faster, Dress4Win is committing to a full migration to a public cloud.

Solution Concept

For the first phase of their migration to the cloud, Dress4Win is moving their development and test environments. They are also building a disaster recovery site because their current infrastructure is at a single location. They are not sure which components of their architecture can be migrated as is and which components need to be changed before migrating them.

Existing Technical Environment

The Dress4Win application is served out of a single data center location. All servers run Ubuntu LTS v16.04.

Databases:

> MySQL: 1 server for user data, inventory, and static data:
>
> - MySQL 5.7
> - 8 core CPUs
> - 128 GB of RAM
> - 2x 5 TB HDD (RAID 1)
>
> Redis: 3 server cluster for metadata, social graph, and caching. Each server consists of:
>
> - Redis 3.2
> - 4 core CPUs
> - 32GB of RAM

Compute:

> 40 Web application servers providing micro-services based APIs and static content.
>
> - Tomcat - Java
> - Nginx
> - 4 core CPUs
> - 32 GB of RAM
>
> 20 Apache Hadoop/Spark servers:
>
> - Data analysis
> - Real-time trending calculations
> - Eight core CPUs
> - 128 GB of RAM
> - 4x 5 TB HDD (RAID 1)
>
> 3 RabbitMQ servers for messaging, social notifications, and events:
>
> - Eight core CPUs
> - 32GB of RAM
>
> Miscellaneous servers:
>
> - Jenkins, monitoring, bastion hosts, and security scanners
> - Eight core CPUs
> - 32GB of RAM

Storage appliances:

- iSCSI for VM hosts

- Fiber channel SAN - MySQL databases

  - 1 PB total storage; 400 TB available

- NAS - image storage, logs, backups

  - 100 TB total storage; 35 TB available

Business Requirements

- Build a reliable and reproducible environment with scaled parity of production.

- Improve security by defining and adhering to a set of security and Identity and Access Management (IAM) best practices for the cloud.

- Improve business agility and speed of innovation through rapid provisioning of new resources.

- Analyze and optimize architecture for performance in the cloud.

Technical Requirements

- Easily create non-production environments in the cloud.

- Implement an automation framework for provisioning resources in cloud. Implement a continuous deployment process for deploying applications to the on-premises data center or cloud.

- Support failover of the production environment to the cloud during an emergency.

- Encrypt data on the wire and at rest.

- Support multiple private connections between the production data center and cloud environment.

Executive Statement

Our investors are concerned about our ability to scale and contain costs with our current infrastructure. They are also concerned that a competitor could use a public cloud platform to offset their up-front investment and free them to focus on developing better features. Our traffic patterns are highest in the mornings and weekend evenings; during other times, 80 percent of our capacity is sitting idle.

Our capital expenditure is now exceeding our quarterly projections. Migrating to the cloud will likely cause an initial increase in spending, but we expect to transition completely before our next hardware refresh cycle. Our total cost of ownership (TCO) analysis over the next five years for a public cloud strategy achieves a cost reduction of 30–50 percent over our current model.

🌐 **Real World Scenario**

Mountkirk Games Case Study

Company Overview

Mountkirk Games makes online, session-based, multiplayer games for mobile platforms. They build all of their games using some server-side integration. Historically, they have used cloud providers to lease physical servers.

Due to the unexpected popularity of some of their games, they have had problems scaling their global audience, application servers, MySQL databases, and analytics tools.

Their current model is to write game statistics to files and send them through an ETL tool that loads them into a centralized MySQL database for reporting.

Solution Concept

Mountkirk Games is building a new game, which they expect to be very popular. They plan to deploy the game's backend on the Google Compute Engine so that they can capture streaming metrics, run intensive analytics, and take advantage of its autoscaling server environment and integrate with a managed NoSQL database.

Business Requirements

- Increase to a global footprint
- Improve uptime (downtime is loss of players)
- Increase efficiency of the cloud resources they use
- Reduce latency to all customers

Technical Requirements

Requirements for Game Backend Platform

1. Dynamically scale up or down based on game activity.
2. Connect to a transactional database service to manage user profiles and game state.
3. Store game activity in a time series database service for future analysis.
4. As the system scales, ensure that data is not lost due to processing backlogs.
5. Run hardened Linux distro.

Requirements for Game Analytics Platform

1. Dynamically scale up or down based on game activity.

2. Process incoming data on the fly directly from the game servers.

3. Process data that arrives late because of slow mobile networks.

4. Allow queries to access at least 10 TB of historical data.

5. Process files that are regularly uploaded by users' mobile devices.

Executive Statement

Our last successful game did not scale well with our previous cloud provider, resulting in lower user adoption and affecting the game's reputation. Our investors want more key performance indicators (KPIs) to evaluate the speed and stability of the game, as well as other metrics that provide deeper insight into usage patterns so that we can adapt the game to target users. Additionally, our current technology stack cannot provide the scale we need, so we want to replace MySQL and move to an environment that provides autoscaling, low-latency load balancing, and frees us up from managing physical servers.

 **Real World Scenario**

TerramEarth Case Study

Company Overview

TerramEarth manufactures heavy equipment for the mining and agricultural industries. About 80 percent of their business is from mining and 20 percent is from agriculture. They currently have over 500 dealers and service centers in 100 countries. Their mission is to build products that make their customers more productive.

Solution Concept

There are 20 million TerramEarth vehicles in operation that collect 120 fields of data per second. Data is stored locally on the vehicle, and it can be accessed for analysis when a vehicle is serviced. The data is downloaded via a maintenance port. This same port can be used to adjust operational parameters, allowing the vehicles to be upgraded in the field with new computing modules.

Approximately 200,000 vehicles are connected to a cellular network, allowing TerramEarth to collect data directly. At a rate of 120 fields of data per second, with 22 hours of operation per day, TerramEarth collects a total of about 9 TB of data per day from these connected vehicles.

Existing Technical Environment

TerramEarth's existing architecture is composed of Linux and Windows-based systems that reside in a single U.S, west coast-based data center. These systems gzip CSV files from the field, upload via FTP, and place the data in their data warehouse. Because this process takes time, aggregated reports are based on data that is three weeks old.

With this data, TerramEarth has been able to stock replacement parts preemptively and reduce unplanned downtime of their vehicles by 60 percent. However, because the data is stale, some customers are without their vehicles for up to four weeks while they wait for replacement parts.

Business Requirements

- Decrease unplanned vehicle downtime to less than one week

- Support the dealer network with more data on how their customers use their equipment to position new products and services better.

- Have the ability to partner with different companies—especially with seed and fertilizer suppliers in the fast-growing agricultural business—to create compelling joint offerings for their customers.

Technical Requirements

- Expand beyond a single data center to decrease latency to the American Midwest and east coast

- Create a backup strategy

- Increase security of data transfer from equipment to the data center

- Improve data in the data warehouse

- Use customer and equipment data to anticipate customer needs

Application 1: Data ingest

A custom Python application reads uploaded data files from a single server and writes to the data warehouse.

Compute

Windows Server 2008 R2

- 16 CPUs

- 128 GB of RAM

- 10 TB local HDD storage

Application 2: Reporting

An off-the-shelf application that business analysts use to run a daily report to see what equipment needs repair. Only 2 analysts of a team of 10 (5 west coast, 5 east coast) can connect to the reporting application at a time.

Compute

Off-the-shelf application. License tied to number of physical CPUs.

- Windows Server 2008 R2

- 16 CPUs

- 32 GB of RAM

- 500 GB HDD

Data warehouse

- A single PostgreSQL server

- RedHat Linux

- 64 CPUs

- 128 GB of RAM

- 4x 6TB HDD in RAID 0

Executive Statement

Our competitive advantage has always been in our manufacturing process, with our ability to build better vehicles for lower cost than our competitors. However, new products with different approaches are constantly being developed, and I'm concerned that we lack the skills to undergo the next wave of transformations in our industry. My goals are to build our skills while addressing immediate market needs through incremental innovations.

Summary

The Google Cloud Professional Architect exam covers several broad areas, including the following:

- Planning a cloud solution
- Managing a cloud solution
- Securing systems and processes
- Complying with government and industry regulations
- Understanding technical requirements and business considerations
- Maintaining solutions deployed to production, including monitoring

These areas require business as well as technical skills. For example, since architects regularly work with nontechnical colleagues, it is important for architects to understand issues such as reducing operational expenses, accelerating the pace of development, maintaining and reporting on service-level agreements, and assisting with regulatory compliance. In the realm of technical knowledge, architects are expected to understand functional requirements around computing, storage, and networking as well as nonfunctional characteristics of services, such as availability and scalability.

The exam includes three case studies, and some exam questions reference the case studies. Questions about the case studies may be business or technical questions.

Exam Essentials

Assume every word matters in case studies and exam questions.   Some technical requirements are stated explicitly, but some are implied in business statements. Review the business requirements as carefully as the technical requirements in each case study. Similarly, when reading an exam question, pay attention to all of the statements. What may look like extraneous background information at first may turn out to be information that you need in order to choose between two options.

Study and analyze case studies before taking the exam.   Become familiar with the case studies before the exam to save time while taking the text. You don't need to memorize the case studies, as you'll have access to them during the test. Watch for numbers that indicate the scale of the problem. If you need to transmit more than 10 Gbps, then you should consider a Cloud Interconnect solution over a VPN solution, which works up to about 3 Gbps.

Understand what is needed in the near term and what may be needed in the future.   For example, in the TerramEarth case study, 200,000 vehicles are equipped with cellular communications equipment that can collect data daily. What would change about your design if all 20 million vehicles in production reported their data daily? This requirement is not stated, and not even implied, but it is the kind of planning for the future that architects are expected to do.

Understand how to plan a migration.   Migrations are high-risk operations. Data can be lost, and services may be unavailable. Know how to plan to run new and old systems in parallel so that you can compare results. Be able to identify lower-risk migration steps so that they can be scheduled first. Plan for incremental migrations.

Know agile software development practices.   You won't have to write code for this exam, but you will need to understand continuous integration/continuous deployment and maintaining development, test, staging, and production environments. Understand what is meant by an infrastructure-as-code service and how that helps accelerate development and deployment.

Keep in mind that solutions may involve non-Google services or applications.   Google has many services, but sometimes the best solution involves a third-party solution. For example, Jenkins and Spinnaker are widely used tools to support continuous integration and deployment. Google Cloud has a code repository, but many developers use GitHub. Sometimes businesses are locked into existing solutions, such as a third-party database. The business may want to migrate to another database solution, but the cost may be too high for the foreseeable future.

Review Questions

1. You have been tasked with interviewing line-of-business owners about their needs for a new cloud application. Which of the following do you expect to find?

   A. A comprehensive list of defined business and technical requirements

   B. That their business requirements do not have a one-to-one correlation with technical requirements

   C. Business and technical requirements in conflict

   D. Clear consensus on all requirements

2. You have been asked by stakeholders to suggest ways to reduce operational expenses as part of a cloud migration project. Which of the following would you recommend?

   A. Managed services, preemptible machines, access controls

   B. Managed services, preemptible machines, autoscaling

   C. NoSQL databases, preemptible machines, autoscaling

   D. NoSQL databases, preemptible machines, access controls

3. Some executives are questioning your recommendation to employ continuous integration/ continuous deployment (CI/CD). What reasons would you give to justify your recommendation?

   A. CI/CD supports small releases, which are easier to debug and enable faster feedback.

   B. CI/CD is used only with preemptible machines and therefore saves money.

   C. CI/CD fits well with waterfall methodology but not agile methodologies.

   D. CI/CD limits the number of times code is released.

4. The finance director has asked your advice about complying with a document retention regulation. What kind of service-level objective (SLO) would you recommend to ensure that the finance director will be able to retrieve sensitive documents for at least the next seven years? When a document is needed, the finance director will have up to seven days to retrieve it. The total storage required will be approximately 100 GB.

   A. High availability SLO

   B. Durability SLO

   C. Reliability SLO

   D. Scalability SLO

5. You are facilitating a meeting of business and technical managers to solicit requirements for a cloud migration project. The term *incident* comes up several times. Some of the business managers are unfamiliar with this term in the context of IT. How would you describe an incident?

   A. A disruption in the ability of a DevOps team to complete work on time

   B. A disruption in the ability of the business managers to approve a project plan on schedule

C. A disruption that causes a service to be degraded or unavailable

D. A personnel problem on the DevOps team

6. You have been asked to consult on a cloud migration project that includes moving private medical information to a storage system in the cloud. The project is for a company in the United States. What regulation would you suggest that the team review during the requirements-gathering stages?

A. General Data Protection Regulations (GDPR)

B. Sarbanes–Oxley (SOX)

C. Payment Card Industry Data Security Standard (PCI DSS)

D. Health Insurance Portability and Accountability Act (HIPAA)

7. You are in the early stages of gathering business and technical requirements. You have noticed several references about needing up-to-date and consistent information regarding product inventory. Inventory is managed on a global scale, and the warehouses storing inventory are located in North America, Africa, Europe, and India. Which managed database solution in Google Cloud would you include in your set of options for an inventory database?

A. Cloud Storage

B. BigQuery

C. Cloud Spanner

D. Microsoft SQL Server

8. A developer at Mountkirk Games is interested in how architects decide which database to use. The developer describes a use case that requires a document store. The developer would rather not manage database servers or have to run backups. What managed service would you suggest the developer consider?

A. Cloud Datastore

B. Cloud Spanner

C. Cloud Storage

D. BigQuery

9. Members of your company's legal team are concerned about using a public cloud service because other companies, organizations, and individuals will be running their systems in the same cloud. You assure them that your company's resources will be isolated and not network-accessible to others because of what networking resource in Google Cloud?

A. CIDR blocks

B. Direct connections

C. Virtual private clouds

D. Cloud Pub/Sub

10. What two business drivers are behind Dress4Win's interest in moving to the cloud?

   A. Insufficient infrastructure capacity and desire to be more agile

   B. Insufficient infrastructure and competitors moving to the cloud

   C. Competitors moving to the cloud and desire to be more agile

   D. Insufficient infrastructure and short-term cost savings

11. Dress4Win is considering replacing its self-managed MySQL database with a managed service. Which Google Cloud service would you recommend that they consider?

   A. Cloud Dataproc

   B. Cloud Dataflow

   C. Cloud SQL

   D. PostgreSQL

12. Which of the following requirements from a customer makes you think the application should run in Compute Engine and not App Engine?

   A. Dynamically scale up or down based on game activity

   B. Connect to a database

   C. Run a hardened Linux distro on a virtual machine

   D. Don't lose data

13. Consider the TerramEarth case study. What aspect of that case study prompts you to consider potentially significant changes to requirements in the future?

   A. Dealers will want more reports about their customers.

   B. Of 20 million pieces of equipment, only 200,000 have cellular connections; 19,800,000 additional pieces of equipment may someday transmit data in real time instead of downloading it in batches.

   C. TerramEarth is in a competitive industry.

   D. TerramEarth would like to partner with other companies to improve overall service to their customers.

14. Mountkirk Games wants to store player game data in a time-series database. Which Google Cloud managed database would you recommend?

   A. Bigtable

   B. BigQuery

   C. Cloud Storage

   D. Cloud Dataproc

15. The game analytics platform for Mountkirk Games requires analysts to be able to query up to 10 TB of data. What is the best managed database solution for this requirement?

   A. Cloud Spanner

   B. BigQuery

   C. Cloud Storage

   D. Cloud Dataprep

Chapter

2

Designing for Business Requirements

THE PROFESSIONAL CLOUD ARCHITECT CERTIFICATION EXAM OBJECTIVES COVERED IN THIS CHAPTER INCLUDE THE FOLLOWING:

- ✓ 1.1   Designing a solution infrastructure that meets business requirements

- ✓ 1.2   Designing a solution infrastructure that meets technical requirements

- ✓ 1.5   Envisioning future solution improvements

One of the things that distinguishes a cloud architect from a cloud engineer is the architect's need to work with *business requirements*. Architects work with colleagues responsible for business strategy, planning, development, and operations. Before architects can begin to design solutions, they need to understand their organization's cloud vision and objectives that the business is trying to achieve. These objectives frame the possible solutions that are acceptable to the business.

When it comes to the Professional Cloud Architect exam, business requirements are pieces of information that will help you determine the most appropriate answer to some of the questions. It is important to remember that questions on the exam may have more than one answer that appears correct, but only one answer is the best solution to the problem posed. For example, a question may ask about a small business application that needs to store data in a relational database, and the database will be accessed by only a few users in a single office. You *could* use the globally scalable relational database Cloud Spanner to solve this problem, but Cloud SQL would be a better fit to the requirements and cost less. If you come across a question that seems to have more than one answer, consider all of the technical *and* business requirements. You may find that more than one option meets the technical or the business requirements, but only one option meets both.

This chapter reviews several key areas where business requirements are important to understand, including the following:

- Business use cases and product strategy
- Application design and cost considerations
- Systems integration and data management
- Compliance and regulations
- Security
- Success measures

Throughout the chapter, I will reference the three case studies used in the Google Professional Cloud Architect exam.

Business Use Cases and Product Strategy

Business requirements may be high-level, broad objectives, or they may be tightly focused specifications of some aspect of a service. *High-level objectives* are tied to strategy, or plan, to meet some vision and objective. These statements give us clues as to what the cloud solution will look like. In fact, we can often estimate a number of technical requirements just from statements about business strategy and product offerings.

Let's look at the three case studies and see what kinds of information can be derived to help formulate a solution.

Dress4Win Strategy

In the Dress4Win case study, the company's objective is to "help their users organize and manage their personal wardrobes using a web app and a mobile application." They are trying to achieve this objective by cultivating "an active social network that connects their users with designers and retailers," which leads to revenue "through advertising, e-commerce, referrals, and a freemium app model."

From these statements, we can derive several facts about any solution.

- This is a consumer application, so the scale of the overall problem is a function of the number of people using the service, the number of designers and retailers participating, and the number of products available.

- The solution includes web and mobile applications.

- The service acts as an intermediary connecting consumers with designers and retailers.

- The application supports advertising. It is not stated, but ads are commonly provided by a third-party service.

- The application supports e-commerce transactions, including purchases, returns, product catalogs, and referrals of customers to designers and retailers.

- The application supports both a free set of features and a premium set of features.

This list of business requirements helps us start to understand or at least estimate some likely aspects of the technical requirements. Here are some examples of technical implications that should be considered based on the facts listed previously:

- This is a consumer, e-commerce application, so it will probably need to support ACID transactions for purchases, returns, account balances, and so forth.

- Product attributes vary depending on the type of products. Shirts may have attributes such as color, size, and material, while belts have those attributes plus length. A NoSQL database, particularly a document database, which supports flexible schemas, may be a good option for a catalog database.

- The mobile app should provide for a good user experience even if connectivity is lost. Data may need to be synchronized between mobile devices and cloud databases.

- Customers, designers, and retailers will have to be authenticated. They will have access to different features of the application, so role-based access controls will be needed.

- On an e-commerce site using payment cards, payment data will need to be protected in compliance with the payment card industry and government regulations.

- E-commerce sites should be highly available in terms of both front-end and backend subsystems.

- Wardrobes are seasonal. Dress4Win may need to scale up during peak purchasing periods, such as the start of summer or winter.

- To have low-latency response times in the application, you may want to store static data, such as the product catalog, on a content delivery network (CDN).

- You should understand where customers are located and investigate any regulations that may apply in different regions. For example, if some customers are in the European Union (EU), you should plan for the GDPR requirements for consumer privacy and limitations on storing EU citizen data outside of the EU.

These are just possible requirements, but it helps to keep them in mind when analyzing a use case. This example shows how many possible requirements can be inferred from just a few statements about the business and product strategy. It also shows that architects need to draw on their knowledge of systems design to anticipate requirements that are not explicitly stated, such as the need to keep application response times low, which in turn may require the use of a CDN.

Mountkirk Games Strategy

Mountkirk Games is a company that makes "online, session-based, multiplayer games for mobile platforms," and it is currently "building a new game, which they expect to be very popular." The company is already using cloud computing. In the Mountkirk Games case study, we see an example of a product strategy that is focused on correcting the limitations of the current solution.

The executive statement notes, "Our last successful game did not scale well with our previous cloud provider, resulting in lower user adoption and affecting the game's reputation. Our investors want more KPIs to evaluate the speed and stability of the game, as well as other metrics that provide deeper insight into usage patterns so that we can adapt the game to target users."

From these statements, we can derive several facts about any solution.

- Scalability is a top concern. Since scalability is a function of the entire solution, we will need to consider how to scale application processing services, storage systems, and analytic services.

- User experience is a top concern because that affects the game's reputation. Games are designed for mobile devices, and players should have a good gaming experience in spite of connectivity problems.

- To ensure a good gaming experience, a user's game should not be disrupted if a Compute Engine instance fails. Load balancing of stateless services and live migration of VMs support this need.

- The company expects the game to be popular, so any solution should scale quickly. The solution will likely include infrastructure-as-code, such as instance templates.

- The game will need to collect performance metrics and store them in a way that allows for KPI reporting. Since the company plans to deploy the game backend on Google Compute Engine, Stackdriver is a good option for monitoring and logging.

- The company will analyze usage patterns. This may require collecting game state data on short intervals. The data will need to be stored in a database that can write with low latency and readily scale. This may be a use case for Bigtable, but more information is required to know for sure.

- Analysts will probably need support for exploratory data analysis and analytic processing. BigQuery would be a good option for meeting this requirement.

- Depending on the type of analysis, the company may want to use Cloud Dataproc for Spark and Hadoop-based analysis. If so, they may want to use Cloud Dataflow to pre-process data before loading it for analysis. Additional information is needed to know for sure.

Here again, we see that business and product strategy can help us understand some likely requirements. There is not enough information in the business requirements to make definitive decisions about technical solutions, but they do allow us to start formulating possible solutions.

TerramEarth Strategy

The TerramEarth business problem is summed up in the executive statement: "Our competitive advantage has always been in our manufacturing process, with our ability to build better vehicles for lower cost than our competitors. However, new products with different approaches are constantly being developed, and I'm concerned that we lack the skills to undergo the next wave of transformations in our industry. My goals are to build our skills while addressing immediate market needs through incremental innovations."

The executive here wants to continue to compete but is concerned that the company does not have the collective skills needed to do so. The objective is to build those skills over time while releasing incremental improvements. Let's break that down into business processes that can support both of those objectives.

It is not clear what skills are needed to continue to innovate, but any skills involving mechanical engineering and manufacturing processes are outside the scope of cloud solution design. If the skills include analytical skills to understand customer needs and equipment performance better, then they fall within the scope of this effort.

"Releasing incremental improvements" fits well with agile software development and continuous integration/continuous deployment practices. Incremental improvements could be targeted at improving the experience for the 500 dealers or at improving the quality of analysis and predictive modeling.

The business focus in this case is on responding to competitive pressures in a market where new products with different approaches are frequently released. The business strategy statement here does not provide as much information about product requirements, but we can anticipate some possible solution components.

- If agile practices are not in place, they will likely be adopted. Solutions will include support for tools such as code repositories and continuous integration/continuous deployment.

- Services that implement the solution should be monitored to help identify problems, bottlenecks, and other issues. Stackdriver may be used for collecting metrics and logging.

- Analytics skills should be developed and supported with data management and analysis services. A data warehouse may be needed to store large amounts of data for use in data analysis, in which case BigQuery would be a good option. Big data analytics platforms, like Spark and Hadoop, may be used by data scientists. AutoML Tables may be useful for building classification models for predicting parts failures.

If this were a real-world use case, architects would gather more information about the specific business objectives. This is a good example of a case study that requires architects to exercise "soft skills," such as soliciting information from colleagues and describing possible solutions to help identify missed requirements.

Business requirements are a starting point for formulating a technical solution. Architects have to apply their knowledge of systems design to map business requirements into possible technical requirements. After that, they can dig into explicit technical requirements to start to formulate technical solutions.

The key point of this section is that business requirements are not some kind of unnecessary filler in the case studies. They provide the broad context in which a solution will be developed. While they do not provide enough detail to identify solution components on their own, they do help us narrow the set of feasible technical solutions. Business requirements can help you rule out options to an exam question. For example, a data storage solution that distributes data across multiple regions by default may meet all technical requirements, but if a business requirement indicates the data to be stored must be located in a specific country, then the correct answer is the one that lets you limit where the data is stored.

Application Design and Cost Considerations

In addition to specifying business and product strategy, business requirements may state things that you should consider in application design, such as a preference for managed services and the level of tolerance for disruptions in processing. Implicit in business requirements is the need to minimize costs while meeting business objectives.

One measure of costs is *total cost of ownership (TCO)*. TCO is the combination of all expenses related to maintaining a service, which can include the following:

- Software licensing costs

- Cloud computing costs, including infrastructure and managed services

- Cloud storage costs
- Data ingress and egress charges
- Cost of DevOps personnel to develop and maintain the service
- Cost of third-party services used in an application
- Charges against missed service-level agreements
- Network connectivity charges, such as those for a dedicated connection between an on-premises data center and Google Cloud

While you will want to minimize the TCO, you should be careful not to try to minimize the cost of each component separately. For example, you may be able to reduce the cost of DevOps personnel to develop and maintain a service if you increase your spending on managed services. Also, it is generally a good practice to find a feasible technical solution to a problem before trying to optimize that solution for costs.

Some of the ways to reduce costs while meeting application design requirements include managed services, preemptible virtual machines, and data lifecycle management. Google also offers sustained uses discounts and reserved VMs, which can help reduce costs.

Managed Services

Managed services are Google Cloud Platform services that do not require users to perform common configuration, monitoring, and maintenance operations. For example, Cloud SQL is a managed relational database service providing MySQL and PostgreSQL databases. Database administration tasks, such as backing up data and patching operating systems, are performed by Google and not by customers using the service. Managed services are good options when:

- Users do not need low-level control over the resources providing the service, such as choosing the operating system to run in a VM.
- Managed services provide a functionality that would be difficult or expensive to implement, such as developing a machine vision application.
- There is little competitive advantage to performing resource management tasks. For example, the competitive advantage that may come from using Apache Spark for analytics stems from the algorithms and analysis methodologies, not from the administration of the Spark cluster.

Architects do not necessarily need to know the details of how managed services work. This is one of their advantages. Architects do not need to develop an expertise in natural language processing to use the Cloud Natural Language API, but they do need to understand what kinds of functions managed services provide. See Table 2.1 for brief descriptions of some of the Google Cloud Platform managed services.

This table is provided to show the breadth of Google Cloud Platform managed services. The services offered change over time. Managed services may be generally available, or they can be in beta. For a list of current services, see the Google Platform Services Summary at `https://cloud.google.com/terms/services`.

TABLE 2.1   Examples of Google Cloud Platform Managed Services

Service Name	Service Type	Description
AutoML Tables	AI and machine learning	Machine learning models for structured data
Cloud AutoML	AI and machine learning	Trains machine learning models
Cloud Inference API	AI and machine learning	Correlations over time-series data
Cloud Speech-to-Text	AI and machine learning	Convert speech to text
Cloud Text-to-Speech	AI and machine learning	Convert text to speech
Natural Language	AI and machine learning	Text analysis, including sentiment analysis and classification
Translation	AI and machine learning	Translate text between languages
BigQuery	Analytics	Data warehousing and analytics
Cloud Datalab	Analytics	Interactive data analysis tool based on Jupyter Notebooks
Cloud Dataprep	Analytics	Explore, clean, and prepare structured data
Dataproc	Analytics	Managed Hadoop and Spark service
Google Data Studio	Analytics	Dashboard and reporting tool
Cloud Data Fusion	Data management	Data integration and ETL tool
Data Catalog	Data management	Metadata management service
Dataflow	Data management	Stream and batch processing
Cloud Spanner	Database	Global relational database

Service Name	Service Type	Description
Cloud SQL	Database	Relational database
Cloud Deployment Manager	Development	Infrastructure-as-code service
Cloud Source Control Repositories	Development	Version control and collaboration service
Cloud Pub/Sub	Messaging	Messaging service
Cloud Composer	Orchestration	Data workflow orchestration service
Bigtable	Storage	Wide column, NoSQL database
Cloud Data Transfer	Storage	Bulk data transfer service
Cloud Memorystore	Storage	Managed cache service using Redis
Cloud Storage	Storage	Managed object storage service

Preemptible Virtual Machines

One way to minimize computing costs is to use *preemptible virtual machines*, which are short-lived VMs that cost about 80 percent less than their nonpreemptible counterparts. Here are some things to keep in mind about preemptible VMs when considering business and technical requirements:

- Preemptible VMs may be shut down at any time by Google. They will be shut down after running for 24 hours.
- GCP will signal a VM before shutting down. The VM will have 30 seconds to stop processes gracefully.
- Preemptible VMs can have local SSDs and GPUs if additional storage and compute resources are needed.
- If you want to replace a preempted VM automatically, you can create a managed instance group for preemptible VMs. If resources are available, the managed instance group will replace the preempted VM.
- Preemptible VMs can be used with some managed services, such as Cloud Dataproc, to reduce the overall cost of the service.

Preemptible VMs are well suited for batch jobs or other workloads that can be disrupted and restarted. They are not suitable for running services that need high availability, such as a database or user-facing service, like a web server.

Preemptible VMs are also not suitable for applications that manage state in memory or on the local SSD. Preemptible VMs cannot be configured to live migrate; when they are shut down, locally persisted data and data in memory are lost. If you want to use pre-emptible VMs with stateful applications, consider using Cloud Memorystore, a managed Redis service for caching data, or using a database to store state.

Data Lifecycle Management

When assessing the application design and cost implications of business requirements, consider how to manage storage costs. Storage options lie on a spectrum from short term to archival storage.

- *Memorystore* is a cache, and data should be kept in cache only if it is likely to be used in the very near future. The purpose of this storage is to reduce the latency of accessing data.

- Databases, like *CloudSQL* and *Datastore*, store data that needs to be persistently stored and readily accessed by an application or user. Data should be stored in the database when it could possibly be queried or updated. When data is no longer required to be queried or updated, it can be exported and stored in object storage.

- In the case of *time-series databases*, data may be aggregated by larger time spans as time goes on. For example, an application may collect performance metrics every minute. After three days, there is no need to query to the minute level of detail, and data can be aggregated to the hour level. After one month, data can be aggregated to the day level. This incremental aggregation will save space and improve response times for queries that span large time ranges.

- *Object storage* is often used for unstructured data and backups. Multiregional and regional storage should be used for frequently accessed data. If data is accessed at most once a month, then Nearline storage can be used. When data is not likely to be accessed more than once a year, then Coldline storage should be used.

Consider how to take advantage of Cloud Storage's lifecycle management features, which allow you to specify actions to perform on objects when specific events occur. The two actions supported are deleting an object or changing its storage class. Multiregional and regional class storage objects can be migrated to either Nearline or Coldline storage. Nearline storage can migrate only to Coldline storage. Lifecycle conditions can be based on the following:

- The age of an object
- When it was created
- The object's storage class
- The number of versions of an object
- Whether or not the object is "live" (an object in nonversions bucketed is "live"; archived objects are not live)

It is worth noting that BigQuery has a two-tiered pricing model for data storage. Active data is data that has been modified in the last 90 days. Long-term data has not been accessed in the last 90 days, and it is billed at a lower rate than active data.

Systems Integration and Data Management

Business requirements can give information that is useful for identifying dependencies between systems and how data will flow through those systems.

Systems Integration Business Requirements

One of an architect's responsibilities is to ensure that systems work together. Business requirements will not specify technical details about how applications should function together, but they will state what needs to happen to data or what functions need to be available to users. Let's review examples of systems integration considerations in the case studies.

Dress4Win Systems Integration

In the Dress4Win case study, the description notes that the company generates revenue through referrals, presumably between customers and designers and retailers. To make referrals, a system must analyze customer data as well as designer and retailer profiles. The results of that analysis generate recommended matches.

The matching application will need to integrate data from customers, retailers, and designers. Most likely, this processing will be done in batch since it is not time sensitive. Also, this kind of analysis is best done with analytic platforms such as Cloud Dataproc or BigQuery, so data will need to flow from the e-commerce transaction system to an analytics system. This could require the use of Cloud Dataflow or Cloud Data Fusion, depending on the specific integration and data preprocessing requirements.

Mountkirk Games Systems Integration

Let's consider how datastores and microservices architectures can influence systems integration.

Online games, like those produced by Mountkirk Games, use more than one type of datastore. Player data, such as the player's in-game possessions and characteristics, could be stored in a document database like Cloud Datastore, while the time-series data could be stored in Bigtable, and billing information may be kept in a transaction processing relational database. Architects should consider how data will be kept complete and consistent across datastores. For example, if a player purchases a game item, then the application needs to ensure that the item is added to the player's possession record in the player database and that the charge is authorized by the payment system. If the payment is not authorized, the possession should not be available to the player.

It is likely that Mountkirk Games uses a microservices architecture. Microservices are single services that implement one single function of an application, such as storing player data or recording player actions. An aggregation of microservices implements an application. Microservices make their functions accessible through application programming interfaces (APIs). Depending on security requirements, services may require that calls to their API functions are authenticated. Services that are accessible only to other trusted game services may not require authentication. High-risk services, such as a payment service, may require more security controls than other services. Cloud Endpoints may help to manage APIs and help secure and monitor calls to microservices.

TerramEarth Systems Integration

From the description of the current system, we can see that on-board applications communicate with a centralized data collection system. Some of the data is collected in batches when vehicles are serviced, and some is collected as it is generated using cellular network communications. TerramEarth works with 500 dealers, and one of the business requirements is to "support the dealer network with more data on how their customers use their equipment to better position new products and services."

As part of planning for envisioning future needs, an architect working with TerramEarth should consider how to support more vehicles sending data directly, eventually retiring the batch data load process in favor of having real-time or near-real-time data uploads for all vehicles. This would require planning an ingest pipeline that could receive data reliably and consistently, and perform any preprocessing necessarily.

Services that store and analyze the data will need to scale to support up to tens of millions of vehicles transmitting data. To accomplish this, consider using a Cloud Pub/Sub queue, which allows decoupling and buffering so that data is not lost if the ingestion services cannot keep up with the rate that new data is received. This will ensure that data is not lost if ingestion services cannot keep up with the rate at which new data is received.

TerramEarth seeks to improve data sharing with dealers so that they can better understand how customers use their equipment. This will require integrating TerramEarth and dealer systems. The architect should gather additional details to understand how best to share data with dealers. For example, an architect may ask, "What features of the data are significant to dealers?" Also, architects should consider how dealers would access the data. Dealer applications could query TerramEarth APIs for data or TerramEarth could send data directly to dealer data warehouses or other reporting platforms.

Each case study has examples of systems integration requirements. When considering these requirements, keep in mind the structure and volume of data exchanged, the frequency of data exchange, the need for authentication, the reliability of each system, how to prevent data loss in the event of a problem with one of the services, and how to protect services from intentional or unintentional bursts in API requests that could overwhelm the receiving services.

Data Management Business Requirements

In addition to using business requirements to understand which systems need to work together, architects can use those requirements to understand data management business requirements. At a minimum, data management considerations include the following:

- How much data will be collected and stored?
- How long will it be stored?
- What processing will be applied to the data?
- Who will have access to the data?

How Much Data Is Stored?

One of the first questions asked about data management is "How much data are we expecting, and at what rate will we receive it?" Knowing the expected volumes of data will help plan for storage.

If data is being stored in a managed service like Cloud Storage, then Google will manage the provisioning of storage space, but you should still understand the volume of data so that you can accurately estimate storage costs and work within storage limits.

It is important to plan for adequate storage capacity. Those responsible for managing storage will also need to know the rate at which new data arrives and existing data is removed from the system. This will give the growth rate in storage capacity.

How Long Is Data Stored?

It is also important to understand how long data will be stored in various storage systems. Data may first arrive in a Cloud Pub/Sub queue, but it is immediately processed by a Cloud Function that removes the data from the queue, transforms the data, and writes it to another storage system. In this case, the data is usually in the queue for a short period of time. If the ingestion process is down, data may accumulate in the Cloud Pub/Sub topic. Since Cloud Pub/Sub is a managed service, the DevOps team would not have to allocate additional storage to the queue if there is a backup of data. GCP will take care of that. They will, however, have to consider how long the data should be retained in the queue. For example, there may be little or no business value in data that is more than seven days old. In that case, the team should configure the Cloud Pub/Sub queue with a seven-day retention period.

If data is stored in Cloud Storage, you can take advantage of the service's lifecycle policies to delete or change the storage class of data as needed. For example, if the data is rarely accessed after 45 days, data can be stored in Nearline or Coldline storage. If the data is accessed once per month or less, the Nearline storage is an appropriate choice. If it is accessed once a year or less, then Coldline storage is an appropriate choice.

When data is stored in a database, you will have to develop procedures for removing data that is no longer needed. In this case, the data could be backed up to Cloud Storage for archiving, or it could be deleted without keeping a copy. You should consider the trade-offs between the possible benefits of having data available and the cost of storing it. For instance, machine learning models can take advantage of large volumes of data, so it may be advisable to archive data even if you cannot anticipate a use for the data at this time.

What Processing Is Applied to the Data?

There are several things to consider about how data is processed. These include the following:

- Distance between the location of stored data and services that will process the data
- Volume of data that is moved from storage to processing services
- Acceptable latency when reading and writing the data
- Stream or batch processing
- In the case of stream processing, how long to wait for late arriving data

The distance between the location of data and where it is processed is an important consideration. This affects both the time it takes to read and write the data as well as, in some cases, the network costs for transmitting the data. If data will be accessed from multiple geographic regions, consider using multiregional storage when using Cloud Storage. If you are storing data in a relational database, consider replicating data to a read-only replica located in a region closer to where the data will be read. If there is a single write instance of the database, then this approach will not improve the time to ingest or update the data.

Understand if the data will be processed in batches or as a stream. Batch processes tend to tolerate longer latencies, so moving data between regions may not create problems for meeting business requirements around how fast the data needs to be processed. If data is now being processed in batch but it will be processed as a stream in the future, consider using Cloud Dataflow, Google's managed Apache Beam service. Apache Beam provides a unified processing model for batch and stream processing.

When working with stream processing, you should consider how you will deal with late arriving and missing data. It is a common practice in stream processing to assume that no data older than a specified time will arrive. For example, if a process collects telemetry data from sensors every minute, a process may wait up to five minutes for data. If the data has not arrived by then, the process assumes that it will never arrive.

Business requirements help shape the context for systems integration and data management. They also impose constraints on acceptable solutions. In the context of the exam, business requirements may infer technical requirements that can help you identify the correct answer to a question.

Compliance and Regulation

Businesses and organizations may be subject to one or more regulations. For example, it is likely that Mountkirk Games accepts payment using credit cards and so is subject to financial services regulations governing payment cards. Part of analyzing business requirements is to understand which, if any, regulations require compliance. Regulations have different requirements, depending on their objectives. Some widely recognized regulations include the following:

- *Health Insurance Portability and Accountability Act (HIPAA)*, which addresses privacy security of medical information in the United States.

- *General Data Protection Regulation (GDPR)*, which defines privacy protections for persons in and citizens of the European Union.

- The *Sarbanes-Oxley (SOX) Act*, which regulates business reporting of publicly traded companies to ensure the accuracy and reliability of financial statements in order to mitigate the risk of corporate fraud. This is a U.S. federal regulation.

- *Children's Online Privacy Protection Act (COPPA)* is a U.S. law that regulates websites that collect personal information to protect children under the age of 13.

- *Payment Card Industry Data Security Standard (PCI DSS)* is an industry security standards that applies to businesses that accept payment cards. The regulation specifies security controls that must be in place to protect cardholders' data.

It is important to understand what regulations apply to the systems you design. Some regulations apply because the business or organization developing cloud applications operates in a particular jurisdiction. HIPAA applies to healthcare providers in the United States. Companies that operate in the state of California in the United States may also subject to the California Consumer Privacy Act when it goes into effect in 2020. If a business operates in North America but has customers in Europe, it may be subject to GDPR.

Some regulations apply by virtue of the industry in which the business or organization operates. HIPAA governs healthcare providers and others with access to protected health information. Banks in the United States are subject to the Financial Services Modernization Act, also known as the Gram-Leach-Bliley Act (GLBA), specifying privacy protections for consumers' nonpublic financial information.

Privacy Regulations

Regulations placed on data are often designed to ensure privacy and protect the integrity of data. A large class of regulations govern privacy. HIPAA, GLBA, GDPR, and a host of national laws are designed to limit how personal data is used and to provide individuals with some level of control over their information. More than 40 countries, including the European Union and Singapore, have privacy regulations. (See https://www.privacypolicies.com/blog/privacy-law-by-country/ for a list of countries and links to additional information.) Industry regulations, like PCI DSS, also include protections for keeping data confidential.

From an architect's perspective, privacy regulations require that we plan on ways to protect data through its entire lifecycle. This begins when data is collected, for example, when a patient enters some medical information into a doctor's scheduling application. Protected data should be encrypted before transmitting it to cloud applications and databases. Data should also be encrypted when stored. This is sometimes called encrypting *data in motion* and *data at rest*.

Access controls should be in place to ensure that only authenticated and authorized persons and service accounts can access protected data. In some cases, applications may need to log changes to data. In those cases, logs must be tamperproof.

Networks and servers should be protected with firewalls and other measures to limit access to servers that process protected data. With Google Cloud, architects and developers can take advantage of the Cloud Identity-Aware Proxy to verify a user's identity in the context of a request to a service and determine whether that operation should be allowed.

Security best practices should be used as well. This includes following the *principle of least privilege,* so users and service accounts have only the permissions that are required to carry out their responsibilities. Also practice *defense in depth.* That principle assumes any security control may be compromised, so systems and data should be protected with multiple different types of controls.

Data Integrity Regulations

Data integrity regulations are designed to protect against fraud. SOX, for example, requires regulated business to have controls on systems that prevent tampering with financial data. In addition, businesses need to be able to demonstrate that they have these controls in place. This can be done with application logs and reports from security systems, such as vulnerability scanners or anti-malware applications.

Depending on regulations, applications that collect or process sensitive data may need to use message digests and digital signing to protect data with tamper-proof protections.

Many of the controls used to protect privacy, such as encryption and blocking mechanisms, like firewalls, are also useful for protecting data integrity.

In addition to stated business requirements, it is a good practice to review compliance and regulations with the business owners of the systems that you design. You will often find that the security protections required by regulations overlap with the controls that are used in general to secure information systems and data.

Security

Information security, also known as infosec and cybersecurity, is a broad topic. In this section, you will focus on understanding high-level security requirements based on business requirements. Chapter 7, "Designing for Security and Legal Compliance," will go into more detail on cloud security measures.

Business requirements for security tend to fall into three areas: confidentiality, integrity, and availability.

Confidentiality

Confidentiality is about limiting access to data. Only users and service accounts with legitimate business needs should have access to data. Even if regulations do not require keeping some data confidential, it is a good practice to protect confidentiality. Using HTTPS instead of HTTP and encrypting data at rest should be standard practice. Fortunately, for GCP users, Google Cloud provides encryption at rest by default.

When we use default encryption, Google manages the encryption keys. This requires the least work from customers and DevOps teams. If there is a business requirement that the customer and not Google manage the keys, you can design for customer-managed encryption keys using Cloud KMS, or you can use customer-supplied encryption keys. In the former case, keys are kept in the cloud. When using customer-supplied keys, they are stored on-premises.

Protecting servers and networks is also part of ensuring confidentiality. When collecting business requirements, look for requirements for additional measures, for example if a particular hardened operating system must be used. This can limit your choice of computing services. Also determine what kind of authentication is required. Will two-factor authentication be needed? Start thinking about roles and permissions. Will custom IAM roles be required? Determine what kinds and level of audit logging are required.

Integrity

Protecting *data integrity* is a goal of some of the regulations discussed earlier, but it is a general security requirement in any business application. The basic principle is that only people or service accounts with legitimate business needs should be able to change data, and then only for legitimate business purposes.

Access controls are a primary tool for protecting data integrity. Google Cloud Platform has defined a large number of roles to grant permissions easily according to common business roles. For example, App Engine has roles for administrators, code viewers, deployers, and others. This allows security administrators to assign fine-grained roles to users and service accounts while still maintaining least privileges.

Server and network security measures also contribute to protecting data integrity.

When collecting and analyzing business requirements, seek to understand the roles that are needed to carry out business operations and which business roles or positions will be assigned those roles. Pay particular attention to who is allowed to view and update data and use separate roles for users who have read-access only.

Availability

Availability is a bit different from confidentiality and integrity. Here the goal is to ensure that users have access to a system. Malicious activities, such as distributed denial-of-service (DDoS) attacks, malware infection, and encrypting data without authorization can degrade availability.

During the requirements-gathering phase of a project, consider any unusual availability requirements. With respect to security, the primary focus is on preventing malicious acts. From a reliability perspective, availability is about ensuring redundant systems and failover mechanisms to ensure that services continue to operate in spite of component failures.

Security should be discussed when collecting business requirements. At this stage, it is more important to understand what the business expects in terms of confidentiality, integrity, and availability. We get into technical and implementation details after first understanding the business requirements.

Success Measures

Businesses and other organizations are moving to the cloud because of its value. Businesses can more efficiently develop, deploy, and run applications, especially when they design in ways that take advantage of the cloud. Decision-makers typically want to measure the value of their projects. This enables them to allocate resources to the more beneficial projects while avoiding others that may not prove worthwhile. Two common ways to measure progress and success are key performance indicators and return on investment.

Key Performance Indicators

KPIs are a measurable value of some aspect of the business or operations that indicates how well the organization is achieving its objectives. A sales department may have total value of sales in the last week as a KPI, while a DevOps team might use CPU utilization as a KPI of efficient use of compute resources.

Project KPIs

Project managers may use KPIs to measure the progress of a cloud migration project. KPIs in that case may include a volume of data migrated to the cloud and no longer stored on-premises, a number of test cases run each day in the cloud instead of on-premises, or the number of workload hours running in the cloud instead of on-premises.

You can see from these examples that KPIs can be highly specific and tailored to a particular kind of project. Often, you will have to define how you will measure a KPI. For example, a workload hour may be defined based on the wall clock time and the number of CPUs dedicated to a workload.

The definition of a KPI should allow for an obvious way to measure the indicator. The details of the definition should be stated early in the project to help team members understand the business objectives and how they will be measured.

Operations KPI

Line-of-business managers may use KPIs to measure how well operations are running. These KPIs are closely aligned with business objectives. A retailer may use total sales revenue, while a telecommunications company may monitor reduction in customer churn, in other words, customers taking their business to a competitor. A financial institution that makes loans might use the number of applications reviewed as a measure of how well the business is running.

For architects, it is important to know how the business will measure the success of a project or operations. KPIs help us understand what is most important to the business and what drives decision-makers to invest in a project or line of business.

Return on Investment

ROI is a way of measuring the monetary value of an investment. ROI is expressed as a percentage, and it is based on the value of some aspect of the business after an investment when compared to its value before the investment. The return, or increase or loss, after an investment divided by the cost of the investment is the ROI. The formula for ROI is as follows:

$$ROI = [(value\ of\ investment - cost\ of\ investment)\ /\ cost\ of\ investment] * 100$$

For example, if a company invests $100,000 in new equipment and this investment generates a value of $145,000, then the ROI is 45 percent.

In cloud migration projects, the investment includes the cost of cloud services, employee and contractor costs, and any third-party service costs. The value of the investment can include the expenses saved by not replacing old equipment or purchasing new equipment, savings due to reduced power consumption in a data center, and new revenue generated by applications and services that scale up in the cloud but were constrained when run on-premises.

Success measures such as KPIs and ROI are a formal way of specifying what the organization values with respect to a project or line of business. As an architect, you should know which success measures are being used so that you can understand how the business measures the value of the systems that you design.

Summary

The first stages of a cloud project should begin with understanding the business use cases and product strategy. This information sets the context for later work on the technical requirements analysis.

One part of business requirements analysis includes application design and cost considerations. Application design considerations include assessing the possible use of managed services and preemptible virtual machines. Data lifecycle management is also a factor in application design.

In addition to business drivers, consider regulations that may apply to your projects. Many regulations are designed to protect individuals' privacy or to ensure the integrity of data to prevent fraud. Compliance with regulations may require additional security controls or application features that otherwise would not be implemented.

Security business requirements can be framed around three objectives: protecting confidentiality, preserving the integrity of data, and ensuring the availability of services, especially with respect to malicious acts that could disrupt services.

Business and other organizations will often monitor the progress of projects and the efficiency and profitability of lines of business using success measures, such as KPIs and ROI.

Exam Essentials

Study the three case studies: Dress4Win, Mountkirk Games, and TerramEarth.   You will have access to the case studies during the exam, but you can save time if you are already familiar with the details of each. Also, think through the implications of the business requirements in order to understand how they constrain technical solution options.

Understand business terms like total cost of ownership (TCO), key performance indicators (KPIs), and return on investment (ROI).   You will almost certainly not have to calculate any of these measures, but you should understand what they measure and why they are used by business executives and analysts.

Learn about Google Cloud Platform managed services and for what purposes they are used.   These services can be used instead of deploying and managing applications and managing servers, storage, networking, and so forth. If a business requirement includes using managed services or reducing the workload on a DevOps team, you may be able to use one or more of these services to solve problems presented on the exam.

Understand the elements of data management.   This includes how much data will be collected and stored, how long it will be stored, what processing will be applied to it, and who will have access to it.

Understand how compliance with regulations can introduce additional business requirements.   Businesses and organizations may be subject to one or more regulations. Part of analyzing business requirements is to understand which, if any, regulations require compliance.

Understand the three main aspects of security with respect to business requirements.   They are confidentiality, integrity, and availability. Confidentiality focuses on limiting access to data to those who have a legitimate business need for it. Integrity ensures that data is not tampered with or corrupted in ways that could enable fraud or other misuse. Availability addresses the need to prevent malicious acts from disrupting access to services.

Know why decision-makers use success measures.   Two well-known success measures are KPIs and ROI. KPIs are measures that are specific to a business operation. ROI is a general measure based on the cost of an investment versus the additional benefit realized because of that investment.

Review Questions

1. In the Dress4Win case study, the volume of data and compute load will grow with respect to what factor?

   A. The number of customers, designers, and retailers

   B. The time the application is running

   C. The type of storage used

   D. Compliance with regulations

2. You have received complaints from customers about long wait times while loading application pages in their browsers, especially pages with several images. Your director has tasked you with reducing latency when accessing and transmitting data to a client device outside the cloud. Which of the following would you use? (Choose two.)

   A. Multiregional storage

   B. Coldline storage

   C. CDN

   D. Cloud Pub/Sub

   E. Cloud Dataflow

3. Mountkirk Games will analyze game players' usage patterns. This will require collecting time-series data including game state. What database would be a good option for doing this?

   A. BigQuery

   B. Bigtable

   C. Cloud Spanner

   D. Cloud Storage

4. You have been hired to consult with a new data warehouse team. They are struggling to meet schedules because they repeatedly find problems with data quality and have to write preprocessing scripts to clean the data. What managed service would you recommend for addressing these problems?

   A. Cloud Dataflow

   B. Cloud Dataproc

   C. Cloud Dataprep

   D. Cloud Datastore

5. You have deployed an application that receives data from sensors on TerramEarth equipment. Sometimes more data arrives than can be processed by the current set of Compute Engine instances. Business managers do not want to run additional VMs. What changes could you make to ensure that data is not lost because it cannot be processed as it is sent from the equipment? Assume that business managers want the lowest-cost solution.

   A. Write data to local SSDs on the Compute Engine VMs.

   B. Write data to Cloud Memorystore, and have the application read data from the cache.

   C. Write data from the equipment to a Cloud Pub/Sub queue, and have the application read data from the queue.

   D. Tune the application to run faster.

6. Your company uses Apache Spark for data science applications. Your manager has asked you to investigate running Spark in the cloud. Your manager's goal is to lower the overall cost of running and managing Spark. What would you recommend?

   A. Run Apache Spark in Compute Engine.

   B. Use Cloud Dataproc with preemptible virtual machines.

   C. Use Cloud Dataflow with preemptible virtual machines.

   D. Use Cloud Memorystore with Apache Spark running in Compute Engine.

7. You are working with a U.S. hospital to extract data from an electronic health record (EHR) system. The hospital has offered to provide business requirements, but there is little information about regulations in the documented business requirements. What regulations would you look to for more guidance on complying with relevant regulations?

   A. GDPR

   B. SOX

   C. HIPAA

   D. PCI DSS

8. What security control can be used to help detect changes to data?

   A. Firewall rules

   B. Message digests

   C. Authentication

   D. Authorization

9. Your company has a data classification scheme for categorizing data as secret, sensitive, private, and public. There are no confidentiality requirements for public data. All other data must be encrypted at rest. Secret data must be encrypted with keys that the company controls. Sensitive and private data can be encrypted with keys managed by a third party. Data will be stored in GCP. What would you recommend in order to meet these requirements while minimizing cost and administrative overhead?

   A. Use Cloud KMS to manage keys for all data.

   B. Use Cloud KMS for secret data and Google default encryption for other data.

   C. Use Google default encryption for all data.

   D. Use a custom encryption algorithm for all data.

10. You manage a service with several databases. The queries to the relational database are increasing in latency. Reducing the amount of data in tables will improve performance and reduce latency. The application administrator has determined that approximately 60 percent of the data in the database is more than 90 days old and has never been queried and does not need to be in the database. You are required to keep the data for five years in case it is requested by auditors. What would you propose to decrease query latency without increasing costs—or at least keeping any cost increases to a minimum?

   A. Horizontally scale the relational database.

   B. Vertically scale the relational database.

   C. Export data more than 90 days old, store it in Cloud Storage Coldline class storage, and delete that data from the relational database.

   D. Export data more than 90 days old, store it in Cloud Storage multiregional class storage, and delete that data from the relational database.

11. Your company is running several custom applications that were written by developers who are no longer with the company. The applications frequently fail. The DevOps team is paged more for these applications than any others. You propose replacing those applications with several managed services in GCP. A manager who is reviewing your cost estimates for using managed services in GCP notes that the cost of the managed services will be more than what they pay for internal servers. What would you recommend as the next step for the manager?

   A. Nothing. The manager is correct—the costs are higher. You should reconsider your recommendation.

   B. Suggest that the manager calculate total cost of ownership, which includes the cost to support the applications as well as infrastructure costs.

   C. Recommend running the custom applications in Compute Engine to lower costs.

   D. Recommend rewriting the applications to improve reliability.

12. A director at Mountkirk Games has asked for your recommendation on how to measure the success of the migration to GCP. The director is particularly interested in customer satisfaction. What KPIs would you recommend?

   A. Average revenue per customer per month

   B. Average time played per customer per week

   C. Average time played per customer per year

   D. Average revenue per customer per year

13. Mountkirk Games is implementing a player analytics system. You have been asked to document requirements for a stream processing system that will ingest and preprocess data before writing it to the database. The preprocessing system will collect data about each player for one minute and then write a summary of statistics about that database. The project manager has provided the list of statistics to calculate and a rule for calculating values for missing data. What other business requirements would you ask of the project manager?

   A. How long to store the data in the database?

   B. What roles and permissions should be in place to control read access to data in the database?

   C. How long to wait for late-arriving data?

   D. A list of managed services that can be used in this project

14. A new data warehouse project is about to start. The data warehouse will collect data from 14 different sources initially, but this will likely grow over the next 6 to 12 months. What managed GCP service would you recommend for managing metadata about the data warehouse sources?

  A. Data Catalog

  B. Cloud Dataprep

  C. Cloud Dataproc

  D. BigQuery

15. You are consulting for a multinational company that is moving its inventory system to GCP. The company wants to use a managed database service, and it requires SQL and strong consistency. The database should be able to scale to global levels. What service would you recommend?

  A. Bigtable

  B. Cloud Spanner

  C. Cloud Datastore

  D. BigQuery

16. TerramEarth has interviewed dealers to better understand their needs regarding data. Dealers would like to have access to the latest data available, and they would like to minimize the amount of data they have to store in their databases and object storage systems. How would you recommend that TerramEarth provide data to their dealers?

  A. Extract dealer data to a CSV file once per night during off-business hours and upload it to a Cloud Storage bucket accessible to the dealer.

  B. Create an API that dealers can use to retrieve specific pieces of data on an as-needed basis.

  C. Create a database dump using the database export tool so that dealers can use the database import tool to load the data into their databases.

  D. Create a user account on the database for each dealer and have them log into the database to run their own queries.

17. Your company has large volumes of unstructured data stored on several network-attached storage systems. The maintenance costs are increasing, and management would like to consider alternatives. What GCP storage system would you recommend?

  A. Cloud SQL

  B. Cloud Storage

  C. Cloud Datastore

  D. Bigtable

18. A customer-facing application is built using a microservices architecture. One of the services does not scale as fast as the service that sends it data. This causes the sending service to wait while the other service processes the data. You would like to change the integration to use asynchronous instead of synchronous calls. What is one way to do this?

A. Create a Cloud Pub/Sub topic, have the sending service write data to the topic, and have the receiving service read from the topic.

B. Create a Cloud Storage bucket, have the sending service write data to the topic, and have the receiving service read from the topic.

C. Have the sending service write data to local drives, and have the receiving service read from those drives.

D. Create a Bigtable database, have the sending service write data to the topic, and have the receiving service read from the topic.

19. A product manager at TerramEarth would like to use the data that TerramEarth collects to predict when equipment will break down. What managed services would you recommend TerramEarth to consider?

A. Bigtable

B. Cloud Dataflow

C. Cloud AutoML

D. Cloud Spanner

Chapter

3

Designing
for Technical
Requirements

**THE PROFESSIONAL CLOUD ARCHITECT
CERTIFICATION EXAM OBJECTIVES
COVERED IN THIS CHAPTER INCLUDE
THE FOLLOWING:**

✓ **1.2 Designing a solution infrastructure that meets
technical requirements**

The Google Cloud Professional Architect exam will test your ability to understand technical requirements that are explicitly stated, as well as implied, in case studies and questions.

Technical requirements may specify a particular hardware or software constraint. For example, an application may need to use a MySQL 5.7 database or be able to transmit 1 GB of data between an on-premises data center and the Google Cloud Platform. Technical requirements do not necessarily specify all of the details that you will need to know. If a question states that a virtual private cloud will have three subnets, then you will have to infer from that statement that the subnets will need to be configured with distinct, nonoverlapping address spaces. It is common for questions about technical requirements to require you to choose among multiple solutions and to understand some unstated implication of the requirement so that you can make a choice among possible solutions.

In this chapter, we will consider three broad categories of technical requirements:

- High availability
- Scalability
- Reliability

We will use the case studies as jumping-off points for discussing these kinds of requirements. We will consider how each of these factors influences the choices we make about compute, storage, networking, and specialized services.

The most important piece of information to take away from this chapter is that availability, scalability, and reliability are not just important at the component or subsystem level but across the entire application infrastructure. Highly reliable storage systems will not confer high reliability on a system if the networking or compute services are not reliable.

High Availability

High availability is the continuous operation of a system at sufficient capacity to meet the demands of ongoing workloads. Availability is usually measured as a percent of time that a system is available and responding to requests with latency not exceeding some certain threshold. Table 3.1 shows the amount of allowed downtime at various *service-level agreement (SLA)* levels. An application with a 99 percent availability SLA can be down for 14.4 minutes per day, while a system with a 99.999 percent availability can be down for less than 1 second per day without violating the SLA.

TABLE 3.1 Example availability SLAs and corresponding downtimes

Percent Uptime	Downtime/Day	Downtime/Week	Downtime/Month
99.00	14.4 minutes	1.68 hours	7.31 hours
99.90	1.44 minutes	10.08 minutes	43.83 minutes
99.99	8.64 seconds	1.01 minutes	4.38 minutes
99.999	864 milliseconds	6.05 seconds	26.3 seconds
99.9999	86.4 milliseconds	604.8 milliseconds	2.63 seconds

High availability SLAs, such as these, have to account for the fact that hardware and software fails. Individual physical components, such as a disk drive running in a particular disk array, may have a small probability of failing in a one-month period. If you are using thousands of drives, then it is much more likely that at least one of them will fail.

When designing high availability applications, you have to plan for failures. Failures can occur at multiple points in an application stack:

- An application bug
- A service that the application depends on is down
- A database disk drive fills up
- A network interface card fails
- A router is down
- A network engineer misconfigures a firewall rule

We can compensate for hardware failures with *redundancy*. Instead of writing data to one disk, we write it to three disks. Rather than have a single server running an application, we create instance groups with multiple servers and load balance workload among them. We install two direct network connections between our data center and the GCP—preferably with two different telecommunication vendors. Redundancy is also a key element of ensuring scalability.

We compensate for software and configuration errors with software engineering and *DevOps* best practices. Code reviews, multiple levels of testing, and running new code in a staging environment can help identify bugs before code is released to production. Canary deployments, in which a small portion of a system's workload is routed to a new version of the software, allows us to test code under production conditions without exposing all users to new code. If there is a problem with the new version of software, it will affect only a portion of the users before it is rolled back. Automating infrastructure deployments, by treating infrastructure as code, reduces the need for manual procedures and the chance to make a mistake when entering commands.

As you design systems with an eye for high availability, keep in mind the role of redundancy and best practices for software development and DevOps.

Compute Availability

The GCP offers several compute services. We'll consider availability in four of these services:

- Compute Engine
- Kubernetes Engine
- App Engine
- Cloud Functions

Each of these services can provide high availability compute resources, but they vary in the amount of effort required to achieve high availability.

High Availability in Compute Engine

High availability in *Compute Engine* is ensured by several different mechanisms and practices.

Hardware Redundancy and Live Migration

At the physical hardware level, the large number of physical servers in the GCP provide redundancy for hardware failures. If a physical server fails, others are available to replace it.

Google also provides *live migration*, which moves VMs to other physical servers when there is a problem with a physical server or scheduled maintenance has to occur. Live migration is also used when network or power systems are down, security patches need to be applied, or configurations need to be modified. Live migration is not available for preemptible VMs, however, but preemptible VMs are not designed to be highly available. At the time of this writing, VMs with GPUs attached are not available to live migrate. Constraints on live migration may change in the future. The descriptions of Google services here are illustrative and designed to help you learn how to reason about GCP services in order to answer exam questions. This book should not be construed as documentation for GCP services.

Managed Instance Groups

High availability also comes from the use of redundant VMs. *Managed instance groups* are the best way to create a cluster of VMs, all running the same services in the same configuration. A managed instance group uses an *instance template* to specify the configuration of each VM in the group. Instance templates specify machine type, boot disk image, and other VM configuration details. If a VM in the instance group fails, another one will be created using the instance template.

Managed instance groups (MIGs) provide other features that help improve availability. A VM may be operating correctly, but the application running on the VM may not be functioning as expected. Instance groups can detect this using an application-specific health check. If an application fails the health check, the managed instance group will create a new instance. This feature is known as *auto-healing*.

Managed instance groups use load balancing to distribute workload across instances. If an instance is not available, traffic will be routed to other servers in the instance group. Instance groups can be configured as regional instance groups. This distributes instances across multiple zones. If there is a failure in a zone, the application can continue to run in the other zones.

Multiple Regions and Global Load Balancing

Beyond the regional instance group level, you can further ensure high availability by running your application in multiple regions and using a global load balancer to distribute workload. This would have the added advantage of allowing users to connect to an application instance in the closest region, which could reduce latency. You would have the option of using the *HTTP(S)*, *SSL Proxy*, or *TCP Proxy* load balancers for global load balancing.

High Availability in Kubernetes Engine

Kubernetes Engine is a managed Kubernetes service that is used for container orchestration. Kubernetes is designed to provide highly available containerized services. High availability in GKE *Kubernetes clusters* comes both from Google's technical processes and from the design of Kubernetes itself.

VMs in a GKE Kubernetes cluster are members of a managed instance group, and so they have all of the high availability features described previously.

Kubernetes continually monitors the state of containers and pods. Pods are the smallest unit of deployment in Kubernetes; they usually have one container, but in some cases a pod may have two or more tightly coupled containers. If pods are not functioning correctly, they will be shut down and replaced. Kubernetes collects statistics, such as the number of desired pods and the number of available pods, which can be reported to Stackdriver.

By default, Kubernetes Engine creates a cluster in a single zone. To improve availability, you can create a regional cluster in GKE, the managed service that distributes the underlying VMs across multiple zones within a region. GKE replicates masters and nodes across zones. Masters are servers that run the Kubernetes control plane, which includes the API server, scheduler, and resource controllers. This provides continued availability in the event of a zone failure. The redundant masters allow the cluster to continue to function even if one of the masters is down for maintenance or fails.

High Availability in App Engine and Cloud Functions

App Engine and *Cloud Functions* are fully managed compute services. Users of these services are not responsible for maintaining the availability of the computing resources. The Google Cloud Platform ensures the high availability of these services.

Of course, App Engine and Cloud Functions applications and functions may fail and leave the application unavailable. This is a case where the software engineering and DevOps best practices can help improve availability.

High Availability Computing Requirements in Case Studies

All three case studies have requirements for high availability computing.

- In the *Mountkirk Games case study*, there is no mention of high availability. This does not mean that it is not required. Given the nature of online games, users expect to be able to continue to play once they start and until they decide to stop. The case study specifies that the backend game engine will run on Compute Engine so that the company can take advantage of autoscaling, a feature of managed instance groups. In addition, they plan to collect streaming metrics and perform intensive analytics so that they can report on KPIs. Without highly available servers to ingest, analyze, and store streaming metrics, data would be lost.

- The *Dress4Win case study* notes that the first phase of their project will focus on moving the development and test environments. These generally do not require the same level of availability as production services. The company is also developing a disaster recovery site that, when in use, would have to meet the same availability SLAs as the production environment.

  There is more discussion about scalability than availability in the Dress4Win case study, but many of the architecture choices that you would make for scalability contribute to high availability.

- In the *TerramEarth case study*, the need for high availability is implied in the business and technical requirements. One of the technical requirements states, "[u]se customer and equipment data to anticipate customer needs." The 200,000 connected vehicles operating 22 hours a day stream a total of 9 TB of data each day. That data would be lost if it could not be ingested.

Storage Availability

Highly available storage is storage that is available and functional at nearly all times. The storage services can be grouped into the following categories:

- Object storage
- File and block storage
- Database services

Let's look at availability in each type of storage service.

Availability vs. Durability

Availability should not be confused with *durability*, which is a measure of the probability that a stored object will be inaccessible at some point in the future. A storage system can be highly available but not durable. For example, in Compute Engine, locally attached storage is highly available because of the way Google manages VMs. If there was a problem with the local storage system, VMs would be live migrated to other physical servers. Locally attached drives are not durable, though. If you need durable drives, you could use Persistent Disk or Cloud Filestore, the fully managed file storage service.

Availability of Object, File, and Block Storage

Cloud Storage is a fully managed object storage service. Google maintains high availability of the service. As with other managed services, users do not have to do anything to ensure high availability.

Cloud Filestore is another managed storage service. It provides filesystem storage that is available across the network. High availability is ensured by Google.

Persistent disks are SSDs and hard disk drives that can be attached to VMs. These disks provide block storage so that they can be used to implement filesystems and database storage. Persistent disks continue to exist even after the VMs shut down. One of the ways in which persistent disks enable high availability is by supporting online resizing. If you find that you need additional storage, you can add storage of up to 64 TB per persistent disk. Also, GCP offers both zone persistent disks and region persistent disks. Regional persistent disks are replicated in two zones within a region.

Availability of Databases

GCP users can choose between running database servers in VMs that they managed or using one of the managed database services.

Self-Managed Databases

When running and managing a database, you will need to consider how to maintain availability if the database server or underlying VM fails. Redundancy is the common approach to ensuring availability in databases. How you configure multiple database servers will depend on the database system you are using.

For example, PostgreSQL has several options for using combinations of master servers, hot standby servers, and warm standby servers. A hot standby server can take over immediately in the event of a master server failure. A warm standby may be slightly behind in reflecting all transactions. PostgresSQL employs several methods for enabling failover, including the following:

- *Shared disk*, in which case multiple databases share a disk. If the master server fails, the standby starts to use the shared disk.

- *Filesystem replication*, in which changes in the master server filesystem are mirrored on the failover server's filesystem.

- *Synchronous multimaster replication*, in which each server accepts writes and propagates changes to other servers.

Other database management systems offer similar capabilities. The details are not important for taking the Professional Cloud Architect exam, but it is important to understand how difficult it is to configure and maintain highly available databases. In contrast, if you were using Cloud SQL, you could configure high availability in the console by checking a Create Failover Replica box.

Managed Databases

GCP offers several managed databases. All have high availability features.

Fully managed and serverless databases, such as *Cloud Datastore* and *BigQuery*, are highly available, and Google attends to all of the deployment and configuration details to ensure high availability.

Cloud Firestore is the next generation Datastore. The exam may mention Cloud Datastore or Cloud Firestore. For the purposes of this book, we can consider the two names synonymous. Always refer to the Google documentation for the latest nomenclature.

The database servers that require users to specify some server configuration options, such as Cloud SQL and *Bigtable*, can be made more or less highly available based on the use of regional replication. For example, in Bigtable, regional replication enables primary-primary replication among clusters in different zones. This means that both clusters can accept reads and writes, and changes are propagated to the other cluster. In addition to reads and writes, regional replication in Bigtable replicates other changes, such as updating data, adding or removing column families, and adding or removing tables.

In general, the availability of databases is based on the number of replicas and their distribution. The more replicas and the more they are dispersed across zones, the higher the availability. Keep in mind that as you increase the number of replicas, you will increase costs and possibly latency if all replicas must be updated before a write operation is considered successful. Also consider if the data storage system you choose is available within a zone or globally.

High Availability Storage Requirements in Case Studies

The technical requirements for Mountkirk Games state that the company currently uses a MySQL database.

The executive statement notes, "replace MySQL and move to an environment that provides autoscaling, low latency load balancing, and that frees us up from managing physical servers." Cloud SQL running MySQL meets the requirements to free the company from managing physical servers, but it does not provide autoscaling. The MySQL database is used for reporting and analytics, so this is a good candidate for BigQuery.

BigQuery is a fully managed database, with load distribution and autoscaling. This meets the requirement to "dynamically scale up or down based on game activity." It also uses SQL as a query language, so users would not have to learn a new query language and existing reporting tools will likely work with BigQuery. BigQuery is also a good option for meeting the requirement to store at least 10 TB of historical data. (Currently, Cloud SQL can store up to 10 TB, which makes BigQuery a good choice).

There is a requirement to "process data that arrives late because of slow mobile networks." This requirement could be satisfied using a common ingestion and preprocessing pattern of writing data to a Cloud Pub/Sub topic, which is read by a Cloud Dataflow process and transformed as needed and then written to BigQuery.

The Dress4Win storage requirements include specifications for database storage, network-attached storage, and storage for the Spark cluster. If they use Cloud SQL instead of a self-managed MySQL server, they can improve storage availability by using regional replicas. Using Cloud Storage will provide highly available storage for images, logs, and backups. If Dress4Win decides to use *Cloud Dataproc* instead of managing its own Spark cluster, then storage availability will be managed by the Google Cloud Platform.

TerramEarth needs to store 9 TB of equipment data per day. This data is time-series data, which means that each record has a time stamp, identifiers indicating the piece of equipment that generated the data, and a series of metrics. Bigtable is a good option when you need to write large volumes of data in real time at low latency. Bigtable has support for regional replication, which improves availability. Regional or zonal persistent disk can be used with Compute Engine VMs. Regional persistent disks provide higher availability if needed.

Network Availability

When network connectivity is down, applications are unavailable. There are two primary ways to improve network availability:

- Use redundant network connections
- Use Premium Tier networking

Redundant network connections can be used to increase the availability of the network between an on-premises data center and google's data center. One type of connection is a *dedicated interconnect*, which can be used with a minimum of 10 Gbps throughput and does not traverse the public Internet. A *Partner Interconnect* is another option. In this case, traffic flows through a telecommunication provider's network, not the Internet. VPNs can also be used when sending data over the Internet is not a problem. You should choose among these options based on cost, security, throughput, latency, and availability considerations.

Data within the GCP can be transmitted among regions using the public Internet or Google's internal network. The latter is available as the *Premium Network Tier*, which costs more than the *Standard Network Tier*, which uses the public Internet. The internal Google network is designed for high availability and low latency, so the Premium Tier should be considered if global network availability is a concern.

High Availability Network Requirements in Case Studies

The case studies do not provide explicit networking requirements other than an implied expectation that the network is always available. The TerramEarth case study notes that cellular networks may be slow or unavailable, and the applications will need to account for late-arriving data.

An architect could inquire about additional requirements that might determine if Premium Tier networking is required or if multiple network connections among on-premises and Google data centers is needed.

Application Availability

Application availability builds on compute, storage, and networking availability. It also depends on the application itself. Designing software for high availability is beyond the scope of this book, and it is not a subject you will likely be tested on when taking the Professional Cloud Architect exam.

Architects should understand that they can use Stackdriver monitoring to monitor the state of applications so that they can detect problems as early as possible. Applications that are instrumented with custom metrics can provide application-specific details that could be helpful in diagnosing problems with an application.

Scalability

Scalability is the process of adding and removing infrastructure resources to meet work-load demands efficiently. Different kinds of resources have different scaling characteristics. Here are some examples:

▪ VMs in a managed instance group scale by adding or removing instances from the group.

▪ Kubernetes scales *pods* based on load and configuration parameters.

▪ NoSQL databases scale horizontally, but this introduces issues around consistency.

▪ Relational databases can scale horizontally, but that requires server clock synchronization if strong consistency is required among all nodes. *Cloud Spanner* uses the *TrueTime service*, which depends on atomic clocks and GPS signals to track time.

As a general rule, scaling stateless applications horizontally is straightforward. Stateful applications are difficult to scale horizontally, and vertical scaling is often the first choice when stateful applications must scale. Alternatively, stateful applications can move state information out of the individual containers or VMs and store it in a cache, like Cloud Memorystore, or in a database. This makes scaling horizontally less challenging.

Remember that different kinds of resources will scale at different rates. Compute-intensive applications may need to scale compute resources at a faster rate than storage. Similarly, a database that supports large volumes that is not often queried may need to scale up storage faster than compute resources. To facilitate efficient scaling, it helps to decouple resources that scale at different rates.

For example, front-end applications are often needed to scale according to how many users are active on the system and how long requests take to process. Meanwhile, the database server may have enough resources to meet peak demand load without scaling up. When resources are difficult to scale, consider deploying for peak capacity. Relational databases, other than Cloud Spanner, and network interconnects are examples of resources that are difficult to scale. In the case of a non-Spanner relational database, you could scale by running the database on a server with more CPUs and memory. This is vertical scaling, which is limited to the size of available instances. For networks, you could add additional interconnects to add bandwidth between sites. Both of these are disruptive operations compared to scaling a stateless application by adding virtual machines to a cluster, which users might never notice.

Scaling Compute Resources

Compute Engine and Kubernetes Engine support automatic scaling of compute resources. App Engine and Cloud Functions *autoscale* as well, but they are managed by the Google Compute Platform.

Scaling Compute in Compute Engine

In Compute Engine, you can scale the number of VMs running your application using managed instance groups, which support autoscaling. *Unmanaged instance groups* do not support autoscaling.

Autoscaling can be configured to scale based on several attributes, including the following:

- Average CPU utilization
- HTTP load balancing capacity
- Stackdriver monitoring metrics

The autoscaler collects the appropriate performance data and compares it to targets set in an autoscaling policy. For instance, if you set the target CPU utilization to 80 percent, then the autoscaler will add or remove VMs from the managed instance group to keep the CPU utilization average for the group close to 80 percent.

When a *Stackdriver agent* is running on VMs in an instance group, you can specify targets for metrics collected by the agent. Some of the metrics collected by the Stackdriver agent are as follows:

- `api_request_count`
- `log_entry_count`
- `memory_usage`
- `uptime`

By default, autoscalers use data from the previous 10 minutes when making decisions about scaling down. This is done to prevent frequent changes to the cluster based on short-term changes in utilization, which could lead to thrashing, or adding and removing VMs in rapid succession.

Before a VM is removed from a group, it can optionally run a shutdown script to clean up. The shutdown script is run on a best-effort basis.

When an instance is added to the group, it is configured according the configuration details in the instance template.

Scaling Compute in Kubernetes Engine

Kubernetes is designed to manage containers in a cluster environment. Recall that containers are an isolation mechanism that allows processes on the same operating system to run with isolated resources. Kubernetes does not scale containers directly; instead, autoscaling is based on Kubernetes abstractions.

The smallest computational resource in Kubernetes is a *pod*. Pods contain containers. Pods run on *nodes*, which are VMs in managed instance groups. Pods usually contain one container, but they can include more. When pods have more than one container, those containers are usually tightly coupled, such as one container running analysis code while the other container runs ancillary services, such as data cleansing services. Containers in the same pod should have the same scaling characteristics since they will be scaled up and down together.

Pods are organized into deployments. A *deployment* is a functioning version of an application. An application may run more than one deployment at a time. This is actually commonly done to roll out new versions of code. A new deployment can be run in a cluster, and a small amount of traffic can be sent to it to test the new code in a production environment without exposing all users to the new code. This is an example of a *canary deployment*. Groups of deployments constitute a *service*, which is the highest level of application abstraction.

Kubernetes can scale the number of nodes in a cluster, and it can scale the number of replicas and pods running a deployment. Kubernetes Engine automatically scales the size of the cluster based on load. If a new pod is created and there are not enough resources in the cluster to run the pod, then the autoscaler will add a node. Nodes exist within *node pools*, which are nodes with the same configuration. When a cluster is first created, the number and type of nodes created become the default node pool. Other node pools can be added later if needed.

When you deploy applications to Kubernetes clusters, you have to specify how many replicas of an application should run. A replica is implemented as a pod running application containers. Scaling an application is changing the number of replicas to meet the demand.

Kubernetes provides for autoscaling the number of replicas. When using autoscaling, you specify a minimum and maximum number of replicas for your application along with a target that specifies a resource, like CPU utilization, and a threshold, such as 80 percent. Since Kubernetes Engine 1.9, you can specify custom metrics in Stackdriver as a target.

One of the advantages of containerizing applications is that they can be run in Kubernetes Engine, which can automatically scale the number of nodes or VMs in a cluster. It can also scale how those cloud resources are allocated to different services and their deployments.

Scaling Storage Resources

Storage resources are virtualized in GCP, and some are fully managed services, so there are parallels between scaling storage and compute resources.

The least scalable storage system is locally attached SSDs on VMs. Up to eight local SSDs can be attached to a VM. Locally attached storage is not considered a persistent storage option. Data will be retained during reboots and live migrations, but it is lost when the VM is terminated or stopped. Local data is lost from preemptible VMs when they are preempted.

Zonal and *regional persistent disks* and *persistent SSDs* can scale up to 64 TB per VM instance. You should also consider read and write performance when scaling persistent storage. Standard disks have a maximum sustained read *IO operations per second (IOPS)* of 0.75 per gigabyte and write IOPs of 1.5 per gigabyte. Persistent SSDs have a maximum sustained read and write IOPS of 30 per gigabyte. As a general rule, persistent disks are well suited for large-volume, batch processing when low cost and high storage volume are important. When performance is a consideration, such as when running a database on a VM, persistent SSDs are the better option.

Adding storage to a VM is a two-step process. You will need to allocate persistent storage and then issue operating system commands to make the storage available to the filesystem. The commands are operating system specific.

Managed services, such as Cloud Storage and BigQuery, ensure that storage is available as needed. In the case of BigQuery, even if you do not scale storage directly, you may want to consider partitioning data to improve query performance. Partitioning organizes data in a way that allows the query processor to scan smaller amounts of data to answer a query. For example, assume that Mountkirk Games is storing summary data about user sessions in BigQuery. The data includes a date indicating the day that the session data was collected. Analysts typically analyze data at the week and month levels. If the data is partitioned by week or month, the query processor would scan only the partitions needed to answer the query. Data that is outside the date range of the query would not have to be scanned. Since BigQuery charges by the amount of data scanned, this can help reduce costs.

Network Design for Scalability

Connectivity between on-premise data centers and Google data centers doesn't scale the way storage and compute scales. You need to plan ahead for what is the upper limit of what will be needed. You should plan for peak capacity, although you may only pay for bandwidth used depending on your provider.

Reliability

Reliability is a measure of the likelihood of a system being available and able to meet the needs of the load on the system. When analyzing technical requirements, it is important to look for reliability requirements. As with availability and scalability, these requirements may be explicit or implicit.

Designing for reliability requires that you consider how to minimize the chance of system failures. For example, we employ redundancy to mitigate the risk of a hardware failure leaving a crucial component unavailable. We also use DevOps best practices to manage risks with configuration changes and when managing infrastructure as code. These are the same practices that we employ to ensure availability.

You also need to consider how to respond when systems do fail. Distributed applications are complicated. A single application may depend on multiple *microservices*, each with a number of dependencies on other services, which may be developed and managed by another team within the organization or may be a third-party service.

Measuring Reliability

There are different ways to measure reliability, but some are more informative than others.

Total system uptime is one measure. This sounds simple and straightforward, but it is not—at least when dealing with distributed systems. Specifically, what measure do you use to determine whether a system is up? If at least one server is available, is a system up? If there was a problem with an instance group in Compute Engine or the pods in a Kubernetes deployment, you may be able to respond to some requests but not others. If your definition of uptime is based on just having one or some percentage of desired VMs or pods running, then this may not accurately reflect user experience with regard to reliability.

Rather than focus on the implementation metrics, such as the number of instances available, reliability is better measured as a function of the work performed by the service. The number of requests that are successfully responded to is a good basis for measuring reliability. *Successful request rate* is the percentage of all application requests that are successfully responded to. This measure has the advantage of being easy to calculate and of providing a good indicator for the user experience.

Reliability Engineering

As an architect, you should consider ways to support reliability early in the design stage. This should include the following:

- *Identifying how to monitor services.* Will they require custom metrics?

- *Considering alerting conditions.* How do you balance the need for early indication that a problem may be emerging with the need to avoid overloading DevOps teams with unactionable alerts?

- *Using existing incident response procedures with the new system.* Does this system require any specialized procedures during an incident? For example, if this is the first application to store confidential, personally identifying information, you may need to add procedures to notify the information security team if an incident involves a failure in access controls.

- *Implementing a system for tracking outages and performing post-mortems* to understand why a disruption occurred.

Designing for reliability engineering requires an emphasis on organizational and management issues. This is different than designing for high availability and scalability, which is dominated by technical considerations. As an architect, it is important to remember that your responsibilities include both technical and management aspects of system design.

Summary

Architects are constantly working with technical requirements. Sometimes these requirements are explicitly stated, such as when a line-of-business manager states that the system will need to store 10 TB of data per day or that the data warehouse must support SQL. In other cases, you have to infer technical requirements from other statements. If a streaming application must be able to accept late-arriving data, this implies the need to buffer data when it arrives and to specify how long to wait for late data.

Some technical requirements are statements of constraints, like requiring that a database be implemented using MySQL 5.7. Other technical requirements require architects to analyze multiple business needs and other constraints in order to identify requirements. Many of these fall into the categories of high availability, scalability, and reliability. Compute, storage, and networking services should be designed to support the levels of availability, scalability, and reliability that the business requires.

Exam Essentials

Understand the differences between availability, scalability, and reliability.   High availability is the continuous operation of a system at sufficient capacity to meet the demands of ongoing workloads. Availability is usually measured as a percentage of time that a system is available. Scalability is the process of adding and removing infrastructure resources to meet workload demands efficiently. Reliability is a measure of how likely it is that a system will be available and capable of meeting the needs of the load on the system.

Understand how redundancy is used to improve availability.   Compute, storage, and network services all use redundancy to improve availability. Clusters of identically configured VMs behind a load balancer is an example of using redundancy to improve availability. Making multiple copies of data is an example of redundancy used to improve storage availability. Using multiple direct connections between a data center and Google Cloud is an example of redundancy in networking.

Know that managed services relieve users of many responsibilities for availability and scalability.   Managed services in GCP take care of most aspects of availability and scalability. For example, Cloud Storage is highly available and scalable, but users of the service do not have to do anything to enable these capabilities.

Understand how Compute Engine and Kubernetes Engine achieve high availability and scalability.   Compute Engine uses managed instance groups, which include instance templates and autoscalers, to achieve high availability and scale to meet application load. Kubernetes is a container orchestration service that provides higher-level abstractions for deploying applications on containers. Pods scale as needed to meet demands on the cluster and on application services.

Understand reliability engineering is about managing risk.   Designing for reliability requires you to consider how to minimize the chance of system failures. For example, architects employ redundancy to mitigate the risk of a hardware failure leaving a crucial component unavailable. Rather than focus on the implementation metrics, such as number of instances available, reliability is better measured as a function of the work performed by the service. The number of requests that are successfully responded to is a good basis for measuring reliability.

Review Questions

1. You are advising a customer on how to improve the availability of a data storage solution. Which of the following general strategies would you recommend?

   A. Keeping redundant copies of the data

   B. Lowering the network latency for disk writes

   C. Using a NoSQL database

   D. Using Cloud Spanner

2. A team of data scientists is analyzing archived data sets. The model building procedures run in batches. If the model building system is down for up to 30 minutes per day, it does not adversely impact the data scientists' work. What is the minimal percentage availability among the following options that would meet this requirement?

   A. 99.99 percent

   B. 99.90 percent

   C. 99.00 percent

   D. 99.999 percent

3. Your development team has recently triggered three incidents that resulted in service disruptions. In one case, an engineer mistyped a number in a configuration file and in the other cases specified an incorrect disk configuration. What practices would you recommend to reduce the risk of these types of errors?

   A. Continuous integration/continuous deployment

   B. Code reviews of configuration files

   C. Vulnerability scanning

   D. Improved access controls

4. Your company is running multiple VM instances that have not had any downtime in the past several weeks. Recently, several of the physical servers suffered disk failures. The applications running on the servers did not have any apparent service disruptions. What feature of Compute Engine enabled that?

   A. Preemptible VMs

   B. Live migration

   C. Canary deployments

   D. Redundant array of inexpensive disks

5. You have deployed an application on an instance group. The application is not functioning correctly. What is a possible outcome?

   A. The application shuts down when the instance group time-to-live (TTL) threshold is reached.

   B. The application shuts down when the health check fails.

    C. The VM shuts down when the instance group TTL threshold is reached and a new VM is started.

    D. The VM shuts down when the health check fails and a new VM is started.

6. Mountkirk Games is growing its user base in North America, Europe, and Asia. Executives are concerned that players in Europe and Asia will have a degraded experience if the game backend runs only in North America. What would you suggest as a way to improve latency and game experience for users in Europe and Asia?

    A. Use Cloud Spanner to have a globally consistent, horizontally scalable relational database.

    B. Create instance groups running the game backend in multiple regions across North America, Europe, and Asia. Use global load balancing to distribute the workload.

    C. Use Standard Tier networking to ensure that data sent between regions is routed over the public Internet.

    D. Use a Cloud Memorystore cache in front of the database to reduce database read latency.

7. What configuration changes are required to ensure high availability when using Cloud Storage or Cloud Filestore?

    A. A sufficiently long TTL must be set.

    B. A health check must be specified.

    C. Both a TTL and health check must be specified.

    D. Nothing. Both are managed services. GCP manages high availability.

8. The finance director in your company is frustrated with the poor availability of an on-premises finance data warehouse. The data warehouse uses a commercial relational database that only scales by buying larger and larger servers. The director asks for your advice about moving the data warehouse to the cloud and if the company can continue to use SQL to query the data warehouse. What GCP service would you recommend to replace the on-premises data warehouse?

    A. Bigtable

    B. BigQuery

    C. Cloud Datastore

    D. Cloud Storage

9. TerramEarth has determined that it wants to use Cloud Bigtable to store equipment telemetry data transmitted over their cellular network. They have also concluded that they want two clusters in different regions. Both clusters should be able to respond to read and write requests. What kind of replication should be used?

    A. Primary–hot primary

    B. Primary–warm primary

    C. Primary–primary

    D. Primary read–primary write

10. Your company is implementing a hybrid cloud computing model. Line-of-business owners are concerned that data stored in the cloud may not be available to on-premises applications. The current network connection is using a maximum of 40 percent of bandwidth. What would you suggest to mitigate the risk of that kind of service failure?

   A. Configure firewall rules to improve availability.

   B. Use redundant network connections between the on-premises data center and Google Cloud.

   C. Increase the number of VMs allowed in Compute Engine instance groups.

   D. Increase the bandwidth of the network connection between the data center and Google Cloud.

11. A team of architects in your company is defining standards to improve availability. In addition to recommending redundancy and code reviews for configuration changes, what would you recommend to include in the standards?

   A. Use of access controls

   B. Use of managed services for all compute requirements

   C. Use of Stackdriver monitoring to alert on changes in application performance

   D. Use of Bigtable to collect performance monitoring data

12. Why would you want to run long-running, compute-intensive backend computation in a different managed instance group than on web servers supporting a minimal user interface?

   A. Managed instance groups can run only a single application.

   B. Managed instance groups are optimized for either compute or HTTP connectivity.

   C. Compute-intensive applications have different scaling characteristics from those of lightweight user interface applications.

   D. There is no reason to run the applications in different managed instance groups.

13. An instance group is adding more VMs than necessary and then shutting them down. This pattern is happening repeatedly. What would you do to try to stabilize the addition and removal of VMs?

   A. Increase the maximum number of VMs in the instance group.

   B. Decrease the minimum number of VMs in the instance group.

   C. Increase the time autoscalers consider when making decisions.

   D. Decrease the time autoscalers consider when making decisions.

14. Dress4Win has just developed a new feature for its social networking service. Customers can upload images of their clothes, create montages from those images, and share them on social networking sites. Images are temporarily saved to locally attached drives as the customer works on the montage. When the montage is complete, the final version is copied to a Cloud Storage bucket. The services implementing this feature run in a managed instance group. Several users have noted that their final montages are not available even though they saved them in the application. No other problems have been reported with the service. What might be causing this problem?

   A. The Cloud Storage bucket is out of storage.

   B. The locally attached drive does not have a filesystem.

C. The users experiencing the problem were using a VM that was shut down by an autoscaler, and a cleanup script did not run to copy the latest version of the montage to Cloud Storage.

D. The network connectivity between the VMs and Cloud Storage has failed.

15. Kubernetes uses several abstractions to model and manage computation and applications. What is the progression of abstractions from the lowest to the highest level ?

A. Pods → Deployments → Services

B. Pods → Services → Deployments

C. Deployments → Services → Pods

D. Deployments → Pods → Services

16. Your development team has implemented a new application using a microservices architecture. You would like to minimize DevOps overhead by deploying the services in a way that will autoscale. You would also like to run each microservice in containers. What is a good option for implementing these requirements in Google Cloud Platform?

A. Run the containers in Cloud Functions.

B. Run the containers in Kubernetes Engine.

C. Run the containers in Cloud Dataproc.

D. Run the containers in Cloud Dataflow.

17. TerramEarth is considering building an analytics database and making it available to equipment designers. The designers require the ability to query the data with SQL. The analytics database manager wants to minimize the cost of the service. What would you recommend?

A. Use BigQuery as the analytics database, and partition the data to minimize the amount of data scanned to answer queries.

B. Use Bigtable as the analytics database, and partition the data to minimize the amount of data scanned to answer queries.

C. Use BigQuery as the analytics database, and use data federation to minimize the amount of data scanned to answer queries.

D. Use Bigtable as the analytics database, and use data federation to minimize the amount of data scanned to answer queries.

18. Line-of-business owners have decided to move several applications to the cloud. They believe the cloud will be more reliable, but they want to collect data to test their hypothesis. What is a common measure of reliability that they can use?

A. Mean time to recovery

B. Mean time between failures

C. Mean time between deployments

D. Mean time between errors

19. A group of business executives and software engineers are discussing the level of risk that is acceptable for a new application. Business executives want to minimize the risk that the service is not available. Software engineers note that the more developer time dedicated to reducing risk of disruption, the less time they have to implement new features. How can you formalize the group's tolerance for risk of disruption?

   A. Request success rate

   B. Uptime of service

   C. Latency

   D. Throughput

20. Your DevOps team recently determined that it needed to increase the size of persistent disks used by VMs running a business-critical application. When scaling up the size of available persistent storage for a VM, what other step may be required?

   A. Adjusting the filesystem size in the operating system

   B. Backing up the persistent disk before changing its size

   C. Changing the access controls on files on the disk

   D. Update disk metadata, including labels

Chapter 4

Designing Compute Systems

**THE PROFESSIONAL CLOUD ARCHITECT
CERTIFICATION EXAM OBJECTIVES
COVERED IN THIS CHAPTER INCLUDE
THE FOLLOWING:**

✓ **1.3   Designing network, storage, and compute resources**

✓ **2.3   Configuring compute systems**

Google Cloud Platform offers several kinds of compute resources that provide varying levels of controls, features, and management support. In this chapter, we will discuss the foundations of designing compute systems. This begins with understanding these four compute services:

- Compute Engine
- App Engine
- Kubernetes Engine
- Cloud Functions

Each of these four services serves different use cases, although there are use cases that would benefit from using two or more of these services. Knowing how to choose among these is an important skill for architects to develop.

Compute resources require varying levels of provisioning, depending on the compute service. We will discuss using preemptible and standard virtual machines in Compute Engine, understanding the difference between App Engine Standard and App Engine Flexible, designing Kubernetes clusters, and deploying Cloud Functions. Network configuration and infrastructure provisioning using an infrastructure-as-code (IaC) approach is also described.

We will also discuss several common design issues, including managing state in distributed systems, designing data flows and pipelines, data integrity, and monitoring and alerting.

Other compute services are available, such as *Anthos* and *Cloud Run*. Additional compute services may be offered in the future as well.

Compute Services and Use Cases

One of the primary drivers for using public clouds such as the Google Cloud Platform is the ability to access compute resources. Consider these use cases:

- Early public clouds provided access to basic virtual machines, but cloud providers have expanded the type of compute services offered. Google Cloud Platform offers *platform-as-a-service (PaaS)* with App Engine.
- The ability to run small functions in response to events without setting up and managing servers for those functions is especially useful in distributed, cloud applications. This capability is available with Cloud Functions.

- Containers are an efficient way to deploy distributed systems based on microservices, but managing a large number of containers quickly becomes a challenge. Google created its own container orchestration system and then released it into open source as Kubernetes. Google Cloud Platform now offers a fully managed Kubernetes service called *Kubernetes Engine* (known as GKE).

For the Google Cloud Professional Architect exam, it is important to know the features and use cases for each of these compute services. Expect to see questions that ask you to choose the correct compute option for particular scenarios.

Compute Engine

Compute Engine is Google's *infrastructure-as-a-service (IaaS)* offering. It is also the building block for other services that run on top of this compute resource. The core functionality provided by Compute Engine is *virtual machines*. Virtual machines (VMs) in Google Cloud Platform are also known as *instances*.

Specifying a Virtual Machine

When creating a VM, you will need to specify several types of information such as machine type, availability status, and enhanced security controls.

Machine Types and Service Accounts

Instances are provisioned by specifying *machine types*, which are differentiated by the number of CPUs and the amount of memory allocated to the instance. Machine types that have balanced CPU and memory are known as *standard instances*. There are also *highmem* and *highcpu* types, which have more memory and CPUs, respectively, than standard machine types. Google has recently added *ultramem* and *megamem* memory-optimized types as well. Users can also specify customized machine types by specifying vCPUs, memory, CPU platform, number of GPUs, and GPU platform.

When creating an instance, you also specify a boot image. You can choose from a set of predefined boot images, or you can create your own based on one of the predefined boot images. When specifying a boot image, you can also specify *standard persistent disk* or *SSD persistent disk* as well as the size of the disk.

Data is encrypted automatically. You can choose to use Google managed keys, or you can manage keys yourself and store them in the cloud by using the *Google Cloud Key Management Service*. If you prefer to manage and store keys outside of GCP, you can use customer-supplied keys.

VMs can have one to eight network interfaces.

A VM also has a service account associated with it. A *service account* is a type of identity. Service accounts have permissions bound to them. The service account enables VMs to perform actions that would otherwise require a user to execute a task. For example, if a service account has permission to write to a Cloud Storage bucket, a process on the VM can write to that bucket using the service account.

If you need to ensure that your VMs run only on physical servers with other VMs from the same project, you can select *sole tenancy* when provisioning instances.

Preemptible Virtual Machines

VMs can be standard or *preemptible*. Standard VMs continue to run until you shut them down or there is a failure in the VM. If a standard VM fails, it will be migrated to another physical server by default. *Preemptible virtual machines* run up to 24 hours before they are shut down by GCP. They can be shut down at any time before then as well. When a preemptible VM is shut down, processes on the instance will have 30 seconds to shut down gracefully.

Shielded VMs

Shielded VMs are instances with enhanced security controls, including the following:

- Secure boot
- vTPM
- Integrity monitoring

Secure boot runs only software that is verified by digital signatures of all boot components using UEFI firmware features. If some software cannot be authenticated, the boot process fails. *Virtual Trusted Platform Module (vTPM)* is a virtual module for storing keys and other secrets. *Integrity monitoring* compares the boot measurements with a trusted baseline and returns true if the results match and false otherwise.

VMs can be created using the cloud console (`console.cloud.google.com`) or by using the GCP command-line utility, `gcloud`. For details on how to do this, see the *Official Google Cloud Certified Associate Cloud Engineer Study Guide* (Sybex, 2019).

VMs can also be created automatically when using instance groups.

Instance Groups

Instance groups are clusters of VMs that are managed as a single unit. GCP supports two kinds of instance groups: managed and unmanaged. *Managed instance groups (MIGs)* contain identically configured instances. The configuration is specified in an instance template. *Unmanaged instance groups* are groups of VMs that may not be identical. They are not provisioned using an instance template. They are used only to support preexisting cluster configurations for load balancing tasks. Unmanaged instance groups are not recommended for new configurations.

An *instance template* defines a machine type, book disk image or container image, network settings, and other properties of a VM. The instance template can be used to create a single instance or a managed group of instances. Instance templates are global resources, so they can be used in any region. If you specify zonal resources in a template, however, they will have to be changed before using the template in another zone.

MIGs provide several advantages, including the following:

- Maintaining a minimal number of instances in the MIG. If an instance fails, it is automatically replaced.

- Autohealing using application health checks. If the application is not responding as expected, the instance is restarted.

- Distribution of instances across a zone. This provides resiliency in case of zonal failures.

- Load balancing across instances in the group.

- Autoscaling to add or remove instances based on workload.

- Auto-updates, including rolling updates and canary updates.

  - *Rolling updates* will update a minimal number of instances at a time until all instances are updated.

  - *Canary updates* allow you to run two versions of instance templates to test the newer version before deploying it across the group.

MIGs should be used when availability and scalability are required for VMs. This is usually the case in production systems.

Compute Engine Use Cases

Compute Engine provides flexible and customizable compute resources. Compute Engine is a good choice for a compute service when you need control over all aspects of a VM, including specifying the operating system, selecting enhanced security controls, and configuring attached storage.

Compute Engine instances can also be created using a container as a base image. In this case, Compute Engine will use a container-optimized operating system. Kubernetes Engine uses Compute Engine instance groups to implement *Kubernetes clusters*. If you prefer to take advantage of advanced container-orchestration features, you should use Kubernetes Engine. App Engine Flexible supports running custom containers in a platform-as-a-service. Kubernetes Engine and App Engine are described in detail later in this chapter.

You can manage all aspects of a VM when deploying Compute Engine instances by logging into instances as root or administrator. From there, you can install additional software, change access controls, and set up users and groups, among other things.

Compute Engine is also a good option when running stateful applications, like databases. You can configure persistent storage tailored to your needs. If you need to support high IOPS, then you can configure instances with SSD persistent disks. If you are deploying a cluster to run batch jobs that are not time sensitive, you could save on costs by using standard persistent disks, which are hard disk drives, instead.

If you need a highly secured environment, then Shielded VMs and sole tenancy can be enabled in Compute Engine instances. You can also manage your own disk encryption keys in Compute Engine. If you prefer to store keys in the cloud, you should use the Google Cloud Key Management Service. You can also store keys on-premises and manage them yourself as well.

App Engine

App Engine is a serverless PaaS compute offering. With App Engine, users do not have to configure servers since it is a fully managed service. They provide application code that is run in the App Engine environment. There are two forms of App Engine: App Engine Standard and App Engine Flexible.

App Engine Standard

App Engine Standard is a PaaS product that allows developers to run their applications in a serverless environment. There are restrictions, however, on the languages that can be used to develop those applications. Currently, App Engine Standard provides the following language-specific runtime environments:

- Go
- Java
- PHP
- Node.js
- Python

Each instance of an application running in App Engine Standard has an instance class that is determined by the CPU speed and the amount of memory. The default instance class is F1, which has a 600 MHz CPU limit and 256 MB of memory. The largest instance class, B8, provides a 4.8 GHz CPU and 2048 MB of memory. Other instance classes are listed at https://cloud.google.com/appengine/docs/standard/.

App Engine Standard is available in two forms: first generation and second generation. Second-generation services offer more memory and more runtimes. There are no plans to deprecate first-generation services at this time.

First-generation App Engine Standard supports Python 2.7, Java 8, PHP 5.5, and Go 1.9. Network access is restricted in some cases. Specifically, Python 2.7, PHP 5.5, and Go 1.9 can access the network only through a URL Fetch API. Java 8 and Go 1.11 both have full access. Python 2.7, PHP 5.5, and Go 1.9 have no filesystem access, but Java 8 and Go 1.11 have read and write access to the /tmp directory.

The second-generation App Engine Standard improves on first-generation capabilities in that it also supports Python 3.7, PHP 7.2 and 7.3, Node.js 8 and 10, Java 11, and Go 1.11 and 1.12 (beta). All languages can use any extension or library, have full access to the network, and have read and write access to the /tmp directory.

App Engine supported languages and features may change. See the Google Cloud App Engine documentation for the most up-to-date list of supported languages and environments along with instance classes.

App Engine Flexible

App Engine Flexible allows developers to customize their runtime environments by using Docker files. By default, the App Engine Flexible environment supports Java 8, Python 2.7 and Python 3.6, Node.js, Ruby, PHP, .NET core, and Go. The Java runtime does not support web-serving frameworks. Developers can customize these runtimes by providing custom Docker *images* or Dockerfiles. Since developers can provide custom containers, they can install custom packages and SSH into the containers. Developers can also specify how much CPU and memory is allocated to each instance.

App Engine Flexible provides health checks and automatically patches the underlying operating system. VMs are run in geographic regions specified by the GCP project containing the App Engine application. Also, VMs are restarted once a week. Operating system maintenance is performed at that time.

App Engine Use Cases

App Engine Standard is a good option when you have an application that is written in one of the supported languages and needs to scale rapidly up or down, depending on traffic. Instance startup time is on the order of seconds. Other the other hand, App Engine Flexible is a good choice when applications are run within a Docker container. App Engine Flexible scales, but startup time of instances is on the order of minutes, not seconds. It is also a good choice when your application uses microservices, when it depends on custom code, or when libraries are not available in App Engine Standard.

The following are the key differences between running containers in App Engine Flexible and running them in Compute Engine:

- App Engine Flexible containers are restarted once per week.
- By default, SSH access is disabled in an App Engine Flexible container, but you can enable it. SSH access is enabled by default in Compute Engine.
- Images in App Engine Flexible are built using the *Cloud Build* service. Images run in Compute Engine may use the Cloud Build service, but it is not necessary.
- The geographic location of App Engine Flexible instances is determined by project settings, and all App Engine Flexible instances are colocated for performance.

App Engine resources are regional, and GCP deploys resources redundantly across all zones in a region.

App Engine includes the *App Engine Cron Service*, which allows developers to schedule tasks to run at regular times or intervals.

In general, applications running in App Engine should be stateless. If state does need to be maintained, store it outside instances in a cache or database.

App Engine provides *Task Queues* to support operations that need to run asynchronously or in the background. Task Queues can use either a push or pull model. Task Queues are well suited for distributing tasks. If you need a publish/subscribe-type messaging service, then *Cloud Pub/Sub* is a good option.

App Engine Flexible provides some support for deploying applications with containers, but for full container orchestration services, consider using Kubernetes Engine.

Kubernetes Engine

Kubernetes Engine is a managed service providing *Kubernetes cluster management* and *Kubernetes container orchestration*. Kubernetes Engine allocates cluster resources, determines where to run containers, performs health checks, and manages VM lifecycles using Compute Engine instance groups.

Kubernetes Cluster Architecture

You can think of Kubernetes from the perspective of the VMs in the cluster or in terms of how applications function within the cluster.

Instances in Kubernetes

A Kubernetes cluster has two types of instances: cluster masters and nodes.

- The *cluster master* runs four core services that are part of the control plane: controller manager, API server, scheduler, and etcd.

    - The *controller manager* runs services that manage Kubernetes abstract components, such as deployments and replica sets.

    - Applications interacting with the Kubernetes cluster make calls to the master using the *API server*. The API server also handles intercluster interactions.

    - The *scheduler* is responsible for determining where to run pods, which are low-level compute abstractions that support containers.

    - *ectd* is a distributed key-value store used to store state information across a cluster.

    - *Nodes* are instances that execute workloads. They communicate with the cluster master through an agent called *kubelet*.

Kubernetes' Organizing Abstractions

Kubernetes introduces abstractions that facilitate the management of containers, applications, and storage services. Some of the most important are the following:

- Pods
- Services
- ReplicaSets
- Deployments
- PersistentVolumes
- StatefulSets
- Ingress

Pods are the smallest computation unit managed by Kubernetes. Pods contain one or more containers. Usually pods have just one container, but if the services provided by two containers are tightly coupled, then they may be deployed in the same container. For example, a pod may include a container running an extraction, transformation, and load process, as well as a container running ancillary services for decompressing and reformatting data. Multiple containers should be in the same pod only if they are functionally related and have similar scaling and lifecycle characteristics.

Pods are deployed to nodes by the scheduler. They are usually deployed in groups or replicas. This provides for high availability, which is especially needed with pods. Pods are ephemeral and may be terminated if they are not functioning properly. One of the advantages of Kubernetes is that it monitors the health of pods and replaces them if they are not functioning properly. Since multiple replicas of pods are run, pods can be destroyed without completely disrupting a service. Pods also support scalability. As load increases or decreases, the number of pods deployed for an application can increase or decrease.

Since pods are ephemeral, other services that depend on them need a way to discover them when needed. Kubernetes uses the service abstraction for this. A *service* is an abstraction with a stable API endpoint and stable IP address. Applications that need to use a service communicate with the API endpoints. A service keeps track of its associated pods so that it can always route calls to a functioning pod.

A *ReplicaSet* is a controller that manages the number of pods running for a deployment. *Deployments* are a type of controller consisting of pods running the same version of an application. Each pod in a deployment is created using the same template, which defines how to run a pod. The definition is called a *pod specification*.

Kubernetes deployments are configured with a desired number of pods. If the actual number of pods varies from the desired state, for example if a pod is terminated for being unhealthy, then the ReplicaSet will add or remove pods until the desired state is reached.

Pods may need access to persistent storage, but since pods are ephemeral, it is a good idea to decouple pods that are responsible for computation from persistent storage, which should continue to exist even after a pod terminates. *PersistentVolumes* is Kubernetes' way of representing storage allocated or provisioned for use by a pod. Pods acquire access to persistent volumes by creating a *PersistentVolumeClaim*, which is a logical way to link a pod to persistent storage.

Pods as described so far work well for stateless applications, but when state is managed in an application, pods are not functionally interchangeable. Kubernetes uses the Stateful set abstraction, which is similar to a deployment. *StatefulSets* are used to designate pods as stateful and assign a unique identifier to them. Kubernetes uses these to track which clients are using which pods and to keep them paired.

An *Ingress* is an object that controls external access to services running in a Kubernetes cluster. An Ingress Controller must be running in a cluster for an Ingress to function.

Kubernetes Engine Use Cases

Kubernetes Engine is a managed server that relieves users of managing their own Kubernetes cluster. Kubernetes is used to allocate compute resources efficiently to a pool of containers running applications. It is essential that applications and services be containerized before they can run in Kubernetes.

Kubernetes is a good platform for deploying microservices. If you prefer to minimize system administration overhead, you could deploy containers using App Engine Flexible. If you prefer to have more control over systems, then Kubernetes is a better option.

Cloud Functions

Cloud Functions is a serverless compute service well suited for event processing. The service is designed to respond to and execute code in response to events within the Google Cloud Platform. For example, if an image file is uploaded to Cloud Storage, a Cloud Function can execute a piece of code to transform the image or record metadata in a database. Similarly, if a message is written to a Cloud Pub/Sub topic, a Cloud Function may be used to operate on the message or invoke an additional process.

Events, Triggers, and Functions

Cloud Functions use three components: events, triggers, and functions. An *event* is an action that occurs in the GCP. Cloud Functions does not work with all possible events in the cloud platform; instead, it is designed to respond to five kinds of events.

- Cloud Storage
- Cloud Pub/Sub
- HTTP
- Firebase
- Stackdriver Logging

For each kind of event, there are different actions to which a Cloud Function can respond.

- *Cloud Storage* has upload, delete, and archive events.
- *Cloud Pub/Sub* recognizes message publishing events.
- *HTTP events* have five actions: GET, POST, PUT, DELETE, and OPTIONS.
- *Firebase* is a mobile application development platform that supports database triggers, remote configuration triggers, and authentication triggers.
- When a message is written to *Stackdriver Logging*, you can have it forwarded to Cloud Pub/Sub, and from there you can trigger a call to a cloud function.

A trigger in Cloud Functions is a specification of how to respond to an event. Triggers have associated functions. Currently, Cloud Functions can be written in Python 3, Go, and Node.js 8 and 10.

Cloud Function Use Cases

Cloud Functions are used for event-driven processing. The code is run in response to a triggering event, like a file being updated in Cloud Storage or a message written to a Cloud

Pub/Sub topic. Here are some specific use cases that demonstrate the range of uses for Cloud Functions:

- When an image is uploaded to a particular Cloud Storage bucket, a function verifies the image file type and converts to the preferred file type if needed.

- When a new version of code is uploaded to a code repository, trigger on a webhook and execute a function that sends a message to other developers who are watching changes to the code.

- When a user of a mobile app initiates a long-running operation, write a message to a Cloud Pub/Sub queue and trigger a function to send a message to the user informing them that the operation will take several minutes.

- When a background process completes, write a message to a Cloud Pub/Sub queue and trigger the execution of a function that sends a message to the initiator of the process notifying them that the operation finished.

- When a database administrator authenticates to a Firebase database, trigger the execution of a function that writes a message to an audit log and sends a message to all other administrators informing them someone has logged in as an administrator.

Notice that each example begins with the word *When*. This is because Cloud Functions are executed in response to things that happen somewhere in GCP. Cloud Functions complement the App Engine Cron Service, which is provided to execute code at regular intervals or at specific times. With these two services, developers can create code that executes as needed without human intervention. Both services also relieve developers of writing a service that would run continually and check if an event occurred and, if it did, then execute some action.

Compute System Provisioning

GCP provides an interactive console as well as a command-line utility for creating and managing compute, storage, and network resources. It also provides the *Deployment Manager* service that allows you to specify infrastructure as code. It is a good practice to define infrastructure as code, since it allows teams to reproduce environments rapidly. It also lends itself to code reviews, version control, and other software engineering practices.

Deployment Manager uses declarative templates that describe what should be deployed. Here is a sample of a template specifying an f1-micro instance that would be created in the us-west1 region using a project with the project ID of `gcp-arch-exam-project`, a boot disk with the Centos 7 operating system installed, and an external IP address on the network interface:

```
resources:
  - type: compute.v1.instance
    name: gcp-arch-exam-vm1
```

```
properties:.
  zone: us-west1-a
  machineType: https://www.googleapis.com/compute/v1/projects/gcp-arch-exam-
project/zones/us-central1-f/machineTypes/f1-micro
  disks:
  - deviceName: boot
    type: PERSISTENT
    boot: true
    autoDelete: true
    initializeParams:
    sourceImage: https://www.googleapis.com/compute/v1/projects/gce-uefi-
images/global/images/family/centos-7
  networkInterfaces:
  - network: https://www.googleapis.com/compute/v1/projects/gcp-arch-exam-
project /global/networks/default
    accessConfigs:
    - name: External NAT
      type: ONE_TO_ONE_NAT
```

Sets of resource templates can be grouped together into deployments. When a deployment is run or executed, all of the specified resources are created.

Additional Design Issues

In addition to considering how you will configure and deploy compute resources, you will need to understand how compute resources interact, how data flows, and how to monitor infrastructure and applications.

Managing State in Distributed Systems

Managing state information is commonplace when designing distributed systems. Stateful systems present a few different kinds of challenges, which you should keep in mind when designing cloud application architectures.

Persistent Assignment of Clients to Instances

Stateful systems keep data about client processes and connections. For example, consider Internet of Things (IoT) sensors on industrial machines.

Every minute a sensor sends metrics on temperature, vibrations, and throughput of the device. The data is stored in a buffer for 10 minutes where it is evaluated for anomalies. The 10 minutes' worth of data that is maintained is state information. For this model to work, a sensor needs to send its data continually to the same server each time data is generated.

One design decision is how to assign sensors to servers. Often, the best solution is to assign a sensor to an instance randomly. This will distribute the workload evenly across a cluster. In practice, it is common to use modulo division on a numeric identifier, like a sensor ID. The divisor is the number of instances. Assuming that you have a cluster with 8 instances, one set of assignments for sensors with IDs 80, 83, 89, and 93 is as follows:

80 mod 8 = 0

83 mod 8 = 3

89 mod 8 = 1

93 mod 8 = 5

A variation on this pattern is to use some form of aggregate-level identifier, such as an account number or group number instead of individual sensor identifiers. For example, assume that in our IoT example each machine has between 10 and 200 sensors. If we assigned sensors to instances based on machine ID, it is possible that some servers would have more load than others. If 300 machines with 200 sensors were assigned to one machine, while 300 machines with 10 sensors were assigned to another, the workload would be skewed to the former.

Horizontally scalable systems function well in GCP. Compute Engine instance groups and Kubernetes Engine clusters can readily add and remove compute resources as needed. When each instance has to store state information, you will need to find a way to distribute work at the application level so that clients can be assigned to a single server. Another option, however, is to move state information off the instances to some other data store.

Persistent State and Volatile Instances

Assigning a client to a server solves the problem of having state information available to the application instance that needs it. Since clients always send data to the same instance, state information is maintained on that instance. No other instance needs to be queried to collect a client's state data in this scenario.

It does not solve the problem of instance volatility, however. What happens when an instance or container becomes unhealthy and shuts down? We could treat this as a high availability problem and use redundant instances. This may be a viable option when there are a small number of instances, but it can quickly become wasteful as the number of instances grows.

A better solution in many cases is to separate the storage of state data from volatile instances. Both in-memory cache and databases are viable options.

In-Memory Cache

In-memory cache, such as *Cloud Memorystore*, which is a managed Redis service, works well when an application needs low-latency access to data. The data in the cache can be persisted using snapshots. If the cache fails, the contents of memory can be re-created using the latest snapshot. Of course, any data changed between the time of the last snapshot and the cache failure is not restored using the snapshot. Additional measures are required. For example, if the data is ingested from a queue, the data could be kept in the queue until it is saved in a snapshot. If snapshots are made once per minute, *the time to live (TTL)* on messages in the queue could be set to two minutes.

Cloud Pub/Sub uses a publish-subscribe model. Once a message is delivered and the delivery is acknowledged, the message is removed from the message queue.

Databases

Another option for moving state data off of volatile instances is to use a database. This has the advantage of persisting data to durable storage. When using a database, the application only needs to define how to read and write data to the database; no additional steps are needed to snapshot caches or manage message queues. A potential disadvantage is that database latency may be higher than cache latency. If latency is a concern, you can use a cache to store database query results so data that is repeatedly queried can be read from the lower-latency cache instead of the higher-latency database.

Another disadvantage is that databases are complicated applications and can be difficult to maintain and tune. GCP offers several managed databases, including Cloud SQL and Cloud Datastore, which reduce the operational burden on developers and operators.

Data Flows and Pipelines

Applications are typically composed of multiple modules or services. Monolithic applications do exist, but they are typically legacy systems. Even when monolithic applications are used, there are some business operations that require multiple steps of processing using multiple applications.

Consider, for example, a health insurance claim, made on behalf of a patient by a healthcare provider. The workflow to process this claim might include the following:

- Verifying the patient and provider data in an eligibility application
- Analyzing the medical procedures performed and assigning a value in a benefits assignment application
- Reviewing the claim and proposed benefit for potential fraud in a compliance review system
- Sending the data to a data warehouse for use by business analysts
- Issuing payment to the provider by a payment processing system
- Sending an explanation of benefits letter to the patient by a patient services application

This insurance claim scenario is an example of how monolithic systems may be used together to implement a workflow to implement a fairly complicated business process. Other workflows are implemented using microservices. For example, when you make a purchase online, the retailer's application may use several microservices, such as the following:

- Checking inventory to verify that the product is available to ship
- Authorizing payment through a third-party payment processor
- Issuing a fulfillment order that is sent to a warehouse where the item will be packaged and shipped
- Sending details of the transaction to a data warehouse for analysis
- Sending a confirmation message to the customer with delivery information

In both the health insurance claim and the online purchase example, multiple applications and services are used to implement a business workflow. When choosing cloud compute resources and designing workflows to meet business requirements, consider how data will flow from one service to the next.

Synchronous and Asynchronous Operations

In some cases, the workflow is simple enough that a synchronous call to another service is sufficient. *Synchronous calls* are calls to another service or function that wait for the operation to complete before returning; *asynchronous calls* do not wait for an operation to complete before returning. Authorizing a credit card for a purchase is often a synchronous operation. The process is usually completed in seconds, and there are business reasons not to proceed with other steps in the workflow until payment is authorized.

In other situations, synchronous calls to services could hold up processing and introduce lag into the system. Consider the online purchase example. Once payment is authorized, the fulfillment order should be created. The system that receives fulfillment orders may experience high load or might have several servers unavailable during update operations. If a synchronous call is made to the fulfillment system, then a disruption in the normal operation of the fulfillment system could cause delays in finishing the purchase transaction with the customer. From a business requirement perspective, there is no need to complete the fulfillment order processing before completing the sales transaction with the customer. This would be a good candidate for an asynchronous operation.

One way to implement asynchronous processing is to buffer data between applications in a message queue. One application writes data to the message queue, and the other application reads it. Writing and reading from message queues are fast operations, so synchronous read and write operations on queues are not likely to introduce delays in processing. If the application that reads from the queue cannot keep up with the rate at which messages are being written, the messages will remain in the queue until the reading application can get to them.

This kind of buffering is especially helpful when the services have different scaling requirements. A spike in traffic on the front end of a web application can be addressed by adding instances. This is especially straightforward when the front-end application is stateless. If the backend depends on a database, then scaling is more difficult. Instead of trying to scale the backend, it's better to allow work to accumulate in a queue and processes that work using the resources in place. This will require more time to complete the work, but it decouples the work that must be done immediately, which is responding to the user, from work that can be done later, such as backend processing.

You have multiple options when implementing workflows and pipelines. You could implement your own messaging system and run it on one of the GCP compute services. You could also deploy a messaging service, such as RabbitMQ, or a streaming log, such as Apache Kafka. If you would like to use a GCP service, consider Cloud Pub/Sub and Cloud Dataflow.

Cloud Pub/Sub Pipelines

Cloud Pub/Sub is a good option for buffering data between services. It supports both push and pull subscriptions.

With a *push subscription*, message data is sent to by HTTP POST request to a push endpoint URL. The push model is useful when a single endpoint processes messages from multiple topics. It's also a good option when the data will be processed by an App Engine Standard application or a Cloud Function. Both of those services bill only when in use, and pushing a message avoids the need to check the queue continually for messages to pull.

With a *pull subscription*, a service reads messages from the topic. This is a good approach when processing large volumes of data and efficiency is a top concern.

Cloud Pub/Sub pipelines work well when data just needs to be transmitted from one service to another or buffered to control the load on downstream services. If you need to process the data, for example applying transformations to a stream of IoT data, then Cloud Dataflow is good option.

Cloud Dataflow Pipelines

Cloud Dataflow is an implementation of the Apache Beam stream processing framework. Cloud Dataflow is fully managed, so you do not have provision and manage instances to process data in stream. The service also operates in batch mode without changes to processing code. Developers can write stream and batch processing code using Java, Python, and SQL.

Cloud Dataflow can be used in conjunction with Cloud Pub/Sub, with Cloud Dataflow being responsible for processing data and Cloud Pub/Sub being responsible for sending messages and buffering data. Cloud Dataflow pipelines often fit into an application's architecture between data ingestion services, like Cloud Pub/Sub and Cloud IoT Core, and storage and analysis services, such as Cloud Bigtable, BigQuery, or Cloud Machine Learning.

Monitoring and Alerting

Stackdriver is GCP's service for collecting metrics, logs, and events. It also has applications for debugging and tracing. As you are designing a system architecture, consider what kinds of metrics and events you want to collect. Some metrics will help you understand utilization. For example, CPU and memory use is helpful in sizing instances. Application-specific events can help you understand application performance with respect to business considerations. For example, you may want to record an event each time a customer adds or removes an item from a shopping cart.

Managed services, like App Engine and Kubernetes Engine, will automatically monitor your applications using Stackdriver. If you are deploying instances in Compute Engine, you will need to install the Stackdriver agent on each instance.

Consider how you will alert. There is little reason to send a notification to a DevOps engineer if it does not provide enough information for them to correct the problem. Alerts should be actionable. If the action to be taken can be automated, like adding an instance if average CPU utilization passes some threshold, then it should be automated. There is no need to alert on these events, although logging information about the change is a good practice.

Summary

GCP offers a number of compute services including Compute Engine, App Engine, Kubernetes Engine, and Cloud Functions. *Compute Engine* is Google's *infrastructure-as-a-service (IaaS)* offering. The core functionality provided by Compute Engine is *virtual machines (VMs)*. *App Engine* is a *platform-as-a-service (PaaS)* compute offering. With App Engine, users do not have to configure servers. They provide application code that is run in the App Engine environment. There are two forms of App Engine: App Engine Standard and App Engine Flexible. *Kubernetes Engine* is a managed service providing *Kubernetes cluster management* and *Kubernetes container orchestration*. Kubernetes Engine allocates cluster resources, determines where to run containers, performs health checks, and manages VM lifecycles using Compute Engine instance groups. *Cloud Functions* is a serverless compute service well suited for event processing. The service is designed to respond to execute code in response to events within the Google Cloud Platform. Other issues to consider when designing infrastructure are managing state in distributed systems, data flows, and monitoring and alerting.

Exam Essentials

Understand when to use different compute services.   GCP compute services include Compute Engine, App Engine, Kubernetes Engine, and Cloud Functions. Cloud Engine is an IaaS offering. You have the greatest control over instances, but you also have the most management responsibility. App Engine is a PaaS that comes in two forms. App Engine Standard uses language-specific sandboxes to execute your applications. App Engine Flexible lets you deploy containers, which you can create using Docker. Kubernetes Engine is a managed Kubernetes service. It is well suited for applications built on microservices, but it also runs other containerized applications. Cloud Functions is a service that allows you to execute code in response to an event on GCP, such as a file being uploaded to Cloud Storage or a message being written to a Cloud Pub/Sub topic.

Understand Compute Engine instances' optional features.   These include the variety of machine types, preemptibility, and Shielded VMs. Also understand how service accounts are used. Understand managed instance groups and their features, such as autoscaling and health checks.

Know the difference between App Engine Standard and App Engine Flexible.   App Engine Standard employs language-specific runtimes, while App Engine Flexible uses containers that can be used to customize the runtime environment. Be familiar with additional services, such as the App Engine Cron Service and Task Queues.

Know the Kubernetes architecture.   Understand the differences between master cluster instances and node instances in Kubernetes. Understand the organizing abstractions, including Pods, Services, ReplicaSets, Deployments, PersistentVolumes, and StatefulSets. Know that an Ingress is an object that controls external access to services running in a Kubernetes cluster.

Review Questions

1. You are consulting for a client that is considering moving some on-premises workloads to the Google Cloud Platform. The workloads are currently running on VMs that use a specially hardened operating system. Application administrators will need root access to the operating system as well. The client wants to minimize changes to the existing configuration. Which GCP compute service would you recommend?

    A. Compute Engine

    B. Kubernetes Engine

    C. App Engine Standard

    D. App Engine Flexible

2. You have just joined a startup that analyzes healthcare data and makes recommendations to healthcare providers to improve the quality of care while controlling costs. You have to comply with privacy regulations. A compliance consultant recommends that your startup control encryption keys used to encrypt data stored on cloud servers. You'd rather have GCP manage all encryption components to minimize your work and infrastructure management responsibilities. What would you recommend?

    A. Use default encryption enabled on Compute Engine instances.

    B. Use Google Cloud Key Management Service to store keys that you create and use them to encrypt storage used with Compute Engine instances.

    C. Implement a trusted key store on premises, create the keys yourself, and use them to encrypt storage used with Compute Engine instances.

    D. Use an encryption algorithm that does not use keys.

3. A colleague complains that the availability and reliability of GCP VMs is poor because their instances keep shutting down with them issuing shutdown commands. No instance has run for more than 24 hours without shutting down for some reason. What would you suggest your colleague check to understand why the instances may be shutting down?

    A. Make sure that the Stackdriver agent is installed and collecting metrics.

    B. Verify that sufficient persistent storage is attached to the instance.

    C. Make sure that the instance availability is not set to preemptible.

    D. Ensure that an external IP address has been assigned to the instance.

4. Your company is working on a government contract that requires all instances of VMs to have a virtual Trusted Platform Module. What Compute Engine configuration option would you enable or disable your instances?

    A. Trusted Module Setting

    B. Shielded VMs

    C. Preemptible VMs

    D. Disable live migration

5. You are leading a lift-and-shift migration to the cloud. Your company has several load-balanced clusters that use VMs that are not identically configured. You want to make as few changes as possible when moving workloads to the cloud. What feature of GCP would you use to implement those clusters in the cloud?

   A. Managed instance groups

   B. Unmanaged instance groups

   C. Flexible instance groups

   D. Kubernetes clusters

6. Your startup has a stateless web application written in Python 3.7. You are not sure what kind of load to expect on the application. You do not want to manage servers or containers if you can avoid it. What GCP service would you use?

   A. Compute Engine

   B. App Engine

   C. Kubernetes Engine

   D. Cloud Dataproc

7. Your department provides audio transcription services for other departments in your company. Users upload audio files to a Cloud Storage bucket. Your application transcribes the audio and writes the transcript file back to the same bucket. Your process runs every day at midnight and transcribes all files in the bucket. Users are complaining that they are not notified if there is a problem with the audio file format until the next day. Your application has a program that can verify the quality of an audio file in less than two seconds. What changes would you make to the workflow to improve user satisfaction?

   A. Include more documentation about what is required to transcribe an audio file successfully.

   B. Use Cloud Functions to run the program to verify the quality of the audio file when the file is uploaded. If there is a problem, notify the user immediately.

   C. Create a Compute Engine instance and set up a cron job that runs every hour to check the quality of files that have been uploaded into the bucket in the last hour. Send notices to all users who have uploaded files that do not pass the quality control check.

   D. Use the App Engine Cron service to set up a cron job that runs every hour to check the quality of files that have been uploaded into the bucket in the last hour. Send notices to all users who have uploaded files that do not pass the quality control check.

8. You have inherited a monolithic Ruby application that you need to keep running. There will be minimal changes, if any, to the code. The previous developer who worked with this application created a Dockerfile and image container with the application and needed libraries. You'd like to deploy this in a way that minimizes your effort to maintain it. How would you deploy this application?

   A. Create an instance in Compute Engine, install Docker, install the Stackdriver agent, and then run the Docker image.

   B. Create an instance in Compute Engine, but do not use the Docker image. Install the application, Ruby, and needed libraries. Install the Stackdriver agent. Run the application directly in the VM, not a container.

   C. Use App Engine Flexible to run the container image. App Engine will monitor as needed.

   D. Use App Engine Standard to run the container image. App Engine will monitor as needed.

9. You have been asked to give a presentation on Kubernetes. How would you explain the difference between the cluster master and nodes?

   A. Cluster masters manage the cluster and run core services such as the controller manager, API server, scheduler, and etcd. Nodes run workload jobs.

   B. The cluster manager is an endpoint for API calls. All services needed to maintain a cluster are run on nodes.

   C. The cluster manager is an endpoint for API calls. All services needed to maintain a cluster are run on nodes, and workloads are run on a third kind of server, a runner.

   D. Cluster masters manage the cluster and run core services such as the controller manager, API server, scheduler, and etcd. Nodes monitor the cluster master and restart it if it fails.

10. External services are not able to access services running in a Kubernetes cluster. You suspect a controller may be down. Which type of controller would you check?

   A. Pod

   B. Deployment

   C. Ingress Controller

   D. Service Controller

11. You are planning to run stateful applications in Kubernetes Engine. What should you use to support stateful applications?

   A. Pods

   B. StatefulPods

   C. StatefulSets

   D. PersistentStorageSets

12. Every time a database administrator logs into a Firebase database, you would like a message sent to your mobile device. Which compute service could you use that would minimize your work in deploying and running the code that sends the message?

   A. Compute Engine

   B. Kubernetes Engine

   C. Cloud Functions

   D. Cloud Dataflow

13. Your team has been tasked with deploying infrastructure for development, test, staging, and production environments in region us-west1. You will likely need to deploy the same set of environments in two additional regions. What service would allow you to use an Infrastructure as code (IaC) approach?

   A. Cloud Dataflow

   B. Deployment Manager

   C. Identity and Access Manager

   D. App Engine Flexible

14. An IoT startup collects streaming data from industrial sensors and evaluates the data for anomalies using a machine learning model. The model scales horizontally. The data collected is buffered in a server for 10 minutes. Which of the following is a true statement about the system?

   A. It is stateful.

   B. It is stateless.

   C. It may be stateful or stateless, there is not enough information to determine.

   D. It is neither stateful nor stateless.

15. Your team is designing a stream processing application that collects temperature and pressure measurements from industrial sensors. You estimate that for the initial release, the application will need 8 to 12 n1-highmem-32 instances. Someone on the team suggests using a Cloud Memorystore cache. What could that cache be used for?

   A. A SQL database

   B. As a memory cache to store state data outside of instances

   C. An extraction, transformation, and load service

   D. A persistent object storage system

16. A distributed application is not performing as well as expected during peak load periods. The application uses three microservices. The first of the microservices has the ability to send more data to the second service than the second service can process and keep up with. This causes the first microservice to wait while the second service processes data. What can be done to decouple the first service from the second service?

   A. Run the microservices on separate instances.

   B. Run the microservices in a Kubernetes cluster.

   C. Write data from the first service to a Cloud Pub/Sub topic and have the second service read the data from the topic.

   D. Scale both services together using MIGs.

17. A colleague has suggested that you use the Apache Beam framework for implementing a highly scalable workflow. Which Google Cloud service would you use?

A. Cloud Dataproc

B. Cloud Dataflow

C. Cloud Dataprep

D. Cloud Memorystore

18. Your manager wants more data on the performance of applications running in Compute Engine, specifically, data on CPU and memory utilization. What Google Cloud service would you use to collect that data?

A. Cloud Dataprep

B. Stackdriver

C. Cloud Dataproc

D. Cloud Memorystore

19. You are receiving alerts that CPU utilization is high on several Compute Engine instances. The instances are all running a custom C++ application. When you receive these alerts, you deploy an additional instance running the application. A load balancer automatically distributes the workload across all of the instances. What is the best option to avoid having to add servers manually when CPU utilization is high?

A. Always run more servers than needed to avoid high CPU utilization.

B. Deploy the instances in a MIG, and use autoscaling to add and remove instances as needed.

C. Run the application in App Engine Standard.

D. Whenever you receive an alert, add two instances instead of one.

20. A retailer has sales data streaming into a Cloud Pub/Sub topic from stores across the country. Each time a sale is made, data is sent from the point of sale to Google Cloud. The data needs to be transformed and aggregated before it is written to BigQuery. What service would you use to perform that processing and write data to BigQuery?

A. Firebase

B. Cloud Dataflow

C. Cloud Memorystore

D. Cloud Datastore

Chapter
5

Designing Storage Systems

THE PROFESSIONAL CLOUD ARCHITECT CERTIFICATION EXAM OBJECTIVES COVERED IN THIS CHAPTER INCLUDE THE FOLLOWING:

✓ **2.2   Configuring individual storage systems**

Storage is an essential component of virtually any cloud-based system. Storage needs can range from long-term archival storage for rarely accessed data to highly volatile, frequently accessed data cached in memory. Google Cloud Platform provides a full range of storage options, such as the following:

- Object storage
- Persistent local and attached storage
- Relational and NoSQL databases

This chapter reviews the key concepts and design criteria that you will need to know to pass the Professional Cloud Architect exam, including data retention and lifecycle management considerations as well as addressing networking and latency issues with storage system design.

Overview of Storage Services

Cloud architects often have to select one or more storage systems when designing an application. Several factors influence the choice of storage system, such as the following:

- Is the data structured or unstructured?
- How frequently will the data be accessed?
- What is the read/write pattern? What is the frequency of reads versus writes?
- What are the consistency requirements?
- Can Google managed keys be used for encryption, or do you need to deploy customer managed keys?
- What are the most common query patterns?
- Does your application require mobile support, such as synchronization?
- For structured data, is the workload analytic or transactional?
- Does your application require low-latency writes?

The answer to these and similar questions will help you decide which storage services to use and how to configure them.

The Google Cloud Choosing a Storage Option Flowchart at
https://cloud.google.com/storage-options/ is an excellent study
aid and guide for choosing among storage options.

Object Storage with Google Cloud Storage

Google Cloud Storage is an object storage system. It is designed for persisting unstructured data, such as data files, images, videos, backup files, and any other data. It is unstructured in the sense that objects, that is, files stored in Cloud Storage, are treated as atomic. When you access a file in Cloud Storage, you access the entire file. You cannot treat it as a file on a block storage device that allows for seeking and reading specific blocks in the file. There is no presumed structure within the file that Cloud Storage can exploit.

Organizing Objects in a Namespace

Also, there is minimal structure for hierarchical structures. Cloud Storage uses buckets to group objects. A *bucket* is a group of objects that share access controls at the bucket level. For example, the service account assigned to a virtual machine may have permissions to write to one bucket and read from another bucket. Individual objects within buckets can have their own access controls as well.

Google Cloud Storage uses a global namespace for bucket names, so all bucket names must have unique names. Object names do not have to be unique. A bucket is named when it is created and cannot be renamed. To simulate renaming a bucket, you will need to copy the contents of the bucket to a new bucket with the desired name and then delete the original bucket.

The following are best practice suggestions for bucket naming:

- Do not use personally identifying information, such as names, email addresses, IP addresses, and so forth in bucket names. That kind of information could be useful to an attacker.

- Follow DNS naming conventions because bucket names can appear in a CNAME record in DNS.

- Use globally unique identifiers (GUIDs) if creating a large number of buckets.

- Do not use sequential names or timestamps if uploading files in parallel. Files with sequentially close names will likely be assigned to the same server. This can create a hotspot when writing files to Cloud Storage.

- Bucket names can also be subdomain names, such as mybucket.example.com.

To create a domain name bucket, you will have to verify that you are the owner of the domain.

The Cloud Storage service does not provide a filesystem. This means that there is no ability to navigate a path through a hierarchy of directories and files. The object store does support a naming convention that allows for the naming of objects in a way that looks similar to the way that a hierarchical filesystem would structure a file path and filename. If you would like to use Google Cloud Storage as a filesystem, the Cloud Storage FUSE open source project provides a mechanism to map from object storage systems to filesystems.

Cloud Storage FUSE

Filesystem in Userspace (FUSE) is a framework for exposing a filesystem to the Linux kernel. FUSE uses a stand-alone application that runs on Linux and provides a filesystem API along with an adapter for implementing filesystem functions in the underlying storage system. *Cloud Storage FUSE* is an open source adapter that allows users to mount Cloud Storage buckets as filesystems on Linux and MacOS platforms.

Cloud Storage FUSE is not a filesystem like NFS. It does not implement a filesystem or a hierarchical directory structure. It does interpret / characters in filenames as directory delimiters.

For example, when using Cloud Storage FUSE, a user could mount a Cloud Storage bucket to a mount point called gcs. The user could then interact with the local operating system to save a file named mydata.csv to /gcs/myproject/mydirectory/mysubirectory. The user could execute the ls command at the command line to list the contents of the simulated mysubdirectory to see the listing for mydata.csv along with any other files with a name prefixed by myproject/mydirectory. The user could then use a gsutil command or cloud console to list the contents of the mounted bucket, and they would see an object named myproject/mydirectory/mysubdirectory.

Cloud Storage FUSE is useful when you want to move files easily back and forth between Cloud Storage and a Compute Engine VM, a local server, or your development device using filesystem commands instead of gsutil commands or the cloud console.

Cloud Storage FUSE is a Google-developed and community-supported open source project under the Apache license. Cloud Storage FUSE is available at https://github.com/GoogleCloudPlatform/gcsfuse/.

Storage Tiers

Cloud Storage offers four tiers or types of storage. It is essential to understand the characteristics of each tier and when it should be used for the Professional Cloud Architect exam. The four types of Cloud Storage are as follows:

- Regional
- Multiregional
- Nearline
- Coldline

Regional storage stores multiple copies of an object in multiple zones in one region. All Cloud Storage options provide high durability, which means the probability of losing an object during any particular period of time is extremely low. Cloud Storage provides 99.999999999 percent (eleven 9s) annual durability.

This level of durability is achieved by keeping redundant copies of the object. *Availability* is the ability to access an object when you want it. An object can be durably stored but unavailable. For example, a network outage in a region would prevent you from accessing an object stored in that region, although it would continue to be stored in multiple zones.

Multiregional storage mitigates the risk of a regional outage by storing replicas of objects in multiple regions. This can also improve access time and latency by distributing copies of objects to locations that are closer to the users of those objects. Consider a user in California in the western United States accessing an object stored in us-west1, which is a region located in the northwest state of Oregon in the United States. That user can expect under 5ms latency with a user in New York, in the United States northeast, and would likely experience latencies closer to 30ms.[1]

Multiregional storage is also known as *geo-redundant storage*. Multiregional Cloud Storage buckets are created in one of the multiregions—asia, eu, or us—for data centers in Asia, the European Union, and the United States, respectively.

The latencies mentioned here are based on public Internet network infrastructure. Google offers two network tiers: Standard and Premium. With *Standard network tier*, data is routed between regions using public Internet infrastructure and is subject to network conditions and routing decisions beyond Google's control. The *Premium network tier* routes data over Google's global high-speed network. Users of Premium tier networking can expect lower latencies.

Nearline and Coldline storage are used for storing data that is not frequently accessed. Data that is accessed less than once in 30 days is a good candidate for *Nearline storage*. Data that is accessed less than once a year is a good candidate for *Coldline storage*. All storage classes have the same latency to return the first byte of data.

Multiregion storage has a 99.95 percent availability SLA. Regional storage has a 99.9 percent availability SLA. Nearline and Coldline storage have 99.9 percent availability SLA in multiregional locations and 99.0 percent availability in regional locations.

Cloud Storage Use Cases

Cloud Storage is used for a few broad use cases.

- Storage of data shared among multiple instances that does not need to be on persistent attached storage. For example, log files may be stored in Cloud Storage and analyzed by programs running in a Cloud Dataproc Spark cluster.

- Backup and archival storage, such as persistent disk snapshots, backups of on-premises systems, and data kept for audit and compliance requirements but not likely to be accessed.

- As a staging area for uploaded data. For example, a mobile app may allow users to upload images to a Cloud Storage bucket. When the file is created, a Cloud Function could trigger to initiate the next steps of processing.

---

[1] Windstream Services IP Latency Statistics, https://ipnetwork.windstream.net/, accessed May 8, 2019.

Each of these examples fits well with Cloud Storage's treatment of objects as atomic units. If data within the file needs to be accessed and processed, that is done by another service or application, such as a Spark analytics program.

Different tiers are better suited for some use cases. For example, Coldline storage is best used for archival storage, but multiregional storage may be the best option for uploading user data, especially if users are geographically dispersed.

As an architect, it is important to understand the characteristics of the four storage tiers, their relative costs, the assumption of atomicity of objects by Cloud Storage, and how Cloud Storage is used in larger workflows.

Network-Attached Storage with Google Cloud Filestore

Cloud Filestore is a network-attached storage service that provides a filesystem that is accessible from Compute Engine and Kubernetes Engine. Cloud Filestore is designed to provide low latency and IOPS, so it can be used for databases and other performance-sensitive services.

Cloud Filestore has two tiers: standard and premium. Table 5.1 shows the performance characteristics of each tier.

TABLE 5.1   Cloud Filestore performance characteristics

Feature	Standard	Premium
Maximum read throughput	100 MB/s (1 TB), 180 MB/s (10+ TB)	1.2 GB/sec
Maximum write throughput	100 MB/s (1 TB), 120 MB/s (10+ TB)	350 MB/s
Maximum IOPS	5,000	60,000
Typical availability	99.9 percent	99.9 percent

Some typical use cases for Cloud Filestore are home directories and shared directories, web server content, and migrated applications that require a filesystem.

Cloud Filestore filesystems can be mounted using operating system commands. Once mounted, file permissions can be changed as needed using standard Linux access control commands, such as chmod.

IAM roles are used to control access to Cloud Filestore administration. The Cloud Filestore Editor role grants administrative permissions to create and delete Cloud Filestore instances. The Cloud Filestore Editor role grants permissions, such as list filestores, and gets their status. The Cloud Filestore Editor role has all the permissions of the Cloud Filestore Viewer.

Databases

Google Cloud provides a variety of database storage systems. The Professional Cloud Architect exam may include questions that require you to choose an appropriate database solution when given a set of requirements. The databases can be broadly grouped in relational and NoSQL databases.

Relational Database Overview

Relational databases are highly structured data stores that are designed to store data in ways that minimize the risk of data anomalies and to support a comprehensive query language. An example of a data anomaly is inserting an employee record into a database department ID that does not exist in the department table. Relational databases support data models that include constraints that help prevent anomalies.

Another common characteristic of relational databases is support for ACID transactions. (ACID stands for atomicity, consistency, isolation, and durability.) NoSQL databases may support ACID transactions as well, but not all do so.

Atomicity

Atomic operations ensure that all steps in a transaction complete or no steps take effect. For example, a sales transaction might include reducing the number of products available in inventory and charging a customer's credit card. If there isn't sufficient inventory, the transaction will fail, and the customer's credit card will not be charged.

Consistency

Consistency, specifically transactional consistency, is a property that guarantees that when a transaction executes, the database is left in a state that complies with constraints, such as uniqueness requirements and referential integrity, which ensures foreign keys reference a valid primary key. When a database is distributed, consistency also refers to querying data from different servers in a database cluster and receiving the same data from each.

For example, some NoSQL databases replicate data on multiple servers to improve availability. If there is an update to a record, each copy must be updated. In the time between the first and last copies being updated, it is possible to have two instances of the same query receive different results. This is considered an inconsistent read. Eventually, all replicas will be updated, so this is referred to as *eventual consistency.*

There are other types of consistency; for those interested in the details of other consistency models, see "Consistency in Non-Transactional Distributed Storage Systems" by Paolo Viotti and Marko Vukolic at https://arxiv.org/pdf/1512.00168.pdf.

Isolation

Isolation refers to ensuring that the effects of transactions that run at the same time leave the database in the same state as if they ran one after the other. Let's consider an example.

Transaction 1 is as follows:

Set A = 2

Set B = 3

Set C = A + B

Transaction 2 is as follows:

Set A = 10

Set B = 5

Set C = A + B

When high isolation is in place, the value of C will be either 5 or 15, which are the results of either of the transactions. The data will appear as if the three operations of Transaction 1 executed first and the three operations of Transaction 2 executed next. In that case, the value of C is 15. If the operations of Transaction 2 execute first followed by the Transaction 1 operations, then C will have the value 5.

What will not occur is that some of the Transaction 1 operations will execute followed by some of the Transaction 2 operations and then the rest of the Transaction 1 operations.

Here is an execution sequence that cannot occur when isolation is in place:

Set A = 2 (from Transaction 1)

Set B = 5 (from Transaction 2)

Set C = A + B (from Transaction 1 or 2)

This sequence of operations would leave C with the assigned the value of 7, which would be an incorrect state for the database to be in.

Durability

The *durability property* ensures that once a transaction is executed, the state of the database will always reflect or account for that change. This property usually requires databases to write data to persistent storage—even when the data is also stored in memory—so that in the event of a crash, the effects of the transactions are not lost.

Google Cloud Platform offers two managed relational database services: Cloud SQL and Cloud Spanner. Each is designed for distinct use cases. In addition to the two managed services, GCP customers can run their own databases on GCP virtual machines.

Cloud SQL

Cloud SQL is a managed service that provides MySQL and PostgreSQL databases.

At the time of this writing, Cloud SQL for SQL Service is in the alpha stage. The status of this product may have changed by the time you read this. In this book, we will only discuss MySQL and PostgreSQL versions of Cloud SQL.

Cloud SQL allows users to deploy MySQL and PostgreSQL on managed virtual servers. GCP manages patching database software, backups, and failovers. Key features of Cloud SQL include the following:

- All data is encrypted at rest and in transit.
- Data is replicated across multiple zones for high availability.
- GCP manages failover to replicas.
- Support for standard database connectors and tools is provided.
- Stackdriver is integrated monitoring and logging.

Cloud SQL is an appropriate choice for databases that will run on a single server. Customers can choose the machine type and disk size for the virtual machine running the database server. Both MySQL and PostgreSQL support the SQL query language.

Relational databases, like MySQL and PostgreSQL, are used with structured data. Both require well-defined schemas, which can be specified using the data definition commands of SQL. These databases also support strongly consistent transactions, so there is no need to work around issues with eventual consistency. Cloud SQL is appropriate for transaction processing applications, such as e-commerce sales and inventory systems.

A limiting factor of Cloud SQL is that databases can scale only vertically, that is, by moving the database to a larger machine. For use cases that require horizontal scalability or support, a globally accessed database, Cloud Spanner, is an appropriate choice.

Cloud Spanner

Cloud Spanner is a managed database service that supports horizontal scalability across regions. This database supports common relational features, such as schemas for structured data and SQL for querying. It supports strong consistency, so there is no risk of data anomalies caused by eventual consistency. Cloud Spanner also manages replication.

Cloud Spanner is used for applications that require strong consistency on a global scale. Here are some examples:

- Financial trading systems require a globally consistent view of markets to ensure that traders have a consistent view of the market when making trades.
- Logistics applications managing a global fleet of vehicles need accurate data on the state of vehicles.
- Global inventory tracking requires global-scale transaction to preserve the integrity of inventory data.

Cloud Spanner provides 99.999 percent availability, which guarantees less than 5 minutes of downtime per year. Like Cloud SQL, all patching, backing up, and failover management is performed by GCP.

Data is encrypted at rest and in transit. Cloud Spanner is integrated with Cloud Identity to support the use of user accounts across applications and with Cloud Identity and Access Management to control authorizations to perform operations on Cloud Spanner resources.

Analytics Database: BigQuery

BigQuery is a managed data warehouse and analytics database solution. It is designed to support queries that scan and return large volumes of data, and it performs aggregations on that data. BigQuery uses SQL as a query language. Customers do not need to choose a machine instance type or storage system. BigQuery is a serverless application from the perspective of the user.

Data is stored in a columnar format, which means that values from a single column in a database are stored together rather than storing data from the same row together. This is used in BigQuery because analytics and business intelligence queries often filter and group by values in a small number of columns and do not need to reference all columns in a row.

BigQuery uses the concept of a job for executing tasks such as loading and exporting data, running queries, and copying data. Batch and streaming jobs are supported for loading data.

BigQuery uses the concept of a *dataset* for organizing tables and views. A dataset is contained in a project. A dataset may have a regional or multiregional location. Regional datasets are stored in a single region such as us-west2 or europe-north1. Multiregional locations store data in multiple regions within either the United States or Europe.

BigQuery provides its own command-line program called *bq* rather than use the gcloud command line. Some of the bq commands are as follows:

cp for copying data

cancel for stopping a job

extract for exporting a table

head for listing the first rows of a table

insert for inserting data in newline JSON format

load for inserting data from AVRO, CSV, ORC, Parquet, and JSON data files or from Cloud Datastore and Cloud Firestore exports

ls for listing objects in a collection

mk for making tables, views, and datasets

query for creating a job to run a SQL query

rm for deleting objects

show for listing information about an object

BigQuery is integrated with Cloud IAM, which has several predefined roles for BigQuery.

dataViewer. This role allows a user to list projects and tables and get table data and metadata.

dataEditor. This has the same permissions as dataViewer, plus permissions to create and modify tables and datasets.

dataOwner. This role is similar to dataEditor, but it can also create, modify, and delete datasets.

metadataViewer. This role gives permissions to list tables, projects, and datasets.

user. The user role gives permissions to list projects and tables, view metadata, create datasets, and create jobs.

jobUser. A jobUser can list projects and create jobs and queries.

admin. An admin can perform all operations on BigQuery resources.

BigQuery is billed based on the amount of data stored and the amount of data scanned when responding to queries, or in the case of flat-rate query billing, the allocation is used based on the size of the query. For this reason, it is best to craft queries that return only the data that is needed, and filter criteria should be as specific as possible.

If you are interested in viewing the structure of a table or view or you want to see sample data, it is best to use the Preview Option in the console or use the bq head command from the command line. BigQuery also provides a --dry-run option for command-line queries. It returns an estimate of the number of bytes that would be returned if the query were executed.

The *BigQuery Data Transfer Service* is a specialized service for loading data from other cloud services, such as Google Ads and Google Ad Managers. It also supports transferring data from Cloud Storage and AWS S3, but these are both are in beta stage at the time of this writing.

GCP provides two managed relational databases and an analytics database with some relational features. Cloud SQL is used for transaction processing systems that do not need to scale beyond a single server. It supports MySQL and PostgreSQL. Cloud Spanner is a transaction processing relational database that scales horizontally, and it is used when a single server relational database is insufficient. BigQuery is designed for data warehousing and analytic querying of large datasets. BigQuery should not be used for transaction processing systems. If data is frequently updated after loading, then one of the other managed relational databases is a better option.

NoSQL Databases

GCP offers three NoSQL databases: Bigtable, Datastore, and Cloud Firestore. All three are well suited to storing data that requires flexible schemas. Cloud Bigtable is a wide-column NoSQL database. Cloud Firestore and Cloud Datastore are document NoSQL databases. Cloud Firebase is the next generation of Cloud Datastore.

Cloud Bigtable

Cloud Bigtable is designed to support petabyte-scale databases for analytic operations, such as storing data for machine learning model building, as well as operational use cases, such as streaming Internet of Things (IoT) data. It is also used for time series, marketing data, financial data, and graph data. Some of the most important features of Cloud Bigtable are as follows:

- Sub 10 ms latency
- Stores petabyte-scale data
- Uses regional replication
- Queried using a Cloud Bigtable–specific command, cbt
- Supports use of Hadoop HBase interface
- Runs on a cluster of servers

Bigtable stores data in tables organized by key-value maps. Each row contains data about a single entity and is indexed by a row key. Columns are grouped into column families, which are sets of related columns. A table may contain multiple column families.

Tables in Bigtable are partitioned into blocks of contiguous rows known as *tablets*. Tablets are stored in the Colossus scalable filesystem. Data is not stored on nodes in the cluster. Instead, nodes store pointers to tablets stored in Colossus. Distributing read and write load across nodes yields better performance than having hotspots where a small number of nodes are responding to most read and write requests.

Bigtable supports creating more than one cluster in a Bigtable instance. Data is automatically replicated between clusters. This is useful when the instance is performing a large number of read and write operations at the same time. With multiple clusters, one can be dedicated to responding to read requests while the other receives write requests. Bigtable guarantees eventual consistency between the replicas.

Cloud Datastore

Cloud Datastore is a managed document database, which is a kind of NoSQL database that uses a flexible JSON-like data structure called a *document*. Some of the key features of Cloud Datastore are as follows:

- ACID transactions are supported.
- It is highly scalable and highly available.
- It supports strong consistency for lookup by key and ancestor queries, while other queries have eventual consistency.
- Data is encrypted at rest.
- It provides a SQL-like query language called GQL.
- Indexes are supported.
- Joins are not supported.

- It scales to zero. Most other database services usually require capacity to be allocated regardless of whether it is consumed.

The terminology used to describe the structure of a document is different than that for relational databases. A table in a relational database corresponds to a *kind* in Cloud Datastore, while a row is referred to as an *entity*. The equivalent of a relational column is a *property*, and a primary key in relational databases is simply called the *key* in Cloud Datastore.

Cloud Datastore is fully managed. GCP manages all data management operations including distributing data to maintain performance. Also, Cloud Datastore is designed so that the response time to return query results is a function of the size of the data returned and not the size of the dataset that is queried.

The flexible data structure makes Cloud Datastore a good choice for applications like product catalogs or user profiles.

Cloud Firestore

Cloud Firestore is the next generation of the GCP-managed document database. Cloud Firestore:

- Is strongly consistent
- Supports document and collection data models
- Supports real-time updates
- Provides mobile and web client libraries

Cloud Firestore supports both a Datastore mode, which is backward compatible with Cloud Datastore, and a Firestore mode. In Datastore mode, all transactions are strongly consistent, unlike Cloud Datastore transactions, which are eventually consistent. Other Cloud Datastore limitations on querying and writing are removed in Firebase Datastore mode.

It's best practice for customers use Cloud Firestore in Datastore mode for new server-based projects. This supports up to millions of writes per second. Cloud Firestore in its native mode is for new web and mobile applications. This provides client libraries and support for millions of concurrent connections.[2]

Caching with Cloud Memorystore

Cloud Memorystore is a managed Redis service. *Redis* is an open source, in-memory data store, which is designed for submillisecond data access. Cloud Memorystore supports up to 300 GB instances and 12 Gbps network throughput. Caches replicated across two zones provide 99.9 percent availability.

As with other managed storage services, GCP manages Cloud Memorystore patching, replication, and failover.

---

[2] https://cloud.google.com/datastore/docs/firestore-or-datastore#in_native_mode.

Cloud Memorystore is used for low-latency data retrieval, specifically lower latency than is available from databases that store data persistently to disk or SSD.

Cloud Memorystore is available in two service tiers: Basic and Standard. Basic Tier provides a simple Redis cache on a single server. Standard Tier is a highly available instance with cross-zone replication and support for automatic failover.

The caching service also has capacity tiers, called M1 through M5. M1 has 1 GB to 4 GB capacity and 3 Gbps maximum network performance. These capacities increase up to M5, which has more than 100 GB cache size and up to 12 Gbps network throughput.

Memorystore caches are used for storing data in nonpersistent memory, particularly when low-latency access is important. Stream processing and database caching are both common use cases for Memorystore.

Data Retention and Lifecycle Management

Data has something of a life as it moves through several stages, including creation, active use, infrequent access but kept online, archived, and deleted. Not all data goes through all of the stages, but it is important to consider lifecycle issues when planning storage systems.

The choice of storage system technology usually does not directly influence data lifecycles and retention policies, but it does impact how the policies are implemented. For example, Cloud Storage lifecycle policies can be used to move objects from Nearline storage to Coldline storage after some period of time. When partitioned tables are used in BigQuery, partitions can be deleted without affecting other partitions or running time-consuming jobs that scan full tables for data that should be deleted.

If you are required to store data, consider how frequently and how fast the data must be accessed.

- If submillisecond access time is needed, use a cache such as Cloud Memorystore.

- If data is frequently accessed, may need to be updated, and needs to be persistently stored, use a database. Choose between relational and NoSQL based on the structure of the data. Data with flexible schemas can use NoSQL databases.

- If data is less likely to be accessed the older it gets, store data in time-partitioned tables if the database supports partitions. Time-partitioned tables are frequently used in BigQuery, and Bigtable tables can be organized by time as well.

- If data is infrequently accessed and does not require access through a query language, consider Cloud Storage. Infrequently used data can be exported from a database, and the export files can be stored in Cloud Storage. If the data is needed, it can be imported back into the database and queried from there.

- When data is not likely to be accessed, but it must still be stored, use the Coldline storage class in Cloud Storage. This is less expensive than multiregional, regional, or Nearline classes of storage.

Cloud Storage provides object lifecycle management policies to make changes automatically to the way objects are stored in the object datastore. These policies contain rules for manipulating objects and are assigned to buckets. The rules apply to objects in those buckets. The rules implement lifecycle actions, including deleting an object and setting the storage class. Rules can be triggered based on the age of the object, when it was created, the number of newer versions, and the storage class of the object.

Another control for data management is *retention policies*. A retention policy uses the Bucket Lock feature of Cloud Storage buckets to enforce object retention. By setting a retention policy, you ensure that any object in the bucket or future objects in the bucket are not deleted until they reach the age specified in the retention policy. This feature is particularly useful for compliance with government or industry regulations. Once a retention policy is locked, it cannot be revoked.

Networking and Latency

Network latency is a consideration when designing storage systems, particularly when data is transmitted between regions with GCP or outside GCP to globally distributed devices. Three ways of addressing network latency concerns are as follows:

- Replicating data in multiple regions and across continents
- Distributing data using Cloud CDN
- Using Google Cloud Premium Network tier

The reason to consider using these options is that the network latency without them would be too high to meet application or service requirements. For some points of reference, note the following:

- Within Europe and Japan, expect 12ms latency.
- Within North America 30–40 ms latency is typical.
- Trans-Atlantic latency is about 70 ms.
- Trans-Pacific latency is about 100 ms.
- Latency between the Europe, Middle East, and Africa (EMEA) region and Asia Pacific is closer to 120 ms.[3]

Data can be replicated in multiple regions under the control of a GCP service or under the control of a customer-managed service. For example, Cloud Storage multiregional storage replicates data to multiple regions. Cloud Spanner distributes data automatically among multiple regions. Cloud Firestore is designed to scale globally. Using GCP services that manage multiregion and global distribution of data is preferred to managing replication at the application level.

Another way to reduce latency is to use GCP's Cloud CDN. This is particularly effective and efficient when distributing relatively static content globally. Cloud CDN maintains

---

[3] https://enterprise.verizon.com/terms/latency/.

a set of globally distributed points of presence around the world. *Points of presence* are where the Google Cloud connects to the Internet. Static content that is frequently accessed in an area can be cached at these edge nodes.

GCP offers two network service tiers. In the Standard Tier, network traffic between regions is routed over the public Internet to the destination device. With the Premium Tier, all data is routed over the Google network up to a point of presence near the destination device. The Premium Tier should be used when high-performance routing, high availability, and low latency at multi-region scales are required.

Summary

GCP provides four types of storage systems: object storage using Cloud Storage, network-attached storage, databases, and caching. Cloud Storage is used for unstructured data that is accessed at the object level; there is no way to query or access subsets of data within an object. Object storage is useful for a wide array of use cases, from uploading data from client devices to storing long-term archives. Network-attached storage is used to store data that is actively processed. Cloud Filestore provides a network filesystem, which is used to share file structured data across multiple servers.

Google Cloud offers several managed databases, including relational and NoSQL databases. The relational database services are Cloud SQL and Cloud Spanner, Cloud SQL is used for transaction processing systems that serve clients within a region and do not need to scale beyond a single server. Cloud Spanner provides a horizontally scalable, global, strongly consistent relational database. BigQuery is a database designed for data warehousing and analytic database applications. The NoSQL managed databases in GCP are Bigtable, Datastore, and Firestore. Bigtable is a wide-column database designed for low-latency writes at petabyte scales. Datastore and Firestore are managed document databases that scale globally. Firestore is the next generation of document storage in GCP and has fewer restrictions than Cloud Datastore.

When designing storage systems, consider data lifecycle management and network latency. GCP provides services to help implement data lifecycle management policies and offers access to the Google global network through the Premium Tier network service.

Exam Essentials

Understand the major types of storage systems available in GCP. These include object storage, persistent local and attached storage, and relational and NoSQL databases. Object storage is often used to store unstructured data, archived data, and files that are treated as atomic units. Persistent local and attached storage provides storage to virtual machines. Relational databases are used for structured data, while NoSQL databases are used when it helps to have flexible schemas.

Cloud Storage has multiple tiers: multiregional, regional, Nearline, and Coldline. Multiregional storage replicates objects across multiple regions, while regional replicates data across zones within a region. Nearline is used for data that is accessed less than once in 30 days. Coldline storage is used for data that is accessed less than once a year.

Cloud Filestore is a network-attached storage service that provides a filesystem that is accessible from Compute Engine and Kubernetes Engine. Cloud Filestore is designed to provide low latency and IOPs so it can be used for databases and other performance-sensitive services.

Cloud SQL is a managed relational database that can run on a single server. Cloud SQL allows users to deploy MySQL and PostgreSQL on managed virtual servers. Database administration tasks, such as patching, backing up, and managing failover are managed by GCP.

Cloud Spanner is a managed database service that supports horizontal scalability across regions. Cloud Spanner is used for applications that require strong consistency on a global scale. Cloud Spanner provides 99.999 percent availability, which guarantees less than 5 minutes of downtime a year. Like Cloud SQL, all patching, backing up, and failover management is performed by GCP.

BigQuery is a managed data warehouse and analytics database solution. BigQuery uses the concept of a dataset for organizing tables and views. A dataset is contained in a project. BigQuery provides its own command-line program called bq rather than use the gcloud command line. BigQuery is billed based on the amount of data stored and the amount of data scanned when responding to queries.

Cloud Bigtable is designed to support petabyte-scale databases for analytic operations. It is used for storing data for machine learning model building, as well as operational use cases, such as streaming Internet of Things (IoT) data. It is also used for time series, marketing data, financial data, and graph data.

Cloud Datastore is a managed document database, which is a kind of NoSQL database that uses a flexible JSON-like data structure called a document. Cloud Datastore is fully managed. GCP manages all data management operations, including distributing data to maintain performance. Also, Cloud Datastore is designed so that the response time to return query results is a function of the size of the data returned and not the size of the dataset that is queried. The flexible data structure makes Cloud Datastore a good choice for applications like product catalogs or user profiles. Cloud Firestore is the next generation of GCP-managed document database.

Cloud Memorystore is a managed Redis service. Redis is an open source, in-memory data store, which is designed for submillisecond data access. Cloud Memorystore supports up to 300 GB instances and 12 Gbps network throughput. Caches replicated across two zones provide 99.9 percent availability.

Cloud Storage provides object lifecycle management policies to make changes automatically to the way that objects are stored in the object datastore. Another control for data management is retention policies. A retention policy uses the Bucket Lock feature of Cloud Storage buckets to enforce object retention.

Network latency is a consideration when designing storage systems, particularly when data is transmitted between regions with GCP or outside GCP to globally distributed devices.   Three ways of addressing network latency concerns are replicating data in multiple regions and across continents, distributing data using Cloud CDN, and using Google Cloud Premium Network tier.

Review Questions

1. You need to store a set of files for an extended period of time. Anytime the data in the files needs to be accessed, it will be copied to a server first, and then the data will be accessed. Files will not be accessed more than once a year. The set of files will all have the same access controls. What storage solution would you use to store these files?

    A. Cloud Storage Coldline

    B. Cloud Storage Nearline

    C. Cloud Filestore

    D. Bigtable

2. You are uploading files in parallel to Cloud Storage and want to optimize load performance. What could you do to avoid creating hotspots when writing files to Cloud Storage?

    A. Use sequential names or timestamps for files.

    B. Do not use sequential names or timestamps for files.

    C. Configure retention policies to ensure that files are not deleted prematurely.

    D. Configure lifecycle policies to ensure that files are always using the most appropriate storage class.

3. As a consultant on a cloud migration project, you have been asked to recommend a strategy for storing files that must be highly available even in the event of a regional failure. What would you recommend?

    A. BigQuery

    B. Cloud Datastore

    C. Multiregional Cloud Storage

    D. Regional Cloud Storage

4. As part of a migration to Google Cloud Platform, your department will run a collaboration and document management application on Compute Engine virtual machines. The application requires a filesystem that can be mounted using operating system commands. All documents should be accessible from any instance. What storage solution would you recommend?

    A. Cloud Storage

    B. Cloud Filestore

    C. A document database

    D. A relational database

5. Your team currently supports seven MySQL databases for transaction processing applications. Management wants to reduce the amount of staff time spent on database administration. What GCP service would you recommend to help reduce the database administration load on your teams?

    A. Bigtable

    B. BigQuery

    C. Cloud SQL

    D. Cloud Filestore

6. Your company is developing a new service that will have a global customer base. The service will generate large volumes of structured data and require the support of a transaction processing database. All users, regardless of where they are on the globe, must have a consistent view of data. What storage system will meet these requirements?

    A. Cloud Spanner

    B. Cloud SQL

    C. Cloud Storage

    D. BigQuery

7. Your company is required to comply with several government and industry regulations, which include encrypting data at rest. What GCP storage services can be used for applications subject to these regulations?

    A. Bigtable and BigQuery only

    B. Bigtable and Cloud Storage only

    C. Any of the managed databases, but no other storage services

    D. Any GCP storage service

8. As part of your role as a data warehouse administrator, you occasionally need to export data from the data warehouse, which is implemented in BigQuery. What command-line tool would you use for that task?

    A. gsutil

    B. gcloud

    C. bq

    D. cbt

9. Another task that you perform as data warehouse administrator is granting authorizations to perform tasks with the BigQuery data warehouse. A user has requested permission to view table data but not change it. What role would you grant to this user to provide the needed permissions but nothing more?

    A. dataViewer

    B. admin

    C. metadataViewer

    D. dataOwner

10. A developer is creating a set of reports and is trying to minimize the amount of data each query returns while still meeting all requirements. What bq command-line option will help you understand the amount of data returned by a query without actually executing the query?

    A. `--no-data`

    B. `--estimate-size`

    C. `--dry-run`

    D. `--size`

11. A team of developers is choosing between using NoSQL or a relational database. What is a feature of NoSQL databases that is not available in relational databases?

    A. Fixed schemas

    B. ACID transactions

    C. Indexes

    D. Flexible schemas

12. A group of venture capital investors have hired you to review the technical design of a service that will be developed by a startup company seeking funding. The startup plans to collect data from sensors attached to vehicles. The data will be used to predict when a vehicle needs maintenance and before the vehicle breaks down. Thirty sensors will be on each vehicle. Each sensor will send up to 5K of data every second. The startup expects to start with hundreds of vehicles, but it plans to reach 1 million vehicles globally within 18 months. The data will be used to develop machine learning models to predict the need for maintenance. The startup is planning to use a self-managed relational database to store the time-series data. What would you recommend for a time-series database?

    A. Continue to plan to use a self-managed relational database.

    B. Use a Cloud SQL.

    C. Use Cloud Spanner.

    D. Use Bigtable.

13. A Bigtable instance increasingly needs to support simultaneous read and write operations. You'd like to separate the workload so that some nodes respond to read requests and others respond to write requests. How would you implement this to minimize the workload on developers and database administrators?

    A. Create two instances, and separate the workload at the application level.

    B. Create multiple clusters in the Bigtable instance, and use Bigtable replication to keep the clusters synchronized.

    C. Create multiple clusters in the Bigtable instance, and use your own replication program to keep the clusters synchronized.

    D. It is not possible to accomplish the partitioning of the workload as described.

14. As a database architect, you've been asked to recommend a database service to support an application that will make extensive use of JSON documents. What would you recommend to minimize database administration overhead while minimizing the work required for developers to store JSON data in the database?

   A. Cloud Storage

   B. Cloud Datastore

   C. Cloud Spanner

   D. Cloud SQL

15. Your Cloud SQL database is close to maximizing the number of read operations that it can perform. You could vertically scale the database to use a larger instance, but you do not need additional write capacity. What else could you try to reduce the number of reads performed by the database?

   A. Switch to Cloud Spanner.

   B. Use Cloud Bigtable instead.

   C. Use Cloud Memorystore to create a database cache that stores the results of database queries. Before a query is sent to the database, the cache is checked for the answer to the query.

   D. There is no other option—you must vertically scale.

16. You would like to move objects stored in Cloud Storage automatically from regional storage to Nearline storage when the object is 6 months old. What feature of Cloud Storage would you use?

   A. Retention policies

   B. Lifecycle policies

   C. Bucket locks

   D. Multiregion replication

17. A customer has asked for help with a web application. Static data served from a data center in Chicago in the United States loads slowly for users located in Australia, South Africa, and Southeast Asia. What would you recommend to reduce latency?

   A. Distribute data using Cloud CDN.

   B. Use Premium Network from the server in Chicago to client devices.

   C. Scale up the size of the web server.

   D. Move the server to a location closer to users.

Chapter

6

Designing Networks

**THE PROFESSIONAL CLOUD ARCHITECT
CERTIFICATION EXAM OBJECTIVES
COVERED IN THIS CHAPTER INCLUDE
THE FOLLOWING:**

✓ **2.2   Configuring network topologies**

The Google Cloud Professional Architect exam includes questions about networking, especially around creating virtual private clouds in GCP and linking on-site data centers to GCP resources using VPNs. Load balancing within regions and globally is also covered on the exam. This chapter will cover all of these issues from an architecture perspective. If you would like to read about implementation details, for example how to set up custom subnets in a VPC, see Chapters 14 and 15 of the *Official Google Cloud Certified Associate Cloud Engineer Study Guide* (Sybex, 2019).

Virtual Private Clouds

VPCs are like a network in a data center; they are network-based organizational structures for controlling access to GCP resources. VPCs organize Compute Engine instances, App Engine Flexible instances, and GKE clusters. They are global resources, so a single VPC can span multiple regions.

You may recall that the resource hierarchy is another construct for grouping and organizing resources. The resource hierarchy uses organizations, folders, and projects to administer billing and organize objects for access controls based on identities. VPCs are used to control network access to resources.

A VPC is associated with a project or an organization, and projects can have multiple VPCs. Resources within a VPC can communicate with other resources in the same VPC, subject to firewall rules. Resources can also communicate with Google APIs and services.

VPC Subnets

A VPC can have subnets in each region in order to provide private addresses to resources in the region. Since the subnets are part of a larger network, they must have distinct IP address ranges. For example, a VPC with three subnets might use the ranges 10.140.10.0/20, 10.140.20.0/20, and 10.140.30.0/20 for the subnets. When a VPC is created, it can automatically create subnets in each region, or you can specify custom subnet definitions for each region that should have a subnet. If subnets are created automatically, their IP ranges are based on the region. All automatic subnets are assigned IP addresses in the 10.nnn.0.0/20 range.

VPCs use routes to determine how to route traffic within the VPC and across subnets. Depending on the configuration of the VPC, the VPC can learn regional routes only or multiregional, global routes.

Shared VPC

Sometimes, it is necessary for resources in different projects to communicate. For example, a data warehouse project may need to access a transactional database in an e-commerce project in order to load e-commerce data into the data warehouse. For organizational reasons, it may be preferable to keep the e-commerce and data warehouse systems in separate projects. Another advantage of Shared VPCs is that you can separate project and network management duties. For example, some administrators may be given privileges to manage network resources, such as firewall rules, while others are given privileges to manage project resources, like instances. One way to allow traffic to flow between instances in each VPC is to use a Shared VPC.

Shared VPCs are comprised of a host project and one or more service projects. The host project contains one or more Shared VPC networks. When a VPC is made a Shared VPC, all of the existing subnetworks become Shared VPC subnets. Service projects are attached to the host project at the project level.

VPC Network Peering

VPC network peering enables different VPC networks to communicate using private IP address space, as defined in RFC 1918. VPC network peering is used as an alternative to using external IP addresses or using VPNs to link networks. The following are three primary advantages of VPC network peering:

- There is lower latency because the traffic stays on the Google network and is not subject to conditions on the public Internet.
- Services in the VPC are inaccessible from the public Internet, reducing the attack surface of the organization.
- There are no egress charges associated with traffic when using VPC network peering.

It is important to note that peered networks manage their own resources, such as firewall rules and routes. This is different from firewall rules and routes in a VPC, which are associated with the entire VPC. Also, there is a maximum of 25 peering connections from a single VPC.

It is important to note that VPC peering can connect VPCs between organizations; VPC sharing does not operate between organizations.

Firewall Rules

Firewall rules control network traffic by blocking or allowing traffic into (ingress) or out of (egress) a network. Two implied firewall rules are defined with VPCs: one blocks all incoming traffic, and the other allows all outgoing traffic. You can change this behavior by defining firewall rules with higher priority. Firewall rules have a priority specified by an integer from 0 to 65535, with 0 being the highest priority and 65535 being the lowest. The two implied firewall rules have an implied priority of 65535, so you can override those by specifying a priority of less than 65535.

In addition to the two implied rules, which cannot be deleted, there are four default rules assigned to the default network in a VPC. These rules are as follows:

default-allow-internal allows ingress connections for all protocols and ports among instances in the network.

default-allow-ssh allows ingress connections on TCP port 22 from any source to any instance in the network. This allows users to ssh into Linux servers.

Default-allow-rdp allows ingress connections on TCP port 3389 from any source to any instance in the network. This lets users use Remote Desktop Protocol (RDP) developed by Microsoft to access Windows servers.

Default-allow-icmp allows ingress ICMP traffic from any source to any instance in the network.

All of these rules have a priority of 65534, the second-lowest priority.

Firewall rules have several attributes in addition to priority. They are as follows:

The direction of traffic. This is either ingress or egress.

The action. This is either allow or deny traffic.

The target. This defines the instances to which the rule applies.

The source. This is for ingress rules or the destination for egress rules.

A protocol specification. This includes TCP, UDP, or ICMP, for example.

A port number. A communication endpoint associated with a process.

An enforcement status. This allows network administrators to disable a rule without having to delete it.

Firewall rules are global resources that are assigned to VPCs, so they apply to all VPC subnets in all regions. Since they are global resources, they can be used to control traffic between regions in a VPC.

IP Addressing and CIDR Blocks

Architects are expected to understand IP addresses and classless inter-domain routing (CIDR) block notation. IP addresses can be specified using either IPv4 or IPv6. IPv4 uses four octets, such as 192.168.20.10. IPv6 uses eight 16-bit blocks, such as FE80:0000:0000:0000:0202:B3FF:FE1E:8329. For the purposes of the exam, understanding IPv4 addressing should be sufficient.

When you create a subnet, you will have to specify a range of IP addresses. Any resource that needs an IP address on that subnet will receive an IP address in that range. Each subnet in a VPC should have distinct, non-overlapping IP ranges.

You can specify an IP range using the CIDR notation. This consists of an IPv4 IP address followed by a /, followed by an integer. The integer specifies the number of bits used to identify the subnet; the remaining bits are used to determine the host address.

For example, if you specified 172.16.0.0/12, this would mean that the first 12 bits of the IP address specify the subnet. This is called the *subnet mask*. The remaining 20 bits are used for host addresses. Since there are 20 bits available, there can be 1,048,574 IP addresses in that range.

GCP users have a few options for linking their GCP networks to external networks, such as an on-premise data center network.

Hybrid-Cloud Networking

Hybrid-cloud networking is the practice of providing network services between an on-premise data center and a cloud. When two or more public clouds are linked together, that is called a *multicloud network*. Multicloud networks may also include private data centers. Typically, architects recommend hybrid-cloud or multicloud environments when there are workloads that are especially well suited to run in one environment over another or when they are trying to mitigate the risk of dependency on a particular cloud service. Here are some examples:

- A batch processing job that uses a custom legacy application designed for a mainframe is probably best run on-premises.
- Ad hoc batch processing, such as transforming a large number of image files to a new format, is a good candidate for a cloud computing environment, especially when low-cost preemptible VMs are available.
- An enterprise data warehouse that is anticipated to grow well into petabyte scale is well suited to run in a cloud service such as BigQuery.

Hybrid-Cloud Design Considerations

When workloads are run in different environments, there is a need for reliable networking with adequate capacity. A data warehouse in the cloud may use cloud and on-premises data sources, in which case the network between the on-premises data center and GCP should have sufficient throughput to transfer data for transformation and load operations performed in the cloud.

In addition to throughput, architects need to consider latency. When running batch processing workflow, latency is less of an issue than when running applications that depend on services in the cloud and in a local data center. A web application running GCP may need to call an application programming interface (API) function running on premises to evaluate some business logic that is implemented in a COBOL application running on a mainframe. In this case, the time to execute the function and the round-trip time transmitting data must be low enough to meet the web application's SLAs.

Reliability is also a concern for hybrid-cloud networking. A single network interconnect can become a single point of failure. Using multiple interconnects, preferably from different providers, can reduce the risk of losing internetwork communications. If the cost of maintaining two interconnects is prohibitive, an organization could use a VPN that runs over the public Internet as a backup. VPNs do not have the capacity of interconnects, but the limited throughput may be sufficient for short periods of time.

Architects also need to understand when to use different network topologies. Some common topologies are as follows:

Mirrored topology. In this topology, the public cloud and private on-premise environments mirror each other. This topology could be used to set up test or disaster recovery environments.

Meshed topology. With this topology, all systems within all clouds and private networks can communicate with each other.

Gated egress topology. In this topology, on-premises service APIs are made available to applications running in the cloud without exposing them to the public Internet.

Gated ingress topology. With this topology, cloud service APIs are made available to applications running on premises without exposing them to the public Internet.

Gated egress and ingress topology. This topology combines gated egress and gated ingress.

Handover topology. In this topology, applications running on premises upload data to a shared storage service, such as Cloud Storage, and then a service running in GCP consumes and processes that data. This is commonly used with data warehousing and analytic services.

Depending on the distribution of workloads, throughput and latency requirements, and topology, an architect may recommend one or more of three options supported in GCP.

Hybrid-Cloud Implementation Options

Hybrid-cloud computing is supported by three types of network links.

- Cloud VPN
- Cloud Interconnect
- Direct peering

Each of these options has advantages that favor their use in some cases. Also, there may be situations where more than one of these options is used, especially when functional redundancy is needed.

Cloud VPN

Cloud VPN is a GCP service that provides virtual private networks between GCP and on-premises networks. Cloud VPN is implemented using IPsec VPNs and supports bandwidths up to 3 Gbps.

Data is transmitted over the public Internet, but the data is encrypted at the origin gateway and decrypted at the destination gateway to protect the confidentiality of data in transit. Encryption is based on the Internet Key Exchange (IKE) protocol.

Cloud Interconnect

The *Cloud Interconnect service* provides high throughput and highly available networking between GCP and on-premises networks. Cloud Interconnect is available in 10 Gbps or 100 Gbps configurations when using a direct connection between a Google Cloud access point and your data center. When using a third-party network provider, called a *Partner Interconnect*, customers have the option of configuring 50 Mbps to 10 Gbps connections.

The advantages of using Cloud Interconnect include the following:

- You can transmit data on private connections. Data does not traverse the public Internet.

- Private IP addresses in Google Cloud VPCs are directly addressable from on-premises devices.

- You have the ability to scale up Direct Interconnects to 80 Gbps using eight 10 Gbps direct interconnects or 200 Gbps using two 100 Gbps interconnects.

- You have the ability to scale up Partner Interconnects to 80 Gbps using eight 10 Gbps partner interconnects.

A disadvantage of Cloud Interconnect is the additional cost and complexity of managing a direct or partnered connection. If low latency and high availability are not required, then using Cloud VPN will be less expensive and require less management.

An alternative to Cloud Interconnect is *direct peering*.

Direct Peering

Network peering is a network configuration that allows for routing between networks.

Direct peering is a form of peering that allows customers to connect their networks to a Google network point of access. This kind of connection is not a GCP service—it is a lower-level network connection that is outside of GCP. It works by exchanging Border Gateway Protocol (BGP) routes, which define paths for transmitting data between networks. It does not make use of any GCP resources, like VPC firewall rules or GCP access controls.

 At the time of this writing, Google Cloud Platform is offering additional networking options in beta. These include a high availability VPN and 100 Gbps Cloud Interconnect. By the time you read this, they may be generally available.

When working with hybrid computing environments, first consider workloads and where they are optimally run and how data is exchanged between networks. This can help you determine the best topology for the hybrid or multicloud network. There are three options for linking networks: interconnect, VPN, and direct peering. Interconnects provide high throughput, low latency, and high availability. VPNs are a lower-cost option that does not require managing site-to-site connections, but throughput is lower. A third, not generally recommended option is direct peering. This is an option when requirements dictate that the connection between networks be at the level of exchanging BGP routes.

Load Balancing

Load balancing is the practice of distributing work across a set of resources. GCP provides five different load balancers for different use cases. To determine which load balancer is an appropriate choice in a given scenario, you will have to consider three factors.

▪ Is the workload distributed to servers within a region or across multiple regions?

▪ Does the load balancer receive traffic from internal GCP resources only or from external sources as well?

▪ What protocols does the load balancer need to support?

The answers to these questions will help you determine when to use each of the five types:

▪ Network TCP/UDP

▪ Internal TCP/UDP

▪ HTTP(S)

▪ SSL Proxy

▪ TCP Proxy

Regional Load Balancing

The two regional load balancers are Network TCP/UDP and Internal TCP/UDP. Both work with TCP and UDP protocols as their names imply.

Network TCP/UDP

The *Network TCP/UDP load balancer* distributes workload based on IP protocol, address, and port. This load balancer uses forwarding rules to determine how to distribute traffic. Forwarding rules use the IP address, protocol, and ports to determine which servers, known as a *target pool*, should receive the traffic.

The Network TCP/UDP is a non-proxied load balancer, which means that it passes data through the load balancer without modification. This load balancer only distributes traffic to servers within the region where the load balancer is configured.

All traffic from the same connection is routed to the same instance. This can lead to imbalance if long-lived connections tend to be assigned to the same instance.

Internal TCP/UDP

The *Internal TCP/UDP load balancer* is the only internal load balancer. It is used to distribute traffic from GCP resources, and it allows for load balancing using private IP addresses. It is a regional load balancer.

Instances of the Internal TCP/UDP load balancer support routing either TCP or UDP packets but not both. Traffic passes through the Internal TCP/UDP load balancer and is not proxied.

The Internal TCP/UDP load balancer is a good choice when distributing workload across a set of backend services that run on a Compute Engine instance group in which all of the backend instances are assigned private IP addresses.

When traffic needs to be distributed across multiple regions, then one of the global load balancers should be used.

Global Load Balancing

The three global load balancers are the HTTP(S), SSL Proxy, and TCP Proxy Load Balancing load balancers. All global load balancers require the use of the Premium Tier of network services.

HTTP(S) Load Balancing

The *HTTP(S) load balancer* is used when you need to distribute HTTP and HTTPS traffic globally, or at least across two or more regions.

HTTP(S) load balancers use forwarding rules to direct traffic to a target HTTP proxy. These proxies then route the traffic to a URL map, which determines which target group to send the request to based on the URL. For example, `https://www.example.com/documents` will be routed to the backend servers that serve that kind of request, while `https://www.example.com/images` would be routed to a different target group.

The backend service then routes the requests to an instance within the target group based on capacity, health status, and zone.

In the case of HTTPS traffic, the load balancer uses SSL certificates that must be installed on each of the backend instances.

SSL Proxy Load Balancing

The *SSL Proxy load balancer* terminates SSL/TLS traffic at the load balancer and distributes traffic across the set of backend servers. After the SSL/TLS traffic has been decrypted, it can be transmitted to backend servers using either TCP or SSL. SSL is recommended. Also, this load balancer is recommended for non-HTTPS traffic; HTTPS traffic should use the HTTP(S) load balancer.

The SSL Proxy load balancers will distribute traffic to the closest region that has capacity. Another advantage of this load balancer is that it offloads SSL encryption/decryption for backend instances.

TCP Proxy Load Balancing

TCP Proxy Load Balancing lets you use a single IP address for all users regardless of where they are on the globe, and it will route traffic to the closest instance.

TCP Proxy load balancers should be used for non-HTTPS and non-SSL traffic.

GCP provides load balancers tailored for regional and global needs as well as specialized to protocols. When choosing a load balancer, consider the geographic distribution of backend instances, the protocol used, and whether the traffic is from internal GCP resources or potentially from external devices.

Summary

VPCs are virtual private clouds that define a network associated with a project. VPCs have subnets. Subnets are assigned IP ranges and all instances within a subnet are assigned IP addresses from its range. VPCs can share resources by setting up Shared VPCs. Shared VPCs have one host project and one or more service projects. VPC network peering enables different VPC networks to communicate using a private IP address space, as defined in RFC 1918. VPC network peering is used as an alternative to using external IP addresses or using VPNs to link networks.

The flow of traffic within a VPC is controlled by firewall rules. Two implied rules allow all outgoing traffic and deny most incoming traffic. Implied rules cannot be deleted, but they can be overridden by higher-priority rules. When subnets are automatically created for a VPC, a set of default rules are created to allow typical traffic patterns, such as using SSH to connect to an instance.

Hybrid-cloud networking is the practice of providing network services between an on-premise data center and a cloud. Design considerations include latency, throughput, reliability, and network topology. Hybrid cloud networks can be implemented using Cloud VPN, Cloud Interconnect, and direct peering.

Load balancing is the practice of distributing work across a set of resources. GCP provides five different load balancers: Network TCP/UDP, Internal TCP/UDP, HTTP(S), SSL Proxy, and TCP Proxy Load Balancing. Choose a load balancer based on regional or multi-regional distribution of traffic, protocol, and internal or external traffic.

Exam Essentials

Understand virtual private clouds.   Virtual private clouds are like a network in a data center; they are network-based organizational structures for controlling access to GCP resources. They are global resources, so a single VPC can span multiple regions. VPCs are global resources. Subnets are regional resources.

Know VPCs may be shared.   Shared VPCs include a host VPC and one or more service VPCs. Shared VPCs are used to make resources in one project accessible to resources in other projects. Another advantage of Shared VPCs is that you can separate project and network management duties.

Know what firewall rules are and how to use them.   Firewall rules control network traffic by blocking or allowing traffic into (ingress) or out of (egress) a network. Two implied rules allow all outgoing traffic and deny most incoming traffic. Implied rules cannot be deleted, but they can be overridden by higher-priority rules. When subnets are automatically created for a VPC, default rules are created to allow typical traffic patterns. These rules include `default-allow-internal`, `default-allow-ssh`, `default-allow-rdp`, and `default-allow-icmp`.

Know CIDR block notation.   You can specify an IP range using the CIDR notation. This consists of an IPv4 IP address followed by a /, followed by an integer. The integer specifies the number of bits used to identify the subnet; the remaining bits are used to determine the host address.

Understand why hybrid-cloud networking is needed.   When workloads are run in different environments, there will be a need for reliable networking with adequate capacity. Key considerations include latency, throughput, reliability, and network topology.

Understand hybrid-cloud connectivity options and their pros and cons.   Three ways to implement hybrid-cloud connectivity are Cloud VPN, Cloud Interconnect, and direct peering. Cloud VPN is a GCP service that provides virtual private networks between GCP and on-premises networks using the public Internet. The Cloud Interconnect service provides high throughput and highly available networking between GCP and an on-premises network using private network connections. Direct peering allows you to create a direct peering connection to Google Cloud edge.

Know the five types of load balancers and when to use them.   The five types of load balancers are: Network TCP/UDP, Internal TCP/UDP, HTTP(S), SSL Proxy, and TCP Proxy. Choosing between these requires understanding if traffic will be distributed within a single region or across multiple regions, which protocols are used, and whether the traffic is internal or external to GCP.

Review Questions

1. Your team has deployed a VPC with default subnets in all regions. The lead network architect at your company is concerned about possible overlap in the use of private addresses. How would you explain how you are dealing with the potential problem?

   A. You inform the network architect that you are not using private addresses at all.

   B. When default subnets are created for a VPC, each region is assigned a different IP address range.

   C. You have increased the size of the subnet mask in the CIDR block specification of the set of IP addresses.

   D. You agree to assign new IP address ranges on all subnets.

2. A data warehouse service running in GCP has all of its resources in a single project. The e-commerce application has resources in another project, including a database with transaction data that will be loaded into the data warehouse. The data warehousing team would like to read data directly from the database using extraction, transformation, and load processes that run on Compute Engine instances in the data warehouse project. Which of the following network constructs could help with this?

   A. Shared VPC

   B. Regional load balancing

   C. Direct peering

   D. Cloud VPN

3. An intern working with your team has changed some firewall rules. Prior to the change, all Compute Engine instances on the network could connect to all other instances on the network. After the change, some nodes cannot reach other nodes. What might have been the change that causes this behavior?

   A. One or more implied rules were deleted.

   B. The `default-allow-internal` rule was deleted.

   C. The `default-all-icmp` rule was deleted.

   D. The priority of a rule was set higher than 65535.

4. The network administrator at your company has asked that you configure a firewall rule that will always take precedence over any other firewall rule. What priority would you assign?

   A. 0

   B. 1

   C. 65534

   D. 65535

5. During a review of a GCP network configuration, a developer asks you to explain CIDR notation. Specifically, what does the 8 mean in the CIDR block 172.16.10.2/8?

   A. 8 is the number of bits used to specify a host address.

   B. 8 is the number of bits used to specify the subnet mask.

   C. 8 is the number of octets used to specify a host address.

   D. 8 is the number of octets used to specify the subnet mask.

6. Several new firewall rules have been added to a VPC. Several users are reporting unusual problems with applications that did not occur before the firewall rule changes. You'd like to debug the firewall rules while causing the least impact on the network and doing so as quickly as possible. Which of the following options is best?

    A. Set all new firewall priorities to 0 so that they all take precedence over other rules.

    B. Set all new firewall priorities to 65535 so that all other rules take precedence over these rules.

    C. Disable one rule at a time to see whether that eliminates the problems. If needed, disable combinations of rules until the problems are eliminated.

    D. Remove all firewall rules and add them back one at a time until the problems occur and then remove the latest rule added back.

7. An executive wants to understand what changes in the current cloud architecture are required to run compute-intensive machine learning workloads in the cloud and have the models run in production using on-premises servers. The models are updated daily. There is no network connectivity between the cloud and on-premises networks. What would you tell the executive?

    A. Implement additional firewall rules

    B. Use global load balancing

    C. Use hybrid-cloud networking

    D. Use regional load balancing

8. To comply with regulations, you need to deploy a disaster recovery site that has the same design and configuration as your production environment. You want to implement the disaster recovery site in the cloud. Which topology would you use?

    A. Gated ingress topology

    B. Gated egress topology

    C. Handover topology

    D. Mirrored topology

9. Network engineers have determined that the best option for linking the on-premises network to GCP resources is by using an IPsec VPN. Which GCP service would you use in the cloud?

    A. Cloud IPsec

    B. Cloud VPN

    C. Cloud Interconnect IPsec

    D. Cloud VPN IKE

10. Network engineers have determined that a link between the on-premises network and GCP will require an 8 Gbps connection. Which option would you recommend?

    A. Cloud VPN

    B. Partner Interconnect

    C. Direct Interconnect

    D. Hybrid Interconnect

11. Network engineers have determined that a link between the on-premises network and GCP will require a connection between 60 Gbps and 80 Gbps. Which hybrid-cloud networking services would best meet this requirement?

    A. Cloud VPN

    B. Cloud VPN and Direct Interconnect

    C. Direct Interconnect and Partner Interconnect

    D. Cloud VPN, Direct Interconnect, and Partner Interconnect

12. The director of network engineering has determined that any links to networks outside of the company data center will be implemented at the level of BGP routing exchanges. What hybrid-cloud networking option should you use?

    A. Direct peering

    B. Indirect peering

    C. Global load balancing

    D. Cloud IKE

13. A startup is designing a social site dedicated to discussing global political, social, and environmental issues. The site will include news and opinion pieces in text and video. The startup expects that some stories will be exceedingly popular, and others won't be, but they want to ensure that all users have a similar experience with regard to latency, so they plan to replicate content across regions. What load balancer should they use?

    A. HTTP(S)

    B. SSL Proxy

    C. Internal TCP/UDP

    D. TCP Proxy

14. As a developer, you foresee the need to have a load balancer that can distribute load using only private RFC 1918 addresses. Which load balancer would you use?

    A. Internal TCP/UDP

    B. HTTP(S)

    C. SSL Proxy

    D. TCP Proxy

15. After a thorough review of the options, a team of developers and network engineers have determined that the SSL Proxy load balancer is the best option for their needs. What other GCP service must they have to use the SSL Proxy load balancer?

    A. Cloud Storage

    B. Cloud VPN

    C. Premium Tier networking

    D. TCP Proxy Load Balancing

Chapter

7

Designing for Security and Legal Compliance

THE PROFESSIONAL CLOUD ARCHITECT
CERTIFICATION EXAM OBJECTIVES
COVERED IN THIS CHAPTER INCLUDE
THE FOLLOWING:

✓ 3.1 Designing for security

✓ 3.2 Designing for legal compliance

Identity and Access Management

The *Identity and Access Management (IAM)* service is designed to allow you to specify what operations specific users can perform on particular resources. This is also described as specifying "who gets to do what on which resources." IAM is the recommended way to control access in most cases. In some limited cases, such as in a development environment, the older primitive roles system may be used. More on that to follow.

The first step to understanding IAM is to understand the abstractions used. The primary elements of IAM are as follows:

- Identities and groups
- Resources
- Permissions
- Roles
- Policies

It is essential to have a solid grasp of these concepts to function as a Google Cloud architect.

Identities and Groups

Identities and groups are entities that are used to grant access permissions to users.

Identities

An *identity* is an entity that represents a person or other agent that performs actions on a GCP resource. Identities are sometimes called *members*. There are several kinds of identities:

- Google account
- Service account
- Cloud Identity domain

Google accounts are used by people and represent people who interact with GCP, such as developers and administrators. These accounts are designated by an email address that is linked to a Google account. For example, jane.doe@gmail.com could be an identity in GCP. The domain of the email does not have to be gmail.com; it just has to be associated with a Google account.

Service accounts are used by applications running in GCP. These are used to give applications their own set of access controls instead of relying on using a person's account for permissions. Service accounts are also designated by email addresses. You can create multiple service accounts for an application, each with its own set of access control capabilities. When you create a service account, you specify a name of the account, such as gcp-arch-exam. IAM will then create an associated email such as gcp-arch-exam@gcp-certs-1 .iam.gserviceaccount.com, where gcp-certs-1 is the project ID of the project hosting the service account. Note that not all service accounts follow this pattern. When App Engine creates a service account, it uses the appspot.gserviceaccount.com domain.

Cloud Identity is an (IaaS) offering. Users who do not have Google accounts or G Suite accounts can use the Cloud Identity service to create an identity. It will not be linked to a Google account, but it will create an identity that can be used when assigning roles and permissions.

Groups

Related to identities are *Google Groups*, which are sets of Google accounts and service accounts. Groups have an associated email address. Groups are useful for assigning permissions to sets of users. When a user is added to a group, that user acquires the permissions granted to the group. Similarly, when a user is removed from the group, they no longer receive permissions from the group. Google Groups do not have login credentials, and therefore they cannot be used as an identity.

G Suite domains are another way to group identities. A *G Suite domain* is one that is linked to a G Suite account; that is, a G Suite account consists of users of a Google service account that bundles mail, Docs, Sheets, and so on for businesses and organizations. All users in the G Suite account are members of the associated group. Like Google Groups, G Suite domains can be used for specifying sets of users, but they are not identities.

Resources

Resources are entities that exist in the Google Cloud platform and can be accessed by users. Resources is a broad category that essentially includes anything that you can create in GCP. Resources include the following:

- Projects
- Virtual machines
- App Engine applications
- Cloud Storage buckets
- Pub/Sub topics

Google has defined a set of permissions associated with each kind of resource. Permissions vary according to the functionality of the resource.

Permissions

A *permission* is a grant to perform some action on a resource. Permissions vary by the type of resource with which they are associated. Storage resources will have permissions related to creating, listing, and deleting data. For example, a user with the `bigquery.datasets .create` permission can create tables in BigQuery. Cloud Pub/Sub has a permission called `pubsub.subscriptions.consume`, which allows users to read from a Cloud Pub/Sub topic.

Here are some examples of other permissions used by Compute Engine:

- `compute.instances.get`
- `compute.networks.use`
- `compute.securityPolicies.list`

Here are some permissions used with Cloud Storage:

- `resourcemanager.projects.get`
- `resourcemanager.projects.list`
- `storage.objects.create`

For the purpose of the exam, it is not necessary to know specific permissions. However, it is important to know that the permissions in IAM are fine-grained; that is, they grant permissions to do limited operations. Usually, for each Google Cloud API endpoint, there is a permission associated with it. There are API endpoints for almost every kind of action that you can take in GCP so that there is basically a one-to-one relationship between the things that you can do and the permissions to do them.

One of the reasons why it is not required to know specific permissions in detail is that GCP administrators do not have to work with them very often. Instead, they work with roles, which are collections of permissions.

Roles

Roles are sets of permissions. One of the most important things to remember about IAM is that administrators grant roles to identities, not permissions. You cannot grant a permission directly to a user—you must grant it by assigning an identity a role.

Roles can be granted to *identities*. An identity can have multiple roles. Roles are granted for projects, folders, or organizations, and they apply to all resources under those. In other words, resources in those projects, folders, or organizations assume those roles when the role applies to the type of resource. For example, roles granted to a project that grants permissions to Compute Engine instances are applied to VM instances in that project.

There are three types of roles.

- Predefined
- Primitive
- Custom

Predefined Roles

Predefined roles are created and managed by GCP. The roles are organized around groups of tasks commonly performed when working with IT systems, such as administering a server, querying a database, or saving a file to a storage system. Roles have names such as the following:

- `roles/bigquery.admin`
- `roles/bigquery.dataEditor`
- `roles/cloudfunction.developer`
- `roles/cloudsql.viewer`

The naming convention is to use the prefix `roles/` followed by the name of the service and a name associated with a person's organizational responsibilities.

For the purpose of the exam, it is important to understand how predefined roles are structured and named. There may be questions about what role is needed to perform a task, but you will likely be able to choose the correct answer based on the service name and the function performed. Some function names are used repeatedly in predefined roles, such as viewer, admin, and editor.

Primitive Roles

GCP did not always have the IAM service. Before IAM was released, permissions were grouped into a set of three roles that are now called *primitive roles*.

- Viewer
- Editor
- Owner

The *Viewer role* grants a user read-only permission to a resource. A user with a Viewer role can see but not change the state of a resource.

The *Editor role* has all of the capabilities of the Viewer role and can also modify the state of the resource. For example, users with the Editor role on a storage system can write data to that system.

The *Owner role* includes the capabilities of the Editor role and can also manage roles and permissions for the resource to which it is assigned. For example, if the owner role is granted on a project to a user, then that user can manage roles and permissions for all resources in the project. The Owner role can also be assigned to specific resources, such as a Compute Engine instance or a Cloud Pub/Sub topic. In those cases, the permissions apply only to that specific resource.

Users with the Owner role can also set up billing.

As a general rule, you should favor the use of predefined roles over primitive roles except in cases where resources are used by a small, trusted group of individuals. A DevOps team working in a development environment is an example of a use case for using primitive roles. Using primitive roles can reduce the administrative overhead of managing access controls.

Custom Roles

When the predefined roles do not fit a particular set of needs, users of GCP can set up their own roles. These are known as *custom roles*. With custom roles, administrators can specify a particular set of permissions. This is useful when you want to ensure that a user has the fewest permissions possible and is still able to perform tasks associated with their role. This is an example of following the principle of least privilege. It is considered a security best practice.

In highly secure production environments, developers may be able to view code (Get) in production but not change it (Set). If developers are deploying code that makes use of Cloud Functions, they could be granted the role roles/cloudfunctions.developer. This role includes several permissions, including cloudfunctions.functions .sourceCodeGet and cloudfunctions.functions.sourceCodeSet. The cloudfunctions .functions sourceCodeGet permission is not a problem, but the developer should not have the cloudfunctions.functions sourceCodeSet permission. In a case like this, you should create a custom role that has all of the permissions of roles/cloudfunctions .developer except cloudfunctions.functions sourceCodeSet.

Policies

In addition to granting roles to identities, you can associate a set of roles and permissions with resources by using policies. A *policy* is a set of statements that define a combination of users and the roles. This combination of users (or *members* as they are sometimes called) and a role is called a *binding*. Policies are specified using JSON.

In the following example from Google's IAM documentation, the role roles/ storage_objectAdmin is assigned to four identities, and the roles/storage_objectViewer is assigned to one identity—a user with the email bob@example.com:

```
{
  "bindings": [
  {
    "role": "roles/storage.objectAdmin",
    "members": [
      "user:alice@example.com",
      "serviceAccount:my-other-app@appspot.gserviceaccount.com",
      "group:admins@example.com",
      "domain:google.com" ]
  },
  {
    "role": "roles/storage.objectViewer",
    "members": ["user:bob@example.com"]
  }
  ]
}
```

Source: https://cloud.google.com/iam/docs/overview

Policies can be managed using the Cloud IAM API, which provides three functions.

- `setIamPolicy` for setting policies on resources
- `getIamPolicy` for reading policies on resources
- `testIamPermissions` for testing whether an identity has a permission on a resource

Policies can be set anywhere in the resource hierarchy, such as at the organization, folder, or project level (see Figure 7.1). They can also be set on individual resources. Policies set at the project level are inherited by all resources in the project, while policies set at the organization level are inherited by all resources in all folders and projects in the organization. If the resource hierarchy is changed, permissions granted by policies change accordingly.

FIGURE 7.1   Google Cloud Platform resource hierarchy

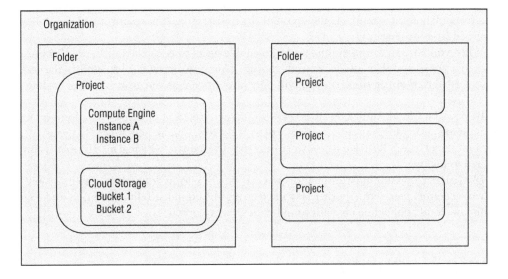

IAM Best Practices

Google recommends several best practices for using IAM securely. For more details, see https://cloud.google.com/iam/docs/using-iam-securely.

Favor predefined roles over primitive roles. Predefined roles are designed to provide all of the permissions needed for a user or service account to carry out a particular set of tasks. Use primitive roles only for small teams that do not need granular permissions or in development and test environments where having broad groups of permissions can facilitate the use of the environment without introducing too much risk. When using predefined roles, assign the most restricted set of roles needed to do a job. For example, if a user only needs to list Cloud Pub/Sub topics, then grant pubsub.topics.list only.

Think in terms of *trust boundaries*, which set the scope of where roles and permissions should apply. For example, if you have three services in an application, consider having three trust boundaries—one for each service. You could use a different service account for each service and assign it just the roles it needs. For example, if only one of the services writes to Cloud Storage, then only that service should have permissions to write to Cloud Storage. If either of the other services is compromised, it will not have permission to write to Cloud Storage and thus limit the amount of damage that can be done.

Review where policies are set in the resource hierarchy. Folders inherit from the organization, and projects inherit from the organization and their containing folders. Policies assigned to a child entity cannot affect its parent entity.

Restrict access to roles that allow a user to administer IAM roles and policies. The `Project IAM Admin` and `Folder IAM Admin` roles allow a user to modify policies but do not grant the permissions needed to read, write, or otherwise administer resources. The effective policy for a resource is the union of the policy set at that resource and the policy inherited from its parent.

When you have to assign multiple roles to enable users to perform a task, grant those roles to a group and then add users to the group. This way, if you need to modify the set of roles needed to perform the task, you will only have to change the group and not each individual user.

Review the Cloud Audit Logs messages for changes to IAM policies. Also, limit access to audit logs using logging roles, such as `roles/logging.viewer` and `roles/logging .privateLogViewer`. Restrict access to `roles/logging.admin`, which gives all permissions related to logging.

IAM gives cloud administrators tools to craft sets of permissions granted to users and service accounts precisely. Another way of ensuring the confidentiality, integrity, and availability of cloud applications is with sound data security practices.

Data Security

GCP provides multiple mechanisms for securing data in addition to IAM policies, which control access to data. Two essential services are encryption and key management.

Encryption

Encryption is the process of encoding data in a way that yields a coded version of data that cannot be practically converted back to the original form without additional information additional information such as a key. We typically distinguish between encryption at rest and encryption in transit.

Encryption at Rest

Google encrypts data at rest by default. You do not have to configure any policy to enable this feature. This applies to all Google data storage services, such as Cloud Storage, Cloud SQL, and Cloud Bigtable. *Encryption at rest* actually occurs at multiple levels.

- At the platform level, database and file data is protected using AES256 and AES128 encryption.
- At the infrastructure level, data is grouped into data chunks in the storage system, and each chunk is encrypted using AES256 encryption.
- At the hardware level, storage devices apply AES256 or AES128 encryption.

At the platform level, distributed filesystems and databases encrypt data. The granularity of encryption can vary across services. For example, Cloud SQL encrypts all data in a database instance with the same key, while Cloud Spanner, Bigtable, and Cloud Firestore encrypt data using the infrastructure encryption mechanism.

When Google Cloud stores data in the storage system, it stores it in subfile chunks that can be up to several gigabytes in size. Each chunk is encrypted with its own key, known as a *data encryption key (DEK)*. If a chunk is updated, a new key is used. Keys are not used for more than one chunk. Also, each chunk has a unique identifier that is referenced by access control lists (ACLs) to limit access to the chunks, which are stored in different locations to make it even more difficult for a malicious actor to piece them together.

In addition to encrypting data that is in chunks, Google also encrypts the data encryption keys using a second key. This is known as *envelope encryption*. The key used to encrypt a DEK is known as a *key encryption key (KEK)*.

In addition to the chunk-level encryption that occurs at the infrastructure level, when blocks of data are written to persistent storage, the storage device encrypts those blocks using either AES128 or AES256. Older devices use AES128, but new storage devices use AES256.

To summarize encryption at rest:

- Data at rest is encrypted by default in Google Cloud Platform.
- Data is encrypted at multiple levels, including the application, infrastructure, and device levels.
- Data is encrypted in chunks. Each chunk has its own encryption key, which is called a data encryption key.
- Data encryption keys are themselves encrypted using a key encryption key.

Google Cloud manages much of the encryption process, including managing keys. This is helpful for users who want Google Cloud to manage all aspects of encryption. In cases where organizations need to manage their own keys, they will have to use one of two key management methods, described in the "Key Management" section.

Before delving into key management, let's look at encryption in transit.

Encryption in Transit

Encryption in transit, also called encryption in motion, is used to protect the confidentiality and integrity of data in the event that the data is intercepted in transit. GCP uses a combination of authenticating sources and encryption to protect data in transit.

Google distinguishes data in transit on the Google network and data in transit on the public Internet. Data within the boundaries of the Google network is authenticated but may not be encrypted. Data outside the physical boundaries of the Google network is encrypted.

Users of applications running in Google Cloud communicate with the application over the Internet. Traffic incoming from users to the Google Cloud is routed to the Google Front End, a globally distributed proxy service. The *Google Front End* terminates HTTP and HTTPS traffic and routes it over the Google network to servers running the application. The Google Front End provides other security services, such as protecting against distributed denial-of-service (DDoS) attacks. Google Front End also implements global load balancers.

All traffic to Google Cloud services is encrypted by default. Google Cloud and the client negotiate how to encrypt data using either *Transport Layer Security (TLS)* or the Google-developed protocol QUIC (in the past, this term stood for Quick UDP Internet Connections, but now the name of the protocol is simply QUIC).

Within the Google Cloud infrastructure, Google uses *Application Layer Transport Security (ALTS)* for authentication and encryption. This is done at layer 7 of the OSI network model.

GCP offers encryption at rest and encryption in transit by default. Cloud users do not have to do anything to ensure that encryption is applied to their data. Users of GCP services can, however, determine how encryption keys are managed.

Key Management

There are many data encryption and key encryption keys in use at any time in the Google Cloud.

Default Key Management

Google manages these keys by default for users. DEKs are stored near the data chunks that they encrypt. There is a separate DEK for each data chunk, but one KEK can be used to encrypt multiple DEKs. The KEKs are stored in a centralized key management service.

The DEKs are generated by the storage service that is storing the data chunk using a common cryptographic library. The DEKs are then sent to the centralized key management service, where they are themselves encrypted using the storage system's KEK. When the storage system needs to retrieve data, it sends the DEK to the key management service, where the calling service is authenticated, and the DEK is decrypted and sent back to the storage system.

Cloud KMS Key Management

Cloud KMS is a hosted key management service in Google Cloud. It enables customers to generate and store keys in GCP. It is used when customers want control over key management but do not need keys to reside on their own key management infrastructure.

Cloud KMS supports a variety of *cryptographic keys*, including AES256, RSA 2048, RSA 3072, RSA 4096, EC P256, and EC P384. It also provides functionality for automatically rotating keys and encrypting DEKs with KEKs. Cloud KMS keys can be destroyed, but there is a 24-hour delay before the key is destroyed in case someone accidentally deletes a key or in the event of a malicious act.

Cloud KMS keys can be used for application-level encryption in GCP services, including Compute Engine, BigQuery, Cloud Storage, and Cloud Dataproc.

Customer-Supplied Keys

A third alternative for key management is *customer-supplied keys*. Customer-supplied keys are used when an organization needs complete control over key management, including storage.

In this model, keys are generated and kept on-premises and used by GCP services to encrypt the customer's data. These keys are passed with other arguments to API function calls. When the keys are sent to GCP, they are stored in memory while being used. Customer-supplied keys are not written to persistent storage.

Encryption and key management are essential components of a comprehensive security regime. Data at rest and in transit are encrypted by default. Keys are managed by default by GCP but can be managed by cloud users. They have two options: Cloud KMS, which is a hosted managed key service that generates and stores keys in the cloud on behalf of a user; the other option is customer-supplied keys, which are managed on-premises and sent to Google as part of API calls. Customer-supplied keys allow customers the greatest amount of control but also require infrastructure and management procedures that are not needed when using default encryption.

Security Evaluation

Cloud users can expend significant time and resources configuring and managing identity management services, access controls, and encryption key management. Without a formal evaluation process, however, they are in the dark about how well these measures protect their systems. Two ways to evaluate the extent of the protection provided by the combination of security measures in place are penetration testing and auditing.

Penetration Testing

Penetration testing is the process of simulating an attack on an information system in order to gain insights into potential vulnerabilities. Penetration tests are authorized by system owners. In some cases, penetration testers know something about the structure of the network, servers, and applications being tested. In other cases, testers start without detailed knowledge of the system that they are probing.

Penetration testing occurs in these five phases:

1. **Reconnaissance** is the phase at which penetration testers gather information about the target system and the people who operate it or have access to it. This could include phishing attacks that lure a user into disclosing their login credentials or details of software running on their network equipment and servers.

2. **Scanning** is the automated process of probing ports and checking for known and unpatched vulnerabilities.

3. **Gaining access** is the phase at which the attackers exploit the information gathered in the first two phases to access the target system.

4. In the **maintaining access** phase, attackers will do things to hide their presence, such as manipulating logs or preventing attacking processes from appearing in a list of processes running on a server.

5. **Removing footprints,** the final phase, involves eliminating indications that the attackers have been in the system. This can entail manipulating audit logs and deleting data and code used in the attack.

During a penetration test, testers will document how they gathered and exploited information, what if any vulnerabilities they exploited, and how they removed indications that they were in the system.

You do not have to notify Google when conducting a penetration test, but you must still comply with the terms of service for GCP.

You can find details on how to perform penetration testing at the Highly Adaptive Cybersecurity Services site at `https://www.gsa.gov/technology/technology-products-services/it-security/highly-adaptive-cybersecurity-services-hacs`, at the Penetration Testing Execution Standard organization at `http://www.pentest-standard .org/index.php/Main_Page`, and at the Open Web Application Security Project at `https://www.owasp.org/index.php/Penetration_testing_methodologies`.

Auditing

Auditing is basically reviewing what has happened on your system. In the case of Google Cloud, there are a number of sources of logging information that can provide background details on what events occurred on your system and who executed those actions.

Your applications should generate logs that identify significant events, especially security-related events. For example, if a new user is granted administrator rights to an application, that should be logged. The Stackdriver Logging Agent will collect logs for widely used services, including syslog, Jenkins, Memcached, MySQL, PostgreSQL, Redis, and Zookeeper. For a full list of logs collected, see `https://cloud.google.com/logging/docs/agent/ default-logs`.

Managed services, like Compute Engine, Cloud SQL, and App Engine, log information to Stackdriver logs.

Cloud Audit Logs is a GCP service that records administrative actions and data operations. Administrative actions that modify configurations or metadata of resources is always logged by Cloud Audit Logs. Data access logs record information when data is created, modified, or read. Data access logs can generate large volumes of data so that it can be configured to collect information for select GCP services.

The logs are saved for a limited period of time. Often, regulations require that audit logs be retained for longer periods of time. Plan to export audit logs from Cloud Audit Logs and save them to Cloud Storage or BigQuery. They can also be written to Cloud Pub/Sub.

Logs are exported from Stackdriver, which supports the following three export methods:

- JSON files to Cloud Storage
- Logging tables to BigQuery datasets
- JSON messages to Cloud Pub/Sub

You can use lifecycle management policies in Cloud Storage to move logs to different storage tiers, such as Nearline and Coldline storage, or delete them when they reach a specified age.

Penetration testing and logging are two recommend practices for keeping your systems secure.

Security Design Principles

As a cloud architect, you will be expected to know security design principles such as separation of duties, least privileges, and defense in depth.

Separation of Duties

Separation of duties (SoD) is the practice of limiting the responsibilities of a single individual in order to prevent the person from successfully acting alone in a way detrimental to the organization. A simple example comes from finance. In a finance department that practices separation of duties, a single person cannot both create a bill to be paid and pay the bill. If they could, then that person could create a false bill in the finance system and then approve its payment. We have similar situations in information technology.

If there is concern that developers should not have the ability to deploy application code to production without first having it reviewed, then the deployment process could be configured to require that another developer review the code before releasing it. In this case, the developer who wrote the code cannot be the one to review it. This kind of practice is used in DevOps organizations that prioritize agility and rapid release of new features. In an organization where security is a higher priority, then developers may not be allowed to deploy code to production at all. Instead, that responsibility is given to a different role.

Sometimes duties extend outside of development or system administration. For example, an organization may require a senior manager to approve giving a root privilege to an account on systems that store sensitive and confidential information. Another person, such as a system administrator, would then actually create the account. In this case, approval and execution are separated.

There are limits to separation of duties. In small organizations, there may not be enough staff to separate duties as much as one would like. For example, if only one person knows how to administer operating systems, then that person would likely have complete access to any part of the system. In such a case, the system administrator could make a malicious change to the operating system and then modify logs to hide those actions. In these cases, other practices, such as third-party audits, can be used to mitigate the risk of malicious activity.

Least Privilege

Least privilege is the practice of granting only the minimal set of permissions needed to perform a duty. IAM roles and permissions are fine-grained and enable the practice of least privilege. Consider, for example, roles associated with App Engine.

`roles/appengine.appAdmin` can read, write, and modify access to all application configuration and settings.

`roles/appengine.appViewer` has read-only access to all application configuration and settings.

`roles/appengine.codeViewer` has read-only access to all application configuration, settings, and deployed source code.

`roles/appengine.deployer` has read-only access to all application configuration and settings and has write access to create a new version but cannot modify existing versions other than deleting versions that are not receiving traffic.

`roles/appengine.serviceAdmin` has read-only access to all application configuration and settings and has write access to module-level and version-level settings but cannot deploy a new version.

Someone who is responsible for auditing App Engine code in production only needs to view code and does not need to change it. They can have only `roles/appengine.codeViewer` and still able to perform their duties. In an organization where developers release code into production but then an application administrator takes over responsibility, developers can be granted `roles/appengine.deployer`, and the application administrator can have `roles/appengine.serviceAdmin`.

The predefined roles in IAM are designed to fit the needs of common roles found in information technology. There is likely to be a predefined IAM role for most organizational roles. If not, you can create a custom role and assign that role the specific privileges required.

The primitive roles—roles/viewer, roles/editor, and roles/owner—are not suitable for implementing the principal of least privilege. These roles grant broad permissions, such as the ability to view all existing resources and data in a project. These may be suitable for some situations, such as a small team development environment, but they should not be used when blanket access to resources is not acceptable.

Defense in Depth

Defense in depth is the practice of using more than one security control to protect resources and data. For example, to prevent unauthorized access to a database, a user attempting to read the data may need to authenticate to the database and must be executing the request from an IP address that is allowed by firewall rules.

Defense in depth prevents an attacker from gaining access to a resource by exploiting a single vulnerability. If an attacker used a phishing scheme to coax a user's login credentials, they could then log in and bypass the protection of the authentication system. With a firewall rule in place to allow traffic only from trusted IP addresses, the attacker could not reach the resource from other IP addresses. The attacker would have to try to spoof an IP address or gain physical access to a location with devices assigned a trusted IP address.

Defense in depth assumes that any security control can be compromised. One might be tempted to think a widely used open source application that has source code available to anyone would have been reviewed so much that any vulnerabilities have been found and corrected. That is not the case. For example, in 2014, the Heartbleed vulnerability was found in OpenSSL, a widely used open source cryptographic software library. The vulnerability allowed attackers to read memory of servers or clients running the compromised version. For more information on Heartbleed, see http://heartbleed.com/.

These security design principles are often used to secure systems, especially when those systems are subject to regulations.

Major Regulations

Governments and industry organizations have developed rules and regulations to protect the privacy of individuals, ensure the integrity of business information, and ensure that a baseline level of security is practiced by organizations using information technology. As a cloud architect, you should understand widely applicable regulations, such as HIPAA/HITECH, which applies to individuals living in the United States, and GDPR, which applies to individuals living in the European Union. Although HIPAA/HITECH and GDPR are different regulations, they have overlapping goals. It is not surprising that similar security controls and practices are often used to comply with both. Two other regulations with which you should be familiar for the Architect exam are SOX and the Children's Online Privacy Protection Act.

Compliance is a shared responsibility of Google and GCP customers. Google is responsible for protecting the physical infrastructure of GCP and lower levels of the GCP platform. Customers are responsible for application-level security, assigning access controls to users, and properly configuring resources.

HIPAA/HITECH

HIPAA is a federal law in the United States that protects individuals' healthcare information. It was enacted in 1996 and updated in 2003 and 2005. HIPAA is a broad piece of legislation, but from a security perspective the most important parts are the HIPAA Privacy Rule and the HIPAA Security Rule.

The *HIPAA Privacy Rule* is a set of rules established to protect a patient's healthcare information. It sets limits on data that can be shared by healthcare providers, insurers, and others with access to protected information. This rule also grants patients the right to review information in their records and request information. For further details on this rule, see `https://www.hhs.gov/hipaa/for-professionals/privacy/index.html`.

The *HIPAA Security Rule* defines standards for protecting electronic records containing personal healthcare information. The rule requires organizations that hold electronic healthcare data to ensure the confidentiality, integrity, and availability of healthcare information, protect against expected threats, and prevent unauthorized disclosures. In practice, this requires security management practices, access control practices, incident response procedures, contingency planning, and evaluation of security measures. For more information on the HIPAA Security rule, see `https://www.hhs.gov/hipaa/for-professionals/security/index.html`.

The *Health Information Technology for Economic and Clinical Health (HITECH) Act* was enacted in 2009, and it includes rules governing the transmission of health information. HITECH extended the application of HIPAA to business associates of healthcare providers and insurers. Business associates that provide services to healthcare and insurance providers must follow HIPAA regulations as well.

When using Google Cloud for data and processes covered by HIPAA, you should know that all of Google Cloud infrastructure is covered under Google's Business Associate Agreement (BAA), and many GCP services are as well, including Compute Engine, App Engine, Kubernetes Engine, BigQuery, Cloud SQL, and many other products. For a complete list, see `https://cloud.google.com/security/compliance/hipaa/`.

For more on HITECH, see `https://www.hhs.gov/hipaa/for-professionals/special-topics/hitech-act-enforcement-interim-final-rule/index.html`.

General Data Protection Regulation

The EU's GDPR was passed in 2016 and began enforcement in 2018. The purpose of this regulation is to standardize privacy protections across the European Union, grant controls to individuals over their private information, and specify security practices required for organizations holding the private information of EU citizens.

GDPR distinguishes controllers and processors. A *controller* is a person or organization that determines the purpose and means of processing personal data. A *processor* is a person or organization that processes data on behalf of a controller. Controllers are responsible for gaining and managing consent of individuals whose data is collected. Controllers direct processors on implementing the wishes of individuals who request access or changes to data. Processors are responsible for securing data and conducting audits to ensure that security practices are functioning as expected.

In the event of a data breach, data processors must notify the controller. Controllers in turn must notify the supervising authority, which varies by country, and individuals whose data was compromised.

For more information on GDPR, see `https://eugdpr.org/`.

Sarbanes-Oxley Act

SOX is a United States federal law passed in 2002 to protect the public from fraudulent accounting practices in publicly traded companies. The legislation includes rules governing financial reporting and information technology controls. SOX has three rules covering destruction and falsification of records, the retention period of records, and the types of records that must be kept.

Under SOX, public companies are required to implement controls to prevent tampering with financial data. Annual audits are required as well. This typically means that companies will need to implement encryption and key management to protect the confidentiality of data and access controls to protect the integrity of data.

For more information on Sarbanes-Oxley, see `https://www.soxlaw.com`.

Children's Online Privacy Protection Act

COPPA is a U.S. federal law passed in 1998 that requires the U.S. Federal Trade Commission to define and enforce regulations regarding children's online privacy. This legislation is primarily focused on children under the age of 13, and it applies to websites and online services that collect information about children.

The rules require online service operators to do the following:

- Post clear and comprehensive privacy policies.

- Provide direct notice to parents before collecting a child's personal information.

- Give parents a choice about how a child's data is used.

- Give parents access to data collected about a child.

- Give parents the opportunity to block collection of a child's data.

- Keep a child's data only so long as needed to fulfill the purpose for which it was created.

- In general, maintain the confidentiality, integrity, and availability of collected data.

Personal information covered by this rule includes name, address, online contact information, telephone number, geolocation data, and photographs.

For more information on COPPA, see `https://www.ftc.gov/tips-advice/business-center/guidance/complying-coppa-frequently-asked-questions`.

ITIL Framework

ITIL, which was formerly known as the *Information Technology Infrastructure Library*, is a set of IT service management practices for coordinating IT activities with business goals and strategies. ITIL specifies 34 practices grouped into three broad areas.

- General management practices, which include strategy, architecture, risk management, security management, and project management

- Service management practices, which include business analysis, service design, capacity and performance management, incident management, and IT asset management

- Technical management practices, which include deployment management, infrastructure management, and software development management

One reason an organization may adopt ITIL is to establish repeatable good practices that span business and technical domains within an organization.

For more on information ITIL, see the following page:

`https://www.tsoshop.co.uk/AXELOS-Global-Best-Practice/ITIL-4/?DI=650015`

Summary

Designing for security and compliance is multifaceted. IAM is used for managing identities, groups, roles, permissions, and related functionality. Predefined roles are preferred over primitive roles in most situations. Policies are used to associate a set of roles and permissions with a resource. Encryption is used to protect data in transit and at rest. Google Cloud encrypts data at rest by default. Google Cloud can manage keys, or customers can manage their own keys. It is strongly suggested that you use security best practices, including separation of duties and defense in depth.

Exam Essentials

Know the key components of the Identity and Access Management service.   The key components of the IAM service include identities and groups, resources, permissions, roles, and policies. Identities can be a Google account, a service account, or a Cloud Identity account. Identities can be collected into Google Groups or G Suite groups.

Understand roles are sets of permissions.   Remember that IAM permissions are granted to roles and roles are granted to identities. You cannot grant a permission directly to an identity. Google has created predefined roles that map to common organizational roles, such as administrators, viewers, and deployers. Predefined roles have all of the permissions someone in that organizational role typically needs to perform their duties. Custom roles can also be created if the predefined roles do not fit your needs.

Primitive roles should be used in limited situations.   Primitive roles are the owner, editor, and viewer. These roles existed prior to IAM and grant course-grained permissions to identities. Primitive roles should be used only in cases where users need broad access, such as developers in a development environment. In general, you should favor predefined roles over primitive roles or custom roles.

Resources are entities in GCP that can be accessed by a user. Access is controlled by IAM.   Resources is a broad category that essentially includes anything that you can create in GCP including projects, virtual machines, storage buckets, and Cloud Pub/Sub topics. Permissions vary by type of resource. Cloud Pub/Sub, for example, has permissions related to writing messages to topics and creating subscriptions. Those permissions would not make sense for other types of resources. Some role patterns are used across entity types, such as admin and viewer.

Policies are used to associate a set of roles and permissions with resources.   A policy is a set of statements that define a combination of users and roles. This combination of users and a role is called a *binding*. Policies are specified using JSON. Policies are used in addition to IAM identity-based access controls to limit access to resources.

Understand the resource hierarchy.   Organizations are at the top of the hierarchy. Organizations contain folders and projects. Folders can contain other folders as well as projects. Access controls assigned to entities in the hierarchy are inherited by entities lower in the hierarchy. Access controls assigned to an entity do not affect entities higher in the hierarchy.

Know that Google encrypts data at rest by default.   Data is encrypted at multiple levels. At the platform level, database and file data is protected using AES256 and AES128 encryption. At the infrastructure level, data is grouped into data chunks in the storage system, and each chunk is encrypted using AES256 encryption. At the hardware level, storage devices apply AES256 or AES128 encryption.

Data at rest is encrypted with a data encryption key (DEK).   The DEK is encrypted with a KEK. Data is encrypted in chunks, and the DEK is kept near the data that it encrypts. The service writing the data has a KEK, which is used to encrypt the DEK. Google manages rotating KEKs.

Understand how Google encrypts data in transit.   Google distinguishes data in transit on the Google network and data in transit in the public Internet. Data within the boundaries of the Google network is authenticated but may not be encrypted. Data outside the physical boundaries of the Google network is encrypted.

Know the three types of key management.   Google provides default key management in which Google generates, stores, and manages keys. With the Cloud KMS Key Management service, customers manage the generation, rotation, and destruction of keys, but the KMS service stores the keys in the cloud. Customer-supplied keys are fully managed and stored on-premises by customers.

Understand the role of penetration testing and auditing.   Both are forms of security evaluation. The goal of penetration testing is to find vulnerabilities in services by simulating an attack by malicious actors. You do not have to notify Google when you perform penetration testing. The purpose of auditing is to ensure that security controls are in place and functioning as expected.

Know security best practices, including separation of duties, least privilege, and defense in depth.   Separation of duties is the practice of limiting the responsibilities of a single individual in order to prevent the person from successfully acting alone in a way detrimental to the organization. Least privilege is the practice of granting only the minimal set of permissions needed to perform a duty. Defense in depth is the practice of using more than one security control to protect resources and data.

Understand how to use security controls to comply with regulations.   Governments and industry organizations have developed rules and regulations to protect the privacy of individuals, ensure the integrity of business information, and make sure that a baseline level of security is practiced by organizations using information technology. Architects should understand the broad requirements of these regulations. Regulations often have common requirements around confidentiality, integrity, and availability.

Review Questions

1. A company is migrating an enterprise application to Google Cloud. When running on-premises, application administrators created user accounts that were used to run background jobs. There was no actual user associated with the account, but the administrators needed an identity with which to associate permissions. What kind of identity would you recommend using when running that application in GCP?

    A. Google-associated account

    B. Cloud Identity account

    C. Service account

    D. Batch account

2. You are tasked with managing the roles and privileges granted to groups of developers, quality assurance testers, and site reliability engineers. Individuals frequently move between groups. Each group requires a different set of permissions. What is the best way to grant access to resources that each group needs?

    A. Create a group in Google Groups for each of the three groups: developers, quality assurance testers, and site reliability engineers. Add the identities of each user to their respective group. Assign predefined roles to each group.

    B. Create a group in Google Groups for each of the three groups: developers, quality assurance testers, and site reliability engineers. Assign permissions to each user and then add the identities to their respective group.

    C. Assign each user a Cloud Identity, and grant permissions directly to those identities.

    D. Create a G Suite group for each of the three groups: developers, quality assurance testers, and site reliability engineers. Assign permissions to each user and then add the identities to their respective group.

3. You are making a presentation on Google Cloud security to a team of managers in your company. Someone mentions that to comply with regulations, the organization will have to follow several security best practices, including least privilege. They would like to know how GCP supports using least privilege. What would you say?

    A. GCP provides a set of three broad roles: owner, editor, and viewer. Most users will be assigned viewer unless they need to change configurations, in which case they will receive the editor role, or if they need to perform administrative functions, in which case they will be assigned owner.

    B. GCP provides a set of fine-grained permissions and predefined roles that are assigned those permissions. The roles are based on commonly grouped responsibilities. Users will be assigned only the predefined roles needed for them to perform their duties.

    C. GCP provides several types of identities. Users will be assigned a type of identity most suitable for their role in the organization.

    D. GCP provides a set of fine-grained permissions and custom roles that are created and managed by cloud users. Users will be assigned a custom role designed specifically for that user's responsibilities.

4. An online application consists of a front-end service, a back-end business logic service, and a relational database. The front-end service is stateless and runs in an instance group that scales between two and five servers. The back-end business logic runs in a Kubernetes Engine cluster. The database is implemented using Cloud SQL PostgreSQL. How many trust domains should be used for this application?

    A. 1.

    B. 2.

    C. 3.

    D. None. These services do not need trust domains.

5. In the interest of separating duties, one member of your team will have permission to perform all actions on logs. You will also rotate the duty every 90 days. How would you grant the necessary permissions?

    A. Create a Google Group, assign roles/logging.admin to the group, add the identity of the person who is administering the logs at the start of the 90-day period, and remove the identity of the person who administered logs during the previous 90 days.

    B. Assign roles/logging.admin to the identity of the person who is administering the logs at the start of the 90-day period, and revoke the role from the identity of the person who administered logs during the previous 90 days.

    C. Create a Google Group, assign roles/logging.privateLogViewer to the group, add the identity of the person who is administering the logs at the start of the 90-day period, and remove the identity of the person who administered logs during the previous 90 days.

    D. Assign roles/logging.privateLogViewer to the identity of the person who is administering the logs at the start of the 90-day period, and revoke the role from the identity of the person who administered logs during the previous 90 days.

6. Your company is subject to several government and industry regulations that require all personal healthcare data to be encrypted when persistently stored. What must you do to ensure that applications processing protected data encrypts it when it is stored on disk or SSD?

    A. Configure a database to use database encryption.

    B. Configure persistent disks to use disk encryption.

    C. Configure the application to use application encryption.

    D. Nothing. Data is encrypted at rest by default.

7. Data can be encrypted at multiple levels, such as at the platform, infrastructure, and device levels. Data may be encrypted multiple times before it is written to persistent storage. At the device level, how is data encrypted in GCP?

    A. AES256 or AES128 encryption

    B. Elliptic curve cryptography

    C. Data Encryption Standard (DES)

    D. Blowfish

8. In GCP, each data chunk written to a storage system is encrypted with a data encryption key. The key is kept close to the data that it encrypts to ensure low latency when retrieving the key. How does GCP protect the data encryption key so that an attacker who gained access to the storage system storing the key could not use it to decrypt the data chunk?

    A. Writes the data encryption key to a hidden location on disk

    B. Encrypts the data encryption key with a key encryption key

    C. Stores the data encryption key in a secure Cloud SQL database

    D. Applies an elliptic curve encryption algorithm for each data encryption key

9. Data can be encrypted at different layers of the OSI network stack. Google Cloud may encrypt network data at multiple levels. What protocol is used at layer 7?

    A. IPSec

    B. TLS

    C. ALTS

    D. ARP

10. After reviewing security requirements with compliance specialists at your company, you determine that your company will need to manage its own encryption keys. Keys may be stored in the cloud. What GCP service would you recommend for storing keys?

    A. Cloud Datastore

    B. Cloud Firestore

    C. Cloud KMS

    D. Bigtable

11. The finance department of your company has notified you that logs generated by any finance application will need to be stored for five years. It is not likely to be accessed, but it has to be available if needed. If it were needed, you would have up to three days to retrieve the data. How would you recommend storing that data?

    A. Keep it in Stackdriver Logging.

    B. Export it to Cloud Storage and store it in Coldline class storage.

    C. Export it to BigQuery and partition it by year.

    D. Export it to Cloud Pub/Sub using a different topic for each year.

12. The legal department in your company notified software development teams that if a developer can deploy to production, then that developer cannot be allowed to perform the final code review before deploying to production. This is an example of which security best practice?

    A. Defense in depth

    B. Separation of duties

    C. Least privilege

    D. Encryption at rest

13. A startup has hired you to advise on security and compliance related to their new online game for children ages 10 to 14. Players will register to play the game, which includes collecting the name, age, and address of the player. Initially, the company will target customers in the United States. With which regulation would you advise them to comply?

A. HIPAA/HITECH

B. SOX

C. COPPA

D. GDPR

14. The company for which you work is expanding from North America to set up operations in Europe, starting with Germany and the Netherlands. The company offers online services that collect data on users. With what regulation must your company comply?

A. HIPAA/HITECH

B. SOX

C. COPPA

D. GDPR

15. Enterprise Self-Storage Systems is a company that recently acquired a startup software company that provides applications for small and midsize self-storage companies. The company is concerned that the business strategy of the acquiring company is not aligned with the software development plans of the software development teams of the acquired company. What IT framework would you recommend the company follow to better align business strategy with software development?

A. ITIL

B. TOGAF

C. Porters Five Forces Model

D. Ansoff Matrix

Chapter

8

Designing for Reliability

THE PROFESSIONAL CLOUD ARCHITECT CERTIFICATION EXAM OBJECTIVES COVERED IN THIS CHAPTER INCLUDE THE FOLLOWING:

- ✓ **4.3** Developing procedures to test the resilience of solutions in production (e.g., DiRT and Simian Army)

- ✓ **6.1** Monitoring/Logging/Alerting solution

- ✓ **6.2** Deployment and release management

- ✓ **6.3** Supporting operational troubleshooting

- ✓ **6.4** Evaluating quality control measures

A reliable system continuously provides its service. Reliability is closely related to availability. *Reliability* is a probability, specifically, the probability that a system will be able to process some specified workload for some period of time. *Availability* is a measure of the percentage of time that a system is functioning and able to meet some specified workload. The difference between reliability and availability is important to keep in mind when thinking about metrics and service-level agreements (SLAs). When thinking broadly about ensuring that services are functioning and, if not, that they can be restored quickly, the two concepts may seem to overlap.

In this book, and for the purposes of the Google Cloud Professional Architect certification exam, we will focus on reliability from a reliability engineering perspective. That is, how do we design, monitor, and maintain services so that they are reliable and available? This is a broad topic that will get a high-level review in this book. For a detailed study of reliability engineering, see the book *Site Reliability Engineering: How Google Runs Production Systems* edited by Betsy Beyer, Chris Jones, Jennifer Petoff, and Niall Richard Murphy (O'Reilly, 2016). Many of the topics presented here, and especially those in the "System Reliability" section of this chapter, are discussed in detail in the SRE book, as it is commonly known.

Improving Reliability with Stackdriver

It is difficult, if not impossible, to provide reliable software services without insights into how that software is functioning. The state of software systems is constantly changing, especially in the cloud, where infrastructure as well as code can change frequently. Also, demands on applications change.

- A new service might be more popular than anticipated, so additional compute infrastructure is needed to meet demand.
- Seasonal variations, such as holiday shopping, can lead to expected high workloads.
- An error in a service may be disrupting a workflow, resulting in a backlog of unprocessed tasks.
- A database runs out of persistent storage and can no longer execute critical transactions.
- The cache hit ratio is dropping for an application because the memory size is no longer sufficient to meet the needs of the service; this does not block operations, but it does slow down workload processing because of increased latency reading data from persistent storage instead of memory.

There are many other ways that things can go wrong in complicated, distributed systems. In addition, even when services are operating as expected, we may be using more resources than needed. Having detailed data about the state of applications and infrastructure can help us maintain reliable and cost-efficient services.

Google Cloud Platform offers *Stackdriver,* a comprehensive set of services for collecting data on the state of applications and infrastructure. Specifically, it supports three ways of collecting and receiving information.

Monitoring. This service is used to help understand performance and utilization of applications and resources.

Logging. This service is used to collect service-specific details about the operations of services.

Alerting. This service is used to notify responsible parties about issues with applications or infrastructure that need attention.

Together, these three components of Stackdriver provide a high degree of observability into cloud systems.

Monitoring with Stackdriver

Monitoring is the practice of collecting measurements of key aspects of infrastructure and applications. Examples include average CPU utilization over the past minute, the number of bytes written to a network interface, and the maximum memory utilization over the past hour. These measurements, which are known as *metrics*, are made repeatedly over time and constitute a time series of measurements.

Metrics

Metrics have a particular pattern that includes some kind of property of an entity, a time range, and a numeric value. GCP has defined metrics for a wide range of entities, including the following:

- GCP services, such as BigQuery, Cloud Storage, and Compute Engine.
- Operating system and application metrics which are collected by Stackdriver agents that run on VMs.
- Anthos, which includes metrics include Kubernetes and Istio metrics
- AWS metrics that measure performance of Amazon Web Service resources, such as EC2 instances.
- External metrics including metrics defined in Prometheus, a popular open source monitoring tool.

In addition to the metric name, value, and time range, metrics can have labels associated with them. This is useful when querying or filtering resources that you are interested in monitoring.

Time Series

A *time series* is a set of metrics recorded with a time stamp. Often, metrics are collected at a specific interval, such as every second or every minute. A time series is associated with a monitored entity. Table 8.1 shows an example of a CPU utilization time series for a VM. Time is shown in epochs, which is the number of seconds that have elapsed since midnight of January 1, 1970, in the UTC time zone, excluding leap seconds.

TABLE 8.1 Example CPU utilization time series for a VM instance

Time	CPU Utilization
1563838664	76
1563838724	67
1563838784	68
1563838844	62
1563838904	71
1563838964	73
1563839024	73
1563839084	61
1563839144	65

Stackdriver Monitoring provides an API for working with time-series metrics. The API supports the following:

- Retrieving time series in a project, based on metric name, resource properties, and other attributes
- Grouping resources based on properties
- Listing group members
- Listing metric descriptors
- Listing monitored entities descriptors

Common ways of working with metrics are using dashboards and alerting.

Dashboards

Dashboards are visual displays of time series. For example, Figure 8.1 shows a simple dashboard with a history of request count and latency of a service.

FIGURE 8.1 Service dashboard showing request count and latency time series data

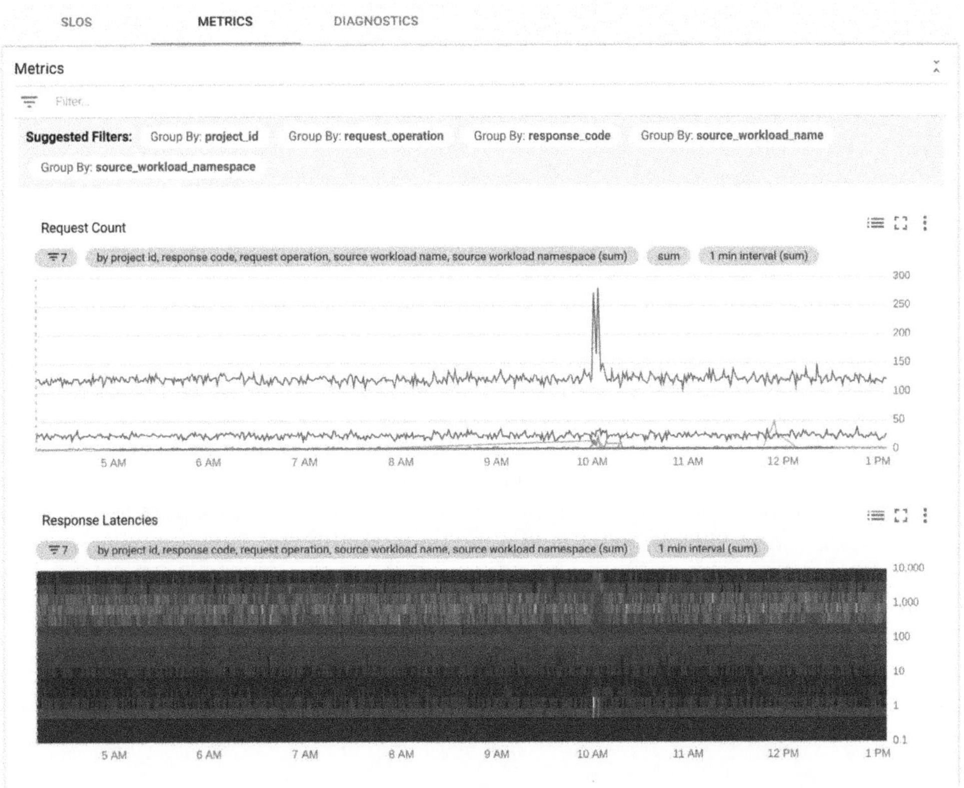

Source: https://cloud.google.com/blog/products/gcp/drilling-down-into-stackdriver-service-monitoring

Dashboards are customized by users to show data that helps monitor and meet service-level objectives or diagnose problems with a particular service. Dashboards are especially useful for determining correlated failures. For example, one dashboard may indicate that you are not meeting your service-level objective of response time for purchase transactions. You might then switch to a dashboard that shows performance metrics for your application server, database, and cache. From there, you could determine which of the main three components of the systems are having performance issues. If, for example, the cache hit rate is unusually low, that can lead to greater IO load on the database, which can increase the latency of purchase transactions. Crafting informative dashboards is often an iterative process. You may know key performance indicators that you should monitor when you first create a service, but over time you may monitor additional metrics. For example, if you had an incident because of a lag in a messaging service, you may want to monitor several metrics of the messaging service to catch potential problems before they occur.

Of course, watching a dashboard for potential problems is not the most efficient use of DevOps engineers' time. Reliable systems also depend on alerting and automation to notify engineers when a problem arises and needs their attention.

Alerting with Stackdriver

Alerting is the process of monitoring metrics and sending notifications when some custom-defined conditions are met. The goal of alerting is to notify someone when there is an incident or condition that cannot be automatically remediated and that puts service-level objectives at risk. If you are concerned about having enough CPU capacity for intermittent spikes in workload, you may want to run your application servers at an average of 70 percent utilization or less. If utilization is greater than 80 percent, then you may want to be notified.

Policies, Conditions, and Notifications

Alerting policies are sets of conditions, notification specifications, and selection criteria for determining resources to monitor.

Conditions are rules that determine when a resource is in an unhealthy state. Alerting users can determine what constitutes an unhealthy state for their resources. Determining what is healthy and what is unhealthy is not always well defined. For example, you may want to run your instances with the highest average CPU utilization possible, but you also want to have some spare capacity for short-term spikes in workload. (For sustained increases in workload, autoscaling should be used to add instances to handle the persistent extra load.)

Finding the optimal threshold may take some experimentation. If the threshold is too high, you may find that performance degrades, and you are not notified. On the other hand, if the threshold is too low, you may receive notifications for incidents that do not warrant your intervention. These are known as *false alerts*. It is important to keep false alerts to a minimum. Otherwise, engineers may suffer "alert fatigue," in which case there are so many unnecessary alerts that engineers are less likely to pay attention to them.

Reducing Alerts

In addition to tuning alerts, reliability can be improved by automatically responding to changes in workload or other conditions. In Compute Engine, an application can run in an instance group of VMs with load balancing and autoscaling enabled. In this case, engineers will need to set thresholds for when to add or remove instances, but using autoscaling can reduce the number of times notifications are sent about VM resources utilization.

A further step toward automation is to use managed services when possible. Instead of running a relational database in Compute Engine to support a data warehouse, you could use BigQuery. In that case, there is no need to monitor servers because it is a serverless product. Of course, there are servers running BigQuery software, but they are managed by Google, which handles monitoring and incident response.

When you are alerted to a condition that needs your attention, you may need to collect information about the state of the system. Logs are excellent sources of such information.

Logging with Stackdriver

Stackdriver Logging is a centralized log management service. Logs are collections of messages that describe events in a system. Unlike metrics that are collected at regular intervals, log messages are written only when a particular type of event occurs. Here are some examples:

- If a new user account is added to an operating system and that account is granted root privileges, a log message with details about that account and who created it may be written to an audit log.

- When a database connection error message is received by an application, the application may write a log message with data about the time and the type of operation that would have been performed.

- Applications running on the Java virtual machine may need to reclaim memory that is no longer in use. This process is called *garbage collection*. Log messages may be written at the start and end of garbage collection.

Stackdriver provides the ability to store, search, analyze, and monitor log messages from a variety of applications and cloud resources. An important feature of Stackdriver Logging is that it can store logs from virtually any application or resource, including GCP resources, other cloud resources, or applications running on premises. The Stackdriver Logging API accepts log messages from any source.

Some of the most important features of Stackdriver Logging are its search and analysis features. In addition to text searching, logs can be easily exported to BigQuery for more structured SQL-based analysis. Logging is also integrated with *Stackdriver Alerting*, so log messages can trigger notifications from the alerting system. Metrics can also be created from log messages, so the functionality of *Stackdriver Monitoring* is available for logs as well.

Applications and resources can create a large volume of log data. Stackdriver Logging will retain log messages for 30 days. If you would like to keep logs for longer, then you can export them to Cloud Storage or BigQuery for longer retention periods.

Logs can also be streamed to Cloud Pub/Sub if you would like to use third-party tools to perform near real-time operations on the log data.

To summarize, Stackdriver provides three essential tools for observing and understanding the state of services: monitoring, alerting, and log management. *Monitoring* collects the basic data about a wide array of resource characteristics and their performance over time. *Alerting* evaluates metric data to determine when some predefined conditions are met, such as high CPU utilization for an extended period of time. *Logging* collects messages about specific events related to application and resource operations. The combination of all three provides a foundation for understanding how complicated systems function and can help improve reliability.

Release Management

Release management is the practice of deploying code and configuration changes to environments, such as production, test, staging, and development environments. It is an integral part of *DevOps*, which combines software engineering and system administration efforts.

In the past, it was common to separate responsibilities for developing software and maintaining it in production. This kind of specialization often helps improve efficiency because individuals can develop skills and knowledge around a narrow domain. In economics, this is known as the *division of labor*. While division of labor can be efficient in many areas, it is less efficient in modern software development environments. Engineers who write code are often the best people to resolve problems with that code in production. Also, with proper tools, software engineers can deploy code to production efficiently so that it does not dramatically cut into the engineers' ability to write code.

Release management is important for reliability because it enables developers to put corrected code into production quickly. There should be no need to wait for some batch release of new code when a bug is found. With release management practices, developers can deploy code frequently and with small changes. This helps get fixes out faster, and it also reduces the risk of introducing new bugs by releasing small changes instead of a large set of changes. When problematic code is released, the same tools that help with deployments can be used to roll back the bad deployments.

Release management tools also provide repositories for capturing information about releases. This can help promote standardized release procedures, which in turn can capture best practices over time and improve overall reliability.

Release management is generally broken down into two core functions: continuous deployment and continuous integration.

Continuous Deployment

Continuous deployment (CD) is the practice of releasing code soon after it is completed and after it passes all tests. CD is an automated process—there is usually no human in the loop. This allows for rapid deployment of code, but since humans other than the developer do not need to review the code prior to release, there is a higher risk of introducing bugs than there would be if a human were in the loop.

In practice, software developers should write comprehensive tests to detect bugs as early as possible. Teams that implement continuous deployment are making a trade-off between fast release of code versus a more thorough review of code. Teams that regularly write comprehensive tests and deploy in small increments find the trade-off favors rapid release. Other teams may find that they optimize their release management practice by having a human quality assurance (QA) engineer review the code and write additional tests.

When a human such as a QA engineer is involved, code may be ready for deployment but not deployed until it is reviewed. This is called *continuous delivery*. Teams that need to guarantee low risks of introducing bugs, or are not as proficient at writing automated tests, may use continuous delivery instead of continuous deployment.

Continuous Deployment Tests

A *test* is a combination of input data and expected output. For example, if you were to test a new calculator function, you might pass the input 2 + 3 to the function and expect to see

5 as the output. There are several different kinds of tests used during deployments. These include the following:

- Unit tests
- Integration tests
- Acceptance tests
- Load testing

Continuous deployment tests promote reliability by reducing the risk that deployed code has errors that can disrupt the functioning of a service.

Unit Tests

A *unit test* is a test that checks the smallest unit of testable code. This could be a function, an API endpoint, or another entry point into a program. Unit tests are designed to find bugs within the smallest unit. In the case of the previous calculator example, the unit test is checking the + operation in the calculator program.

Integration Tests

Integration tests test a combination of units. For example, a RESTful API endpoint may receive a string expression that is passed to the calculator program. The purpose of an integration test is to ensure that the API endpoint properly passes the data to the calculator, receives the results, and returns the results to the caller. Even in this simple example, a number of things can go wrong. The API may pass a string that exceeds the maximum string size accepted by the calculator. The calculator may return its results in a data type that is incompatible with the data type the API function expects. These kinds of bugs are not likely to be caught with simple unit tests.

Integration tests can happen at multiple levels, depending on the complexity of the applications being tested. Testing a low-level API may only test the endpoint code and a single function called by that endpoint. In a more complicated scenario, an integration test can check an API endpoint that calls another API that runs some business logic on a server, which in turn has to query a database.

Acceptance Tests

Unit tests and integration tests help developers ensure that their code is functioning as they expect and want. *Acceptance tests* are designed to assure business owners of the system that the code meets the business requirements of the system. A system can pass rigorous unit and integration tests and still fail to meet business requirements. For example, a code release may have unintentionally disabled some functionality that is unrelated to the code change, or a developer may have forgotten to code a necessary feature. If a developer forgets to include a feature, they are not likely to add a test for that feature.

Load Testing

Load testing is used to understand how a system will perform under a particular set of conditions. A load test creates workloads for the system. This can be as simple as a series of API calls in a fixed time interval. It could also put a heavier-than-expected load on a system. This is useful for testing autoscaling within a cluster and rate limiting or other defensive measures within an application.

Load testing may find bugs that were not uncovered during integration testing. For example, under normal integration testing, a database may have no problem keeping up with the query load. Under heavy loads, the database may not be able to respond to all queries within a reasonable period of time. In that case, the connection will time out. This is a well-understood potential error, so the function should check for it. If it does not, the function could return an error to the code that called it, which in turn could then generate another error that is returned to its calling code. The pattern of returning errors can continue all the way up the application stack. Load testing is especially important when a system may be subject to spiking workloads.

Deployment Strategies

There are a number of different ways that engineers can deploy code to production systems. In many cases, applications run a collection of servers, which each run the application. Also, applications often have a single endpoint that all clients access. For example, an online retailer may have hundreds of servers running its catalog application, but all clients using that catalog use a URL that points to a load balancer for the application. Since many cloud applications are distributed like this, engineers have several options for updating the software on each server.

- Complete deployment
- Rolling deployment
- Canary deployment
- Blue/Green deployment

Complete Deployment

A *complete deployment* updates all instances of the modified code at once. This was a common practice with teams that used waterfall methodologies. It is still the only option in some cases, for example, in the case of a single server running a monolithic application. The other deployment strategies are generally preferred because they reduce the risk of introducing problematic code to all users at once or because they mitigate that risk by providing for rapid switch to the previously running code.

Rolling Deployment

A *rolling deployment* incrementally updates all servers over a period of time. For example, in a 10-server cluster, a deployment may be released to only one server at first. After a period of time, if there are no problems detected, a second server will be updated. This process continues until all of the servers are updated.

An advantage of rolling deployments is that you expose only a subset of users to the risk of disruptive code. In this example, assuming a balanced distribution of users, only 10 percent of the users were exposed to the initial deployment.

Canary Deployment

In a *canary deployment*, engineers release new code, but no traffic is routed to it at first. Once it is deployed, engineers route a small amount of traffic to the deployment. As time passes, if no problems are found, more traffic can be routed to the servers with the newly deployed code.

With a canary deployment, you may want to choose users randomly to route to the new version of code, or you may have criteria for choosing users. A web service that offers a free and paid version of its product may prefer to route free users to new deployments rather than expose paying customers to freshly released code.

Blue/Green Deployment

A *Blue/Green deployment* strategy uses two production environments, named Blue and Green. There are configured identically. At any point in time, one of them (for instance, Green) is the active production environment processing a live workload. The other (in other words, Blue) is available to deploy updated versions of software or new services where those changes can be tested. When testing is complete, workload is shifted from the current environment (Green) to the recently updated environment (Blue).

Blue/Green deployments mitigate the risk of a bad deployment by allowing developers and DevOps engineers to switch between environments quickly. For example, after testing the Blue environment, the workload is routed to the Blue environment. A sudden spike in workload reveals a bug in a service that causes a lag in processing a particular transaction. As soon as the problem is detected, which should be quickly because the environments should be instrumented so that DevOps engineers can monitor key service levels, the workload can be routed back to the Green environment.

If a deployment is completely stateless, then switching between the Blue/Green deployments can operate as just described. In reality, applications often require some kind of state management, such as recording data in a relational database. In this case, it is possible for the Blue and Green environments each to have databases with different information. DevOps engineers and developers will need to have a strategy for addressing this.

One approach is to have a single database that is used by both deployments. If there are only changes to the stateless application layer, then both the Blue and Green deployments can write to the same database. If you need to switch deployments, both will have access to the same data. When the database itself needs to be changed, it is a good practice to use a script to update the database schema to support both the current and the new application versions. Then test and verify that the database changes are correct before switching the application layer to the new environment. Once both the application and database changes are working correctly in the new environment, another database refactoring script can be run to remove any database structures from the older version of the database that are no longer needed.

Continuous deployment is the process of moving code to an environment, such as staging or production. A closely related process is continuous integration.

Continuous Integration

Continuous integration (CI) is the practice of incorporating new code into an established code base as soon as it is complete. For example, a software engineer may have a new algorithm to reduce the time and CPU required to perform a calculation. The code change is isolated to a single function. The software engineers tested the change in their local development and environment and are ready to perform the final tests and release the code to the staging environment.

If the software engineers had to build and compile the code manually, execute tests, and then deploy the code to the production environment for each change, it would make sense to wait until there were multiple changes and then release the code. After all, each of those steps can be time-consuming, and a software engineer's time should be maximized for developing features and services. Bundling multiple changes to code and releasing them as a batch was a common practice before the advent of DevOps. Today, we understand that continually integrating changes into baseline code and then testing and releasing that code is a faster and more efficient way to build software.

Software engineers are able to integrate new code continuously into the production code base because of automated tools.

Tools include version control and test and build tools such as GitHub and Cloud Source Repository. *GitHub* is a widely used open source code repository, and *Cloud Source Repository* is Google Cloud's version control system. Developers can more easily collaborate when they all use a single repository that can keep track of changes to every component in a system. GitHub and Cloud Source Repository support other common practices, such as automatically executing tests or other checks such as verifying stylistic coding conventions. Lint, for example, is the first static code analyzer developed for C. Today there are static code checkers for the many commonly used programming languages.

Jenkins is a widely used CI tool that builds and tests code. Jenkins supports plugins to add functionality, such as integration with a particular version control system or support for different programming languages. *Google Cloud Build* is a GCP service that provides software building services, and it is integrated with other GCP services, such as Cloud Source Repository.

CI and continuous deployment are widely used practices that contribute to systems reliability by enabling small, incremental changes to production systems while providing mechanisms to quickly roll back problematic changes that disrupt service functionality.

Systems Reliability Engineering

While there are many aspects of systems engineering that we could discuss, this section focuses on building systems that are resilient to excessive loads and cascading failures.

Overload

One thing that service designers cannot control is the load that users may want to place on a system at any time. It is a good practice to assume that, at some point, your services will have more workload coming in than they can process. This can happen for a number of reasons, including the following:

- An external event, such as a marketing campaign that prompts new customers to start using a service
- An external event, such as an organizational change in a customer's company that triggers an increase in the workload that they send to your service
- An internal event, such as a bad deployment that causes an upstream service to generate more connection requests than ever generated previously
- An internal event, such as another development team releasing a new service that works as expected but puts an unexpected load on your service

While software engineers and site reliability engineers (SREs) cannot prevent overloads, they can decide how to respond to them.

One factor to consider when responding to overload is the criticality of an operation. Some operations may be considered more important than others and should always take precedence. Writing a message to an audit log, for example, may be more important from a business perspective than responding to a user query within a few seconds. For each of the following overload responses, be sure to take criticality into account when applying these methods.

Shedding Load

One of the simplest ways to respond to overload is to shed or drop data that exceeds the system's capacity to deal with it. A naïve load-shedding strategy would start dropping data as soon as some monitoring condition is met, for example if CPU utilization exceeds some percentage for a period of time or if there are more connection requests than there are available connections in a connection pool. This approach may be easy to implement, but it is something of a crude tool: it does not take into account criticality or variations in service-level agreements with users.

A variation on this approach is to categorize each type of operation or request that can be placed on a service according to criticality. The service can then implement a shedding mechanism that drops lower criticality requests first for some period of time. If overload continues, the next higher category of critical operations can be shed. This can continue until there is no longer an overload condition or until the highest-priority operations are being dropped.

Another approach is to consider service-level agreements with various users. The load from customers who use a service for free may be dropped before the load of paying customers. A business may define a specific volume of workload allowed for a customer based on the amount of money the customer pays for the service. Once the customer exceeds that limit, for example 10,000 requests per minute, future requests are dropped until the next time period starts.

Software engineers can also use statistics to help decide when to shed requests. For example, a time series of measurements from an array of IoT devices may send data every 10 seconds. If there is little variation between the measurements, an ingest service could randomly drop data without significantly affecting the accuracy of aggregate statistics. This approach could be used to sample the input stream to estimate descriptive statistics, such as the mean and standard deviation of the measurements over a period of time.

Degrading Quality of Service

Depending on the nature of a service, it may be possible to provide partial or approximate results.

For example, a service that runs a distributed query over multiple servers may return only the results from some of the servers instead of waiting for servers that are taking too long to respond.

Alternatively, a service could use a sample of data rather than the entire population of data points to estimate the answer to a query. For instance, a data warehouse query that ranks sales regions by total sales last month could sample 10 percent of all sales data to create a sorted list of regions. Assuming that the sample is random and that the data is normally distributed, the ranking based on the sample is likely to be the same as the ranking that would be generated if every data point in the population were considered.

An advantage of responding to overload with a degraded service is that the service provides results rather than errors. This requires some planning on the part of software engineers to accommodate degraded or partial results. This approach does not work in all cases. There is no approximately completing a transaction, for example.

Upstream Throttling

Rather than having a service shed load or return approximate results, a calling service can slow down the rate at which it makes requests. This is known as *upstream throttling*. A client of a service can detect that calls to a service are returning errors or timing out. At that point, the calling service can cache the requests and wait until performance of the downstream service recovers. This requires planning on the part of software engineers, who must have a mechanism to hold requests. Alternatively, the client can shed requests instead of saving them to process at a later time.

Shedding is a good strategy if the data is time sensitive and no longer valuable after some period of time. Consider a downstream process that displays a chart of data from IoT devices for the previous 30 minutes. Data that arrived 30 minutes late would not be displayed and could be discarded without adversely affecting the quality of the visualizations.

When late-arriving data is still of value, then that data can be cached in the calling service or in an intermediate storage mechanism between the calling service and the called service. Message queues, like Cloud Pub/Sub, are often used to decouple the rate at which a service makes a request on another service and the rate at which the downstream service processes those requests.

One way to implement upstream throttling is to use the *Circuit Breaker pattern*. This design pattern uses an object that monitors the results of a function or service call. If the number of errors increases beyond a threshold, then the service stops making additional requests. This is known as *tripping* the circuit breaker. Since the calling service stops sending new requests, the downstream service may be able to clear any backlog of work without having to contend with additional incoming requests. The circuit breaker function waits some random period of time and then tries to make a request. If the request succeeds, the function can slowly increase the rate of requests while monitoring for errors. If there are few errors, then the calling service can continue to increase the rate of calls until it is back to normal operating rates.

Cascading Failures

Cascading failures occur when a failure in one part of a distributed system causes a failure in another part of the system, which in turn causes another failure in some other service, and so on. For example, if a server in a cluster fails, additional load will be routed to other servers in the cluster. This could cause one of those servers to fail, which in turn will further increase the load on the remaining healthy servers.

Consider the example of a database failure. Imagine that a relational database attempts to write data to persistent storage but the device is full. The low-level data storage service that tries to find a block for the data fails to find one. This failure cascades up the database software stack to the code that issued the corresponding INSERT operation. The INSERT operation in turn returns an error to the application function that tried to write the data. That application code detects the error and decides to retry the operation every 10 seconds until it succeeds or until it tries six times and fails each time. Now imagine that multiple calls to the database are failing and responding with the same strategy of retrying. Now the application is held up for up to an additional 60 seconds for each transaction. This slows the processing of that service's workload. This causes a backlog of requests that in turn causes other services to fail. This kind of ripple effect of failures is a significant risk in distributed systems.

Cascading failures are often caused by resource exhaustion. Too much load is placed on system resources like memory, CPU, or database connections until those resources run out. At that point, services start to fail. A common response to this is to limit the load on failing services.

One way to deal with cascading failures is to use the Circuit Breaker design pattern described earlier. This can reduce the load of services and give them a chance to catch up on their workloads. It also gives calling services a chance to degrade gracefully by implementing a degraded quality-of-service strategy.

Another way to deal with cascading failures is to degrade the quality of service. This conserves resources, such as CPU, by reducing the amount of resources allocated to each service call.

When there is a risk of a cascading failure, the best one can hope for may be to contain the number and range of errors returned while services under stress recover.

To prevent cascading failures, load test services and autoscale resources. Be sure to set autoscaling parameters so that resources are added before failures begin. Also, consider the time that is required to bring a resource online. Plan for some period of time between when the need to scale is detected and the time that resource becomes available. Also consider when to release resources when the load drops. If you are quick to drop resources, you may find that you have to add resources again when the load increases slightly. Adding and releasing resources in quick succession, known as *thrashing*, should be avoided. It is better to have spare capacity in resources rather than try to run resources at capacity.

Testing for Reliability

Testing is an important part of ensuring reliability. There are several kinds of tests, and all should be used to improve reliability. Testing for reliability includes practices used in CI/CD but adds others as well. These tests may be applied outside of the CI/CD process. They include the following:

- Unit tests
- Integration tests
- System tests
- Reliability stress test

Unit Tests

Unit tests are the simplest type of test. They are performed by software developers to ensure that the smallest unit of testable code functions as expected. As described in the discussion of CI/CD, these tests are often automated and performed before code is released into an environment outside the engineer's development environment.

Integration Tests

Integration tests determine whether functional units operate as expected when used together. For example, an integration test may be used to check that an API function with a SQL query executes properly when executed against a staging database.

System Tests

Systems tests include all integrated components and test whether an entire system functions as expected. These usually start with simple "sanity checks" that determine whether all of the components function under the simplest conditions. Next, additional load is placed on the system using a performance test. This should uncover any problems with meeting expected workloads when the system is released to production. A third type of system test is a *regression test*. These are designed to ensure that bugs that have been corrected in the past are not reintroduced to the system at a later time. Developers should create tests that check for specific bugs and execute each of those during testing.

Reliability Stress Tests

Reliability stress tests place increasingly heavy load on a system until it breaks. The goal of these tests is to understand when a system will fail and how it will fail. For example, will excessive load trigger failures in the database before errors in the application layer? If the memory cache fails, will that immediately trigger a failure in the database? Stress tests are useful for understanding cascading failures through a system. This can help guide your monitoring strategy so that you are sure to monitor components that can trigger cascading failures. It can also inform how you choose to invest development time to optimize reliability by focusing on potentially damaging cascading failures.

Another form of stress testing uses *chaos engineering* tools such as Simian Army, which is a set of tools developed by Netflix to introduce failures randomly into functioning systems in order to study the impact of those failures. This is an example of the practice of chaos engineering. For more on Simian Army, see `https://medium.com/netflix-techblog/the-netflix-simian-army-16e57fbab116`.

Incident Management and Post-Mortem Analysis

Incidents are events that entail a significant adverse impact on a service's ability to function. An incident may occur when customers cannot perform a task, retrieve information, or otherwise use a system that should be available. Incidents may have a narrow impact, such as just affecting internal teams that depend on a service, or they can have broad impact, such as affecting all customers. Incidents are not minor problems that adversely affect only a small group, for example, a single team of developers. Incidents are service-level disruptions that impact multiple internal teams or external customers.

Incident management is a set of practices that are used to identify the cause of a disruption, determine a response, implement the corrective action, and record details about the incident and decisions made in real time. When an incident occurs, it is good practice to do the following:

- Identify an incident commander to coordinate a response.
- Have a well-defined operations team that analyzes the problems at hand and makes changes to the system to correct or remediate the problem.
- Maintain a log of actions taken, which is helpful during post-mortem analysis.

The goal of incident management is to correct problems and restore services to customers or other system users as soon as possible. There should be less focus on why the problem occurred or identifying who is responsible than on solving the immediate problem.

After an incident is resolved, it is a good practice to conduct a *post-mortem analysis*. During a post-mortem meeting, engineers share information about the chain of events that led to the incident. This could be something as simple as a bad deployment or resource exhaustion, or it could be more complicated, such as a failure in a critical service, for instance, DNS name resolution or an unexpected combination of unlikely events that alone would not have been problematic but together created a difficult-to-predict set of circumstances that led to the incident.

The goal of a post-mortem analysis is to identify the causes of an incident, understand why it happened, and determine what can be done to prevent it from happening again. Post-mortems do not assign blame; this is important for fostering an atmosphere of trust and honesty needed to ensure that all relevant details are understood. Post-mortems are opportunities to learn from failures. It is important to document conclusions and decisions for future reference.

Summary

Reliability is a property of systems that measures the probability that a service will be available for a period of time. Several factors contribute to creating and maintaining reliable systems, including monitoring systems using metrics, logs, and alerts.

Continuous integration and continuous deployment are commonly used practices for managing the release of code. These practices reduce risk by emphasizing the frequent release of small changes. The use of automation helps to reduce the risk that a bad deployment will disrupt services for too long.

Systems reliability engineering is a set of practices that incorporates software engineering practices with operations management. These practices recognize that failures will occur, and the best way to deal with those failures is to set well-defined service-level objectives and service-level indicators, monitor systems to detect indications of failure, and learn from failures using techniques such as post-mortem analysis. Systems should be architected to anticipate problems, such as overloading and cascading failures. Testing is an essential part of promoting highly reliable systems.

Exam Essentials

Know the role of monitoring, logging, and alerting in maintaining reliable systems.   Monitoring collects metrics, which are measurements of key attributes of a system, such as utilization rates. Metrics are often analyzed in a time series. Logging is used to record significant events in an application or infrastructure component. Alerting is the process of sending notifications to human operators when some condition is met indicating that a problem needs human intervention. Conditions are often of the form that a resource measurement exceeds some threshold for a specified period of time.

Understand continuous deployment and continuous integration.   CD/CI is the practice of releasing code soon after it is completed and after it passes all tests. This allows for rapid deployment of code. Continuous integration is the practice of incorporating code changes into baseline code frequently. Code is kept in a version control repository that is designed to support collaboration among multiple software engineers.

Know the different kinds of tests that are used when deploying code.   These include unit tests, integration tests, acceptance tests, and load testing. Unit tests check the smallest unit of functional code. Integration tests check that a combination of units function correctly together. Acceptance tests determine whether code meets the requirements of the system. Load testing measures how well the system responds to increasing levels of load.

Understand that systems reliability engineering is a practice that combines software engineering practices with operations management to reduce risk and increase the reliability of systems. The core tenets of systems reliability engineering include the following:

- Automating systems operations as much as possible
- Understanding and accepting risk and implementing practices that mitigate risk
- Learning from incidents
- Quantifying service-level objectives and service-level indicators
- Measuring performance

Know that systems reliability engineering includes design practices, such as planning for overload, cascading failures, and incident response. Overload is when a workload on a system exceeds the capabilities of the system to process the workload in the time allowed. Ways of dealing with overload include load shedding, degrading service, and upstream or client throttling. Cascading failures occur when a failure leads to an action that causes further failures. An example is that in response to a failure in a server in a cluster, a load balancer shifts additional workload to the remaining healthy servers, causing them to fail due to overload. Incident response is the practice of controlling failures by using a structured process to identify the cause of a problem, correct the problem, and learn from the problem.

Know testing is an important part of reliability engineering. There are several kinds of tests, and all should be used to improve reliability. Testing for reliability includes practices used in CI/CD but adds others as well, particularly stress testing. These tests may be applied outside of the CI/CD process.

Review Questions

1. As an SRE, you are assigned to support several applications. In the past, these applications have had significant reliability problems. You would like to understand the performance characteristics of the applications, so you create a set of dashboards. What kind of data would you display on those dashboards?

   A. Metrics and time-series data measuring key performance attributes, such as CPU utilization

   B. Detailed log data from syslog

   C. Error messages output from each application

   D. Results from the latest acceptance tests

2. After determining the optimal combination of CPU and memory resources for nodes in a Kubernetes cluster, you want to be notified whenever CPU utilization exceeds 85 percent for 5 minutes or when memory utilization exceeds 90 percent for 1 minute. What would you have to specify to receive such notifications?

   A. An alerting condition

   B. An alerting policy

   C. A logging message specification

   D. An acceptance test

3. A compliance review team is seeking information about how your team handles high-risk administration operations, such as granting operating system users root privileges. Where could you find data that shows your team tracks changes to user privileges?

   A. In metric time-series data

   B. In alerting conditions

   C. In audit logs

   D. In ad hoc notes kept by system administrators

4. Release management practices contribute to improving reliability by which one of the following?

   A. Advocating for object-oriented programming practices

   B. Enforcing waterfall methodologies

   C. Improving the speed and reducing the cost of deploying code

   D. Reducing the use of stateful services

5. A team of software engineers is using release management practices. They want developers to check code into the central team code repository several times during the day. The team also wants to make sure that the code that is checked in is functioning as expected before building the entire application. What kind of tests should the team run before attempting to build the application?

   A. Unit tests

   B. Stress tests

   C. Acceptance tests

   D. Compliance tests

6. Developers have just deployed a code change to production. They are not routing any traffic to the new deployment yet, but they are about to send a small amount of traffic to servers running the new version of code. What kind of deployment are they using?

   A. Blue/Green deployment

   B. Before/After deployment

   C. Canary deployment

   D. Stress deployment

7. You have been hired to consult with an enterprise software development that is starting to adopt agile and DevOps practices. The developers would like advice on tools that they can use to help them collaborate on software development in the Google Cloud. What version control software might you recommend?

   A. Jenkins and Cloud Source Repositories

   B. Syslog and Cloud Build

   C. GitHub and Cloud Build

   D. GitHub and Cloud Source Repositories

8. A startup offers a software-as-a-service solution for enterprise customers. Many of the components of the service are stateful, and the system has not been designed to allow incremental rollout of new code. The entire environment has to be running the same version of the deployed code. What deployment strategy should they use?

   A. Rolling deployment

   B. Canary deployment

   C. Stress deployment

   D. Blue/Green deployment

9. A service is experiencing unexpectedly high volumes of traffic. Some components of the system are able to keep up with the workload, but others are unable to process the volume of requests. These services are returning a large number of internal server errors. Developers need to release a patch as soon as possible that provides some relief for an overloaded relational database service. Both memory and CPU utilization are near 100 percent. Horizontally scaling the relational database is not an option, and vertically scaling the database would require too much downtime. What strategy would be the fastest to implement?

   A. Shed load

   B. Increase connection pool size in the database

   C. Partition the workload

   D. Store data in a Pub/Sub topic

10. A service has detected that a downstream process is returning a large number of errors. The service automatically slows down the number of messages it sends to the downstream process. This is an example of what kind of strategy?

   A. Load shedding

   B. Upstream throttling

   C. Rebalancing

   D. Partitioning

Chapter

9

Analyzing and Defining Technical Processes

**THE PROFESSIONAL CLOUD ARCHITECT
CERTIFICATION EXAM OBJECTIVES
COVERED IN THIS CHAPTER INCLUDE
THE FOLLOWING:**

✓ 4.1   Analyzing and defining technical processes

As an architect, you will participate in several kinds of technical processes, including some that we discussed in the previous chapters, such as continuous integration/continuous deployment and post-mortem analysis. In this chapter, we will look at those processes and others, including software development lifecycle planning, testing, and validation, as well as business continuity and disaster recovery planning.

The purpose of this chapter is to describe technical processes with a focus on how they relate to business objectives. For a discussion of more technical aspects, such as the role of tools like Jenkins in continuous integration/continuous deployment, see Chapter 8, "Designing for Reliability."

Software Development Lifecycle Plan

The *software development lifecycle (SDLC)* is a series of steps that software engineers follow to create, deploy, and maintain complicated software systems. SDLC consists of seven phases.

1. Analysis
2. Design
3. Development
4. Testing
5. Deployment
6. Documentation
7. Maintenance

Each phase focuses on a different aspect of software development. The "cycle" in SDLC refers to the fact that even after software is created and deployed, the process of understanding business requirements and developing software to meet those needs continues.

Analysis

Software development begins with requirements. There is some problem that needs to be solved. Some problems are relatively narrow and lend themselves to obvious solutions. For example, addressing a new business requirement, such as enabling the ordering of new types of products, is pretty straightforward. Developing a system to maintain electronic patient records while enabling secure integration with other medical and insurance systems is a massive undertaking. The purpose of the analysis phase is to do the following:

- Identify the scope of the problem to address

- Evaluate options for solving the problem

- Assess the cost benefit of various options

Analysis begins with understanding the problem to be solved.

Scoping the Problem to Be Solved

At this point, the focus is on the business or organizational problem that is to be solved. This requires a combination of domain knowledge about the problem area and software and systems knowledge to understand how to frame a solution. Domain knowledge is often provided by people with direct experience with the requirements. For example, someone with experience in insurance claims processing can describe the workflow that claims processors use and where changes to the workflow could help improve operations. Domain experts with broad knowledge can help identify key aspects of requirements and contribute to efforts to define the scope of a problem.

Evaluating Options

Once the scope of the problem is decided, you should consider options for solving the problem. There may be multiple ways to address a business need, from modifying an existing system to building a new service from scratch. A common question at this stage is, "Should the organization buy a software solution or build one?" *Commercial off-the-shelf software (COTS)* is a term that you may hear to describe existing software solutions.

The advantages of buying software or using a service include the following:

- Faster time to solution since you do not have to build an application

- Allows developers to focus on other business requirements for which there are no good "buy" options

- The purchased software or service likely comes with support

There are disadvantages to buying software, and these can include potentially high licensing costs and the inability to customize the software or service to your specific needs.

If you decide to build your own solution, then you may have the option of modifying an existing application or building a new one from scratch. In these cases, it is important to consider how much modification is needed to make an existing application meet the business requirements. Also consider the lifecycle of the existing application that you would be modifying. Is it a mature, stable application that is well supported? Has the application been deprecated, or is it receiving only minimal support? How well is the application designed; specifically, can it be readily modified to meet the business requirements? Modifying an existing application may be the fastest option for getting a solution into production, but it may also constrain your design choices. For example, if you are modifying a distributed Java application, it is probably best to continue to code in Java and not try to create a module written for the .NET platform.

Building from scratch allows you full control over architecture and systems design choices. However, it may require a significant investment of time and software engineering resources. One of the factors to consider at this point is the opportunity cost of having software engineers work on one project versus another. If you have to choose between implementing a new service that will give your company a competitive advantage in the market or developing a custom workflow tool to support back-office operations, it's probably a better idea to build the competitive feature and use an existing open source or commercial workflow tool.

Cost-Benefit Analysis

Another task in the analysis phase is to consider the costs and benefits of undertaking the project as scoped. The *opportunity cost* described earlier is one example of a cost-benefit consideration. In addition to the opportunity cost of software engineers' time, there is also the financial cost of developing an application.

As an architect, you may be asked to help develop a cost justification for a project. The purpose of this is to allow decision-makers to compare the relative value of different kinds of projects. For example, if instead of developing a new application the logistics department could use the funds to add new, more efficient vehicles to the company's fleet. Which is the better choice? The answer to that question may be decided using measures such as *return on investment (ROI)*, which measures the value, or return, of making an investment.

If at the end of the analysis phase you decide to move ahead with developing software, you will move into the design phase of the SDLC.

Design

In the design phase, you map out in detail how the software will be structured and how key functions will be implemented. The design phase can often be broken into two subphases: high-level design and detailed design.

High-Level Design

During the *high-level design* phase, the major subcomponents of a system are identified. For example, in the case of an insurance claims processing system, the high-level design may include the following:

- An ingest system that receives data on insurance claims from clients

- A data validation system that performs preliminary checks to ensure that all needed information is included

- A business logic backend that evaluates claims against the patient's policy to determine benefits

- A customer communication service that sends letters describing the claim and benefits

- A management reporting component that provides details on the volume of claims processed, backlog of claims to be processed, and other key performance indicators

During high-level design, you will identify the interface between components. This is especially important in microservice architectures or other forms of distributed systems. RESTful interfaces are commonly used with microservices, although GraphQL is an increasingly popular alternative for designing APIs.

If large volumes of data are passed between services, then APIs may not be the most effective interface. Instead, a messaging system, such as Cloud Pub/Sub, may be used. Instead of making a synchronous API call to another service, you can write data to a Cloud Pub/Sub topic, and the receiving service can read it from there. This is a commonly used pattern for decoupling components. The client writing data may experience a spike in load and write more messages than the consuming service can process. In that case, the messages will remain in the queue until the reading service can consume them. This allows the first service to keep up with the workload without requiring the downstream service to keep up at the same pace. This is especially important when the client service can readily scale up, as is the case with stateless web interfaces, but the consuming service cannot readily scale up, for example when writing to a relational database that can only vertically scale.

Detailed Design

Detailed design focuses on how to implement each of the subcomponents. During this phase, software engineers decompose components into modules and lower-level functions that will implement the capabilities of the system. This includes defining data structures, algorithms, security controls, and logging, as well as user interfaces.

As noted earlier, you will probably work with people with deep domain knowledge during the analysis phase. In the detailed design phase, it can help to work with people who will use the system directly. Again, looking at the insurance claim processing example, a domain expert may understand the overall workflow, but a person who spends their workday entering insurance claim data can help identify the requirements for user interface design.

When defining the scope of the problem to be solved, it is important to enlist the help of people with different roles relative to the system. This is especially the case when designing the user interface, which is part of a broader *user experience (UX)*.

During the high-level or detailed design phase, developers may choose libraries, frameworks, or other supporting software for use in the application. For example, if an application will perform a high volume of mathematical calculations, the team may decide to standardize on a particular math library. Similarly, if the application will be built using *object-oriented design*, developers might choose an *Object Relations Mapper (ORM)* to facilitate developing code to interface with a relational database.

Development and Testing

During development, software engineers create software artifacts that implement a system. This can include application code, which implements functionality, and configuration files, which specify environment-specific details, such as file locations or environment variables.

Today, developers often use tools to help with development. These include integrated development environments, code editors, static analysis tools, and database administration tools. They also use version control systems, such as GitHub and Cloud Source Repositories, to support collaboration.

A key component of the development process is testing. In Chapter 8, we discussed different kinds of testing. In the development phase of the SDLC, unit testing and integration testing are commonly performed. Developers have a choice among testing tools to help with these processes. Some are language specific, while others help with a subset of testing, such as API tests.

Documentation

There are three distinct kinds of documentation with regard to software systems:

- Developer documentation
- Operations documentation
- User documentation

 Not all software development lifecycle frameworks include documentation, but for completeness it is included here.

Developer documentation is designed for software engineers who will be working with code. Much developer documentation is in the form of inline comments within the code. This kind of documentation is especially helpful when the purpose or logic of a function or procedure is not obvious. Function or procedure-level documentation should be included for all nontrivial units of code. Other forms of developer documentation include design documents that outline the higher-level details of how a system operates.

Operations documentation consists of instructions used by system administrators and DevOps engineers to deploy and maintain system operations. A *runbook*, for example, includes instructions on how to set up and run a service or application. It may contain troubleshooting advice as well. Operations documentation is important when responsibility for maintaining functioning systems is distributed across a team of developers. In those cases, developers may have to resolve a problem with a part of the code they had never worked on. In times like that, it helps to have a set of best practices and checklists from which to work.

User documentation explains how to use an application. This kind of documentation is written for people who use the system, not necessarily the developers of the system. With the advent of agile software practices, the features of a system can change rapidly, and user documentation should be updated on the same schedule.

Maintenance

Maintenance is the process of keeping software running and up to date with business requirements.

In the past, it was common practice to have a developers' pass of an application for a system administrator to deploy and maintain. With agile software practices, it is common for developers to maintain their own code.

Maintenance includes configuring monitoring, alerting, and logging. *Monitoring* collects data on application and infrastructure performance. This gives developers visibility into how their applications are functioning. *Alerting* is used to notify system administrators or developers of a condition that needs human intervention. *Logging* is used to collect detailed information about the state of the system over time. Software engineers control the details of information saved in log messages, but system administrators can often control the level of detail that is saved.

It is important for architects to understand the software development lifecycle, even if they do not code on a day-to-day basis. The boundaries between development and systems administration are blurring. In the cloud, it is now possible to configure infrastructure by specifying a description in a configuration file. Systems like Terraform, which is used to deploy and modify infrastructure, and Puppet and Chef, which are used to configure software on servers, allow developers to treat infrastructure configuration as code. Architects have substantial roles in the early phases of the SDLC, especially during analysis and high-level design. They also contribute to setting standards for tools, such as version-controlled systems and CI/CD platforms.

Continuous Integration/Continuous Development

CI/CD is the process of incorporating code into a baseline of software, testing it, and if the code passes tests, releasing it for use. A technical discussion of CI/CD can be found in Chapter 8. Here, we will discuss why it is used and some alternative approaches that you may encounter as an architect.

A key benefit of CI/CD is that new features can be rolled out quickly for use by customers. In the past, new features may have been bundled together and released as part of a major update. For example, developers of an application may have released updates every six months. This was a common practice when software was purchased and shipped on magnetic media. The cost of continuous deployment in that situation would have been prohibitive, including the cost of having system administrators constantly updating their deployed systems.

Today, CI/CD is a practical option because tools help developers roll out code quickly and also because much of the software we deploy nowadays is delivered to users as a service. For most cloud applications, there is no need to install new versions of code because we use a SaaS platform. This means that developers can deploy their code to servers in a data center or cloud platform, and users of the service get access to the latest code as soon as it is deployed.

This is not always true. Developers sometimes selectively release new capabilities to customers using a mechanism called *feature flags*.

CI/CD works well when code can be validated using automated tests. While this is the case for many business systems, CI/CD may not be appropriate for some *safety critical software systems*, for example, software used with medical devices or used in aviation, factory automation, or autonomous vehicles. In these cases, the software may need to pass rigorous validation procedures that include human review. *Business-critical software* and *security-critical software* may also have more demanding testing requirements, but those may be able to be incorporated into the CI/CD process. It is not uncommon, for example, to require a human code review before code is pushed from a version control system to the CI/CD tool for deployment.

CI/CD is a widely used alternative to waterfall methodology approaches of batching changes into infrequent bulk updates. CI/CD, however, should be implemented with sufficient testing and human review as required based on software safety and criticality characteristics.

Troubleshooting and Post-Mortem Analysis Culture

Complicated and complex systems fail and sometimes in ways that we do not anticipate. There are a number of ways to respond to this reality.

We can extend more effort to ensure that our software is correct. Formal methods, such as refinements from specification and the use of theorem provers, are appropriate for safety critical systems. In other cases, these formal methods can be too costly and slow down the release of new features more than is warranted by business requirements.

Chaos engineering, which is the practice of introducing failures into a system to better understand the consequences of those failures and identify unanticipated failure modes, is another approach. Obviously, chaos engineering cannot be used in safety critical or security critical systems, but it is a useful tool for many business applications. Netflix's *Simian Army* is a collection of chaos engineering tools that introduce failures at various levels of infrastructure from instances to availability zones.

Another way to accommodate failures is to learn as much as possible from them. This is part of the philosophy behind post-mortem culture in software development. There are two types of post-mortems: one for incidents and another for projects.

Incident Post-Mortems

An *incident* is an event that disrupts a service. Incidents can be fairly limited in scope. For example, a service may lag and not meet service-level objectives for a few minutes. This may impact a small number of customers, but there is no data loss or significant loss of functionality. At the other end of the spectrum are incidents that impact large numbers of customers and entail data loss. This can occur in the event of a severe error, such as a configuration change that leads to a cascading failure, or the loss of access to a zone for an application that is not designed for failover within a region or globally. An *incident post-mortem* is a review of the causes of an incident, assessment of the effectiveness of responses to the incident, and discussions of lessons learned.

Learning from Minor Incidents

Minor incidents in themselves may not provide much opportunity to learn—at least from a single incident. A period of lag in application processing can happen for many reasons, from network failures to resource saturation. If such an incident happens once, it may be caused by factors that are unlikely to occur again, such as a hardware failure in a network device. If we encounter a series of minor incidents, however, there may be a systemic problem present that can be expected to continue if it is not addressed.

In the application lag example, a misconfigured load balancer may not be distributing load optimally across nodes in an instance group that leads to processing lag for some nodes. This may not be as serious as some other incidents, but it should be corrected. This type of incident is an opportunity to evaluate procedures for making configuration changes and verifying that configuration files are correct. A simple typo in the name of a configuration parameter may trigger a warning message that the parameter is unknown, but the configuration process continues. The result could be that the parameter that you had intended to set to a custom value uses the default parameter value instead.

Once you have identified this kind of problem, you could follow up with a couple of remediations. You could, for example, develop a static code analysis script that checks that parameter names are all in a list of valid parameter names. Alternatively, or in addition, you could set an alert on the corresponding log file to send a notification to a DevOps engineer when a parameter warning message appears in the configuration log.

Minor incidents can help you to identify weak spots in your procedures without significant adverse effects on system users. Major incidents are also learning opportunities, but they come with a higher cost.

Learning from Major Incidents

When a large portion of users are adversely affected by a disruption in service or there is a loss of data, then we are experiencing a major incident. The first thing to do in a major incident is to restore service. This may involve a number of people with different responsibilities, such as software developers, network engineers, and database administrators. Chapter 8 includes a discussion of good practices for responding to major incidents. In this chapter, the focus is how to learn from these incidents.

Major incidents in complex systems frequently occur when two or more adverse events occur at or near the same time. If one node in a distributed database runs out of disk space at the same time that a hardware failure causes a network partition, then the impact will be worse than if either of those occurred in isolation. In this example, the impact of the problem in one node cannot be remediated by shifting database traffic to another node because part of the network is down. This combination of failures can be foreseen, but as architects we should assume that there will be failure modes that we do not anticipate.

Major incidents can be valuable learning opportunities, but they need to be treated as such. Engineers responding to an incident should follow established procedures, such as identifying an incident manager, notifying business owners, and documenting decisions and steps taken to correct the problem.

A *timeline of events* is helpful after the fact for understanding what was done. A timeline that includes notes about the reasoning behind a decision is especially helpful. Note taking is not the highest priority during an incident, but capturing as much detail as possible should be a goal. These do not need to be formal, well-structured notes. A thread on a team message channel can capture details about how the team thought through the problem and how they tried to solve it.

After the incident is resolved, the team should review the response. The goal of the review is to understand what happened, why it happened, and how it could be prevented in the future. A post-mortem review is definitely not about assigning blame. Engineers should feel free to disclose mistakes without fear of retribution. This is sometimes called a *blameless culture*. Complex systems fail even when we all do our best, so in many cases there is no one to blame. In other cases, we make mistakes. Part of the value of an experienced engineer is the lessons they have learned by making mistakes.

Project Post-Mortems

Another type of post-mortem that is sometimes used in software engineering is a *project post-mortem*. These are reviews of a project, that review the way work was done. The goal in these post-mortems is to identify issues that might have slowed down work or caused problems for members of the team.

Project post-mortems are helpful for improving team practices. For example, a team may decide to include additional integration testing before deploying changes to the most complicated parts of an application. They may also change how they document decisions, so all team members know where to find answers to questions about issues discussed in the past.

Like incident post-mortems, project post-mortems should be blameless. The goal of these reviews is to improve a team's capabilities.

IT Enterprise Processes

Large organizations need ways to manage huge numbers of software projects, operational systems, and expanding infrastructures. Over time, IT professionals have developed good practices for managing information technology systems at an enterprise level. As an architect, you should be aware of these kinds of processes because they can inform architecture choices and impose requirements on the systems you design. One of the most comprehensive sets of IT enterprise practices is known as ITIL.

ITIL, which initially stood for Information Technology Infrastructure Library, is a set of service management practices. These practices help with planning and executing IT operations in a coordinated way across a large organization. *ISO/IEC 20000* is an international standard for IT service management that is similar to ITIL. ITIL and ISO/IEC 20000 may be helpful for large organizations, but small organizations may find that the overhead of the recommended practices outweighs the benefits.

The ITIL model is organized around four dimensions.

Organizations and people: This dimension is about how people and groups contribute to IT processes.

Information and technology products: This dimension relates to information technology services within an organization.

Partners and suppliers: These are external organizations that provide information technology services.

Value streams and processes: These are the activities executed to realize the benefits of information technologies.

ITIL also organizes management practices into three groups:

General management practices: These practices include strategy, portfolio, and architecture management.

Service management practices: These practices include business analysis, service catalog management, availability management, and service desk management.

Technical management practices: These practices are related to deployment management, infrastructure and platform management, and software development management.

Architects working with large enterprises may need to work within the ITIL, ISO/ICE 20000, or similar enterprise IT processes. The most important thing to know about these practices is that they are used to manage and optimize a wide array of IT operations and tasks. For architects accustomed to thinking about servers, load balancers, and access controls, it is helpful to keep in mind the challenges of coordinating a large and diverse portfolio of services and infrastructure.

The current version of ITIL is ITIL 4, and the definitive documentation about it is available here:

https://www.tsoshop.co.uk/Business-and-Management/
AXELOS-Global-Best-Practice/ITIL-4/

ISO/ICE 20000 is defined by the International Organization for Standards. The definitive ISO/IEC 20000 guide is available here:

https://www.iso.org/standard/51986.html

Business Continuity Planning and Disaster Recovery

Another enterprise-scale process to which architects contribute is *business continuity planning*. This is planning for keeping business operations functioning in the event of a large-scale natural or human-made disaster. A part of business continuity planning is planning for operations of information systems throughout, or despite the presence of disasters. This is called *disaster recovery*.

Business Continuity Planning

Business continuity planning is a broad challenge. It tries to answer the question, "How can we keep the business operating in the event of large-scale disruption of services on which our business depends?" Large-scale disruptions include extreme weather events, such as Category 5 hurricanes, or other disasters, such as 7.0 magnitude or greater earthquakes. These kinds of events can cause major community-scale damage to power, water, transportation, and communication systems. To enable business operations to continue in spite of such events requires considerable planning. These include defining the following:

- Disaster plan
- Business impact analysis
- Recovery plan
- Recovery time objectives

A *disaster plan* documents a strategy for responding to a disaster. It includes information such as where operations will be established, which services are the highest priority, what personnel are considered vital to recovery operations, and plans for dealing with insurance carriers and maintaining relations with suppliers and customers.

A *business impact analysis* describes the possible outcomes of different levels of disaster. Minor disruptions, such as localized flooding, may shut down offices in a small area. In that case, employees who are available to work can be assigned to other offices, and their most important data can be restored from cloud backups. A major disruption that includes loss of power to a data center may require a more extreme response, such as deploying infrastructure to GCP and replicating all services in the cloud. Business impact analysis includes cost estimates as well.

The *recovery plan* describes how services will be restored to normal operations. Once key services, such as power and access to physical infrastructure, are restored, business can start to move operations back to their usual location. This may be done incrementally to ensure that physical infrastructure is functioning as expected.

The recovery plan will also include *recovery time objectives (RTO)*. These prioritize which services should be restored first and the time expected to restore them.

Disaster Recovery

Disaster recovery (DR) is the subset of business continuity planning that focuses specifically on IT operations. DR starts with planning. Teams responsible for services should have plans in place to be able to deploy their services in a production environment other than the one they typically use. For example, if a service usually runs in an on-premises data center, the team should have a plan for running that service in the cloud. The plan should include scripts configured for the disaster recovery environment.

The DR plan should also include a description of roles for establishing services in the DR environment. The process may require a DevOps engineer, a network engineer, and possibly a database administrator, for example. DR plans should have procedures in place for replicating access controls of the normal operating environment. Someone should not have a different set of roles and permissions in the DR environment than they do in the normal production environment.

DR plans should be tested by executing them as if there were a disaster. This can be time-consuming, and some might argue that focusing on delivering features is a higher priority, but DR planning must include testing. Depending on the type of business or organization, there may be industry or government regulations that require specific DR planning and other activities.

A DR plan should have clear guidance on when to switch to a DR environment. For example, if a critical service cannot be restored within a specified period of time, that service is started in the DR environment. In the event that two or more critical services are not functioning in the normal production environment, then all services may be switched to the DR environment. The criteria for switching to a DR environment is a business decision. It may be informed by the organization's risk tolerance, existing service-level agreements with customers, and expected costs for running a DR environment and then restoring to a normal production environment.

For architects, business continuity planning sets the boundaries for establishing disaster plans for IT services and infrastructure. Architects may be called on to contribute to disaster planning. A common challenge is restoring a service in DR to a state as close as possible to the last good state of the system in the production environment. This can require keeping database replicas in a DR environment and copying committed code to a backup repository each time the production version control system is updated.

Business continuity planning and DR should be considered when defining the architecture of systems. DR planning is not something that can be added on after a system is designed, or at least not optimally done so. Organizations may have to choose between comprehensive DR plans that incur high costs and less comprehensive plans that cost less but result in degraded service. Architects can help business decision-makers understand the costs and trade-offs of various DR scenarios.

Summary

Cloud architects contribute to and participate in a wide range of technical and business processes. Some are focused on individual developers and small teams. The software development lifecycle is a series of phases developers go through to understand business requirements, plan the architecture of a solution, design a detailed implementation, develop the code, deploy for use, and maintain it.

Some software development projects can use highly automated CI/CD procedures. This allows for rapid release of features and helps developers catch bugs or misunderstood requirements faster than batch updates that were common in the past.

As systems become more complicated and fail in unanticipated ways, it is important to learn from those failures. A post-mortem analysis provides the means to learn from minor and major incidents in a blameless culture.

Large enterprises with expansive portfolios of software employ additional organization-level processes in order to manage dynamic IT and business environments. ITIL is a well-established set of enterprise practices for managing the general, service, and technical aspects of an organization's IT operations.

Business continuity planning is the process of preparing for major disruptions in an organization's ability to deliver services. Disaster planning is a subset of business continuity planning and focuses on making IT services available in the event of a disaster.

Exam Essentials

Understand that information systems are highly dynamic and individual developers, teams, businesses, and other organizations use technical processes to manage the complexity of these environments. Technical processes have been developed to help individual developers to entire organizations function and operate in a coordinated fashion. SDLC processes focus on creating, deploying, and maintaining code. Other processes include CI/CD, post-mortem analysis, and business continuity planning.

Know that the first stage of the SDLC is analysis. This involves identifying the scope of the problem to address, evaluating options for solving the problem, and assessing the costs/benefits of various options. Options should include examining building versus buying. Cost considerations should include the opportunity costs of developers' time and the competitive value of the proposed software development effort.

Understand the difference between high-level and detailed design. High-level design focuses on major subcomponents of a system and how they integrate. Architecture decisions, such as when to use asynchronous messaging or synchronous interfaces, are made during the high-level design. Detailed design describes how subcomponents will be structured and operate. This includes decisions about algorithms and data structures. Decisions about frameworks and libraries may be made during either high-level or detailed design.

Know the three kinds of documentation. Developer documentation is for other software engineers to help them understand application code and how to modify it. Operations documentation is for DevOps engineers and system administrators so that they can keep systems functioning. A runbook is documentation that describes steps to run an application and correct operational problems. User documentation is for users of the system, and it explains how to interact with the system to have it perform the functions required by the user.

Understand the benefits of CI/CD. CI/CD is the process of incorporating code into a baseline of software, testing it, and if the code passes tests, releasing it for use. A key benefit of CI/CD is that new features can be rolled out for use by customers quickly. This may not always be an option. For example, safety critical software may require substantial testing and validation before it can be changed.

Know what a post-mortem is and why it is used. Post-mortems are reviews of incidents or projects with the goal of improving services or project practices. Incidents are disruptions to services. Major incidents are often the result of two or more failures within a system. Post-mortems help developers better understand application failure modes and learn ways to mitigate risks of similar incidents. Post-mortems are best conducted without assigning blame.

Understand that enterprises with large IT operations need enterprise-scale management practices. Large organizations need ways to manage large numbers of software projects, operational systems, and expanding infrastructures. Over time, IT professionals have developed good practices for managing information technology systems at an enterprise level. One of the most comprehensive sets of IT enterprise practices is ITIL.

Know why enterprises use business continuity planning and disaster recovery planning. These are ways of preparing for natural or human-made disasters that disrupt an organization's ability to deliver services. Disaster planning is a component of business continuity planning. Disaster planning includes defining the criteria for declaring a disaster, establishing and switching to a DR environment, and having a plan for restoring normal operations. DR plans should be tested regularly.

Review Questions

1. A team of early career software engineers has been paired with an architect to work on a new software development project. The engineers are anxious to get started coding, but the architect objects to that course of action because there has been insufficient work prior to development. What steps should be completed before beginning development according to SDLC?

    A. Business continuity planning

    B. Analysis and design

    C. Analysis and testing

    D. Analysis and documentation

2. In an analysis meeting, a business executive asks about research into COTS. What is this executive asking about?

    A. Research related to deciding to build versus buying a solution

    B. Research about a Java object relational mapper

    C. A disaster planning protocol

    D. Research related to continuous operations through storms (COTS), a business continuity practice

3. Business decision-makers have created a budget for software development over the next three months. There are more projects proposed than can be funded. What measure might the decision-makers use to choose projects to fund?

    A. Mean time between failures (MTBF)

    B. Recovery time objectives (RTO)

    C. Return on investment (ROI)

    D. Marginal cost displacement

4. A team of developers is working on a backend service to implement a new business process. They are debating whether to use arrays, lists, or hash maps. In what stage of the SDLC are these developers at present?

    A. Analysis

    B. High-level design

    C. Detailed design

    D. Maintenance

5. An engineer is on call for any service-related issues with a service. In the middle of the night, the engineer receives a notification that a set of APIs is returning HTTP 500 error codes to most requests. What kind of documentation would the engineer turn to first?

    A. Design documentation

    B. User documentation

    C. Operations documentation

    D. Developer documentation

6. As a developer, you write code in your local environment, and after testing it, you commit it or write it to a version control system. From there it is automatically incorporated with the baseline version of code in the repository. What is the process called?

    A. Software continuity planning

    B. Continuous integration (CI)

    C. Continuous development (CD)

    D. Software development lifecycle (SDLC)

7. As a consulting architect, you have been asked to help improve the reliability of a distributed system with a large number of custom microservices and dependencies on third-party APIs running in a hybrid cloud architecture. You have decided that at this level of complexity, you can learn more by experimenting with the system than by studying documents and code listings. So, you start by randomly shutting down servers and simulating network partitions. This is an example of what practice?

    A. Irresponsible behavior

    B. Integration testing

    C. Load testing

    D. Chaos engineering

8. There has been a security breach at your company. A malicious actor outside of your company has gained access to one of your services and was able to capture data that was passed into the service from clients. Analysis of the incident finds that a developer included a private key in a configuration file that was uploaded to a version control repository. The repository is protected by several defensive measures, including role-based access controls and network-level controls that require VPN access to reach the repository. As part of backup procedures, the repository is backed up to a cloud storage service. The folder that stores the backup was mistakenly granted public access privileges for up to three weeks before the error was detected and corrected. During the post-mortem analysis of this incident, one of the objectives should be to

    A. Identify the developer who uploaded the private key to a version control repository. They are responsible for this incident.

    B. Identify the system administrator who backed up the repository to an unsecured storage service. They are responsible for this incident.

    C. Identify the system administrator who misconfigured the storage system. They are responsible for this incident.

    D. Identify ways to better scan code checked into the repository for sensitive information and perform checks on cloud storage systems to identify weak access controls.

9. You have just been hired as a cloud architect for a large financial institution with global reach. The company is highly regulated, but it has a reputation for being able to manage IT projects well. What practices would you expect to find in use at the enterprise level that you might not find at a startup?

    A. Agile methodologies

    B. SDLC

    C. ITIL

    D. Business continuity planning

10. A software engineer asks for an explanation of the difference between business continuity planning and DR planning. What would you say is the difference?

    A. There is no difference; the terms are synonymous.

    B. They are two unrelated practices.

    C. DR is a part of business continuity planning, which includes other practices for continuing business operations in the event of an enterprise-level disruption of services.

    D. Business continuity planning is a subset of disaster recovery.

11. In addition to ITIL, there are other enterprise IT process management frameworks. Which other standard might you reference when working on enterprise IT management issues?

    A. ISO/ICE 20000

    B. Java Coding Standards

    C. PEP-8

    D. ISO/IEC 27002

12. A minor problem repeatedly occurs with several instances of an application that causes a slight increase in the rate of errors returned. Users who retry the operation usually succeed on the second or third attempt. By your company's standards, this is considered a minor incident. Should you investigate this problem?

    A. No. The problem is usually resolved when users retry.

    B. No. New feature requests are more important.

    C. Yes. But only investigate if the engineering manager insists.

    D. Yes. Since it is a recurring problem, there may be an underlying bug in code or weakness in the design that should be corrected.

13. A CTO of a midsize company hires you to consult on the company's IT practices. During preliminary interviews, you realize that the company does not have a business continuity plan. What would you recommend they develop first with regards to business continuity?

    A. Recovery time objectives (RTO)

    B. An insurance plan

    C. A disaster plan

    D. A service management plan

14. A developer codes a new algorithm and tests it locally. They then check the code into the team's version control repository. This triggers an automatic set of unit and integration tests. The code passes, and it is integrated into the baseline code and included in the next build. The build is released and runs as expected for 30 minutes. A sudden spike in traffic causes the new code to generate a large number of errors. What might the team decide to do after the post-mortem analysis of this incident?

    A. Fire the developer who wrote the algorithm

    B. Have at least two engineers review all of the code before it is released

    C. Perform stress tests on changes to code that may be sensitive to changes in load

    D. Ask the engineering manager to provide additional training to the engineer who revised the algorithm

15. Your company's services are experiencing a high level of errors. Data ingest rates are dropping rapidly. Your data center is located in an area prone to hurricanes, and these events are occurring during peak hurricane season. What criteria do you use to decide to invoke your disaster recovery plan?

    A. When your engineering manager says to invoke the disaster recovery plan

    B. When the business owner of the service says to invoke the disaster recovery plan

    C. When the disaster plan criteria for invoking the disaster recovery plan are met

    D. When the engineer on call says to invoke the disaster recovery plan

Chapter

10

Analyzing and Defining Business Processes

**THE PROFESSIONAL CLOUD ARCHITECT
CERTIFICATION EXAM OBJECTIVES
COVERED IN THIS CHAPTER INCLUDE
THE FOLLOWING:**

✓ 4.2   Analyzing and defining business processes

Architects perform a variety of roles, many of which tap into their technical skills and experience. Others require an understanding of business processes, especially with regard to working with and influencing business decision-makers. The Google Cloud Professional Architect Exam may include questions that require you to apply reason about business aspects, like stakeholder influence and portfolio management. This chapter outlines several key business processes, including the following:

- Stakeholder management
- Change management
- Team skill management
- Customer success management
- Cost management

Architects are valued both for their breadth and depth of knowledge. That knowledge base should include an understanding of how managers and business executives function and how to work with them.

Stakeholder Management

A *stakeholder* is someone or some group with an interest in a business initiative. There are many kinds of stakeholders involved with IT projects, including employees, contractors, consultants, project managers, program managers, business process owners, compliance officers, external partners, and vendors. Stakeholder management begins with understanding the relationship between interest and influence, the scope of stakeholder interests, and processes for managing stakeholders.

Interests and Influence

A stakeholder has an interest when the outcome of an initiative, like a software development project, may affect the stakeholder. When a stakeholder has influence, that stakeholder can help direct the outcomes of an initiative.

Stakeholders have varying degrees of interest. For example, a business process owner who is funding a project has financial interests around costs as well as technical interests around functionality and reliability. A compliance officer, however, has more narrow interests around ensuring that the project meets regulation requirements around privacy and security. Interests come in several forms, such as the following:

- Financial interests around costs and benefits of an initiative
- Organizational interests, such as the priority in which projects will be funded and completed
- Personnel interests that include assignment of engineers to a project and opportunities for career advancement
- Functional interests, such as another team of engineers who want the new service to include some specific API functions

Interests describe what a stakeholder wants. *Influence* describes the stakeholder's ability to get it.

Stakeholders also have varying degrees of influence. The people responsible for funding a project and the managers of the software developers on the team can exercise significant influence throughout the course of a project over a broad range of topics. Others have significant influence over a narrow range. An information security engineer, for example, may have the authority to block the release of code if it contains security vulnerabilities, but not if the release breaks a non-security-related feature. In other cases, stakeholders have marginal interests and marginal influence. A team of developers for a related product that will use a new service under development but who do not pay for that service may be of limited influence. They may, for example, have an opportunity to offer suggestions about the design of the new services API but cannot dictate final design decisions.

Interest and influence should be understood relative to a particular initiative, which can range from project to portfolio levels of an organization.

Projects, Programs, and Portfolios

Businesses and organizations have strategies that define their purpose or goals. Those strategies are implemented by executing a variety of initiatives. There is no fixed hierarchy of initiatives, but a common organizational structure uses three levels:

- Projects
- Programs
- Portfolios

A *project* is an initiative focused on completing some organizational task. Projects have budgets specifying the funding available for the project. They also have schedules that describe the expected timeframe for completing the project. Projects also have resources, which include employees, contractors, and consultants assigned to the project. Resources may also include infrastructure, such as access to computing and storage services that are paid for by another entity in the organization.

Projects can be part of programs. *Programs* are initiatives designed to achieve some business goal. For example, a financial institution may have a program to increase the number of home equity loans held by the company. To achieve this goal, the business owners will need to work across a variety of departments, including marketing, compliance, and software development. There may be multiple projects required to meet the goal. In the home equity loan example, there may be a project within the marketing department to determine an advertising plan, while software developers will be charged with updating existing loan origination software to improve ease of use.

Portfolios are groups of projects and programs that collectively implement a business or organization's strategy.

Stakeholders can have interest and influence at any level. A project manager has significant influence over a project and moderate influence over a program, but little or no influence over a portfolio. A senior vice president responsible for a portfolio is responsible for all projects and programs in that portfolio. That person has both interests and influence over the entire portfolio, but much of the influence that person can exercise is often delegated to program and project managers.

Stages of Stakeholder Management

Architects often have influence over projects and portfolios because of their knowledge. Their interests should be centered around achieving the business goal while building quality, reliable, functional software systems. As a stakeholder, architects often work with and influence other stakeholders.

When starting a new project or program, you should consider how you will manage stakeholders with respect to your role on the projects. The four basic stages of stakeholder management are as follows:

- Identifying stakeholders
- Determining their roles and scope of interests
- Developing a communications plan
- Communicating with and influencing stakeholders

Some stakeholders are obvious, such as the business owner of a project or the information security team that reviews all project plans from a compliance perspective. Others may be less obvious, such as other engineering teams with an interest in the functionality that new software may deliver.

Architects can learn about roles and scope of interests from formal project documentation, but that is usually limited to obvious stakeholders. You should work with program and project managers to understand who else may have an interest in an initiative and determine their scope of interests. If someone has an interest in your project, they will likely make their interests known at some point, so it is best to identify them as early as possible so that you can maintain communications with them.

A *communication plan* is an important element of stakeholder management. The plan may include publishing updates to a project site or holding regular status update meetings. The way that information is communicated will vary across projects, but it is important to have a communication mechanism in place so that stakeholders can stay informed.

The communication mechanisms are also a means of influencing stakeholders. For example, as an architect you may post a whitepaper advocating for a particular architectural approach. The purpose is to make business owners aware of a key technical decision that needs to be made while demonstrating to engineers that the proposed approach is the best option for the project.

- It is important to note that architects often have to influence many different stakeholders, not just the stakeholders above them in an organizational hierarchy.

- For more on stakeholder management, see the Association for Project Management body of knowledge documentation, especially "Stakeholder Management," here:

    https://www.apm.org.uk/body-of-knowledge/delivery/
    integrative-management/stakeholder-management/

Change Management

Organizations, teams, and individuals frequently experience change. Businesses change strategies in response to new opportunities. Teams respond to changes in project plans. Individuals change teams and departments. Change is so common and has such a pervasive effect on organizations that people have developed methods for managing change. As an architect, you will likely be exposed to various levels of change, from those changes that affect individuals all the way up to enterprise-scale changes.

Reasons for Change

There are many reasons for change, and those reasons differ for individuals, teams and groups, and enterprises.

Individuals can experience change for reasons that they bring upon themselves or because of external changes. Choosing to switch teams, take a new job, or change career paths are examples of self-directed changes. If a company reorganizes, a colleague leaves a team, or collaborators are moved to a new office, then those are examples of externally motivated changes.

Similarly, teams or departments can change. Team members leave, and others join. Management reassigns responsibilities based on changing business needs. Competition can prompt changes in organizational strategy that in turn leads to changes in programs and projects.

Enterprises can experience change, too. Automakers are dealing with the advent of autonomous vehicles. Traditional media companies are facing new forms of competition from social media. Manufacturers are adapting new kinds of technologies that require new sets of skills from workers. These are examples of technology-driven changes. Change may be prompted by new regulatory conditions, such as the introduction of HIPAA to the United States healthcare market or the GDPR to the European Union. Economic factors, such as the Great Recession from December 2007 to June 2009, can disrupt a wide range of businesses.

For architects, understanding the reason for changes can help you understand stakeholders' interests and inform a longer-term view than you might have had if you considered only project implementation details.

Digital Transformation

Digital transformation is a term used to describe the widespread adoption of digital technology to transform the way that companies create products and deliver value to customers. Digital transformation initiatives often adopt the use of web technologies, cloud computing, mobile devices, big data technologies, IoT, and artificial intelligence (AI). According to a survey by the McKinsey & Company consulting firm, 80 percent of respondents say their organizations have engaged in digital transformation efforts between 2013 and 2018. That same study found that digital transformations are more difficult to manage and less likely to succeed than other kinds of changes. McKinsey & Company also found that common traits of successful digital transformation efforts included knowledgeable leaders, ability to build workforce capabilities, enabling new ways of working, and good communications.

Source: https://www.mckinsey.com/business-functions/organization/our-insights/unlocking-success-in-digital-transformations

---

Change Management Methodologies

Business consultants and academic researchers have developed a number of change management methodologies, but for the purposes of the Google Cloud Professional Architect Exam, we will discuss just one. The goal here is to understand what change management is and how an architect might go about managing change.

The *Plan-Do-Study-Act* methodology of change management was developed by Walter Shewhart, an engineer and statistician, and later popularized by W. Edwards Deming, engineer and management consultant. This methodology is a reframed version of the scientific method for organizational management. It includes four stages.

Plan: When a change experiment is developed, predictions made, and various possible results outlined

Do: When the experiment is carried out, and the results are collected

Study: When results are compared to predictions, and other learning opportunities are identified

Act: When a decision is about using the results of the experiment, for example, by changing a workflow or implementing a new standard

This approach leaves much for the practitioner to decide. What should be measured when conducting an experiment? If this is an experiment that affects individuals, how will the impact on them be measured? What are the criteria for determining when to act and implement changes based on the experiment results? Since the reasons for change are so varied, methodologies can only outline high-level steps. As an architect, you will likely participate in organizational changes. Even if a formal methodology is not used, it may help to understand that there are ways to manage change.

For more on change management, see The W. Edwards Deming Institute Blog, especially the article "Change Management—Post Change Evaluation and Action," here:

https://blog.deming.org/2018/11/
change-management-post-change-evaluation-and-action/

Team Skill Management

Architects are leaders and have a role in developing the skills of engineers, system administrators, engineering managers, and others involved in software development and operations. Organizations often have formal management structures that include project managers, engineering managers, and product managers. They are responsible for ensuring that work is organized and executed. They also typically have some responsibility to help individuals and teams develop their skills.

Architects typically have a wide range of experience and are knowledgeable about a broad range of technical topics. They can contribute to team skill development by doing the following:

- Defining skills needed to execute programs and projects defined by organization strategy
- Identifying skill gaps on a team or in an organization
- Working with managers to develop plans to develop skills of individual contributors
- Helping recruit and retain people with the skills needed by the team
- Mentoring engineers and other professionals

In addition to helping develop internal skill sets, architects may be called on to help engage with customers.

Customer Success Management

Customer success management is another set of soft skills that helps architects succeed. The goal of *customer success management* is to advance the goals of the business by helping customers derive value from the products and services their company provides.

There are four basic stages of customer success management.

- Customer acquisition
- Marketing and sales
- Professional services
- Training and support

Customer acquisition is the practice of engaging new customers. This starts with identifying potential customers. This can be done using broad sweep tactics, such as mining social networks for individuals with certain roles in companies. It may be more targeted, for example, by collecting contact information from people who download a white paper from your company website. The fact that a person was interested enough in the topic is an indicator that the person may be interested in related products.

Businesses dedicate significant resources to *marketing and sales.* These are efforts to communicate with customers and convince them to engage with the business. Architects are not likely to have too much direct involvement with customer acquisition or marketing and sales unless they are in a small organization where they take on multiple roles. Architects, however, may be called on to support other types of customer success management.

Professional services are basically consulting services. Customers may buy or license a software and service and want to integrate it with the existing set of applications. For example, a retail company may buy a business intelligence suite of tools specifically designed for their industry. The company that sold that service may have a team of consultants who are experienced with integrating the set of tools with commonly used retail systems. These consultants may want to consult with architects on the best ways to integrate services, especially when the integration will involve multiple systems and a complicated infrastructure.

Enterprise customers will expect *training and support* from their service vendors. Architects may assist with establishing training programs for customers and help set up support teams, including tools to manage support calls and track customer questions and issues.

For more on customer success management, see the recommended readings and other resources at the Customer Success Association website here:

https://www.customersuccessassociation.com/library/
the-definition-of-customer-success/

Cost Management

Cost management is another business domain with which architects should be familiar. This domain is more than accounting, and it begins with planning that is guided by business strategies and established programs that implement those strategies. The main areas of cost management are as follows:

- Resource planning
- Cost estimating

- Cost budgeting
- Cost control

Resource planning is the first step of cost control. It involves identifying projects and programs that require funding and prioritizing their needs. You may also consider the time required to complete projects and the relative benefit of the project when planning for resources.

Once programs and projects have been prioritized, you can start to estimate the costs of the top priority initiatives. *Cost estimating* should take into account several types of costs, including the following:

- Human resources costs, including salary and benefits
- Infrastructure, such as cloud computing and storage costs
- Operational costs, such as supplies
- Capital costs, such as investments in new equipment

Cost budgeting is the stage of cost management where decisions are made about how to allocate funds. Stakeholders may exercise their influence during budget discussions to promote their projects and programs. Ideally, the budgeting process results in a spending plan that maximizes the overall benefits to the organization.

The final stage of cost management is *cost control*, that is, when funds are expended. Enterprises often have approval processes in place for projects to follow. When starting a new project, project managers or other project leaders may need to work with accounting and procurement teams to set up project budgets and get approval for purchases. Finance departments will often provide managers with reports detailing budget allocations and expenditures.

 For more on project management and cost controls, see the Project Management Institute web page at https://www.pmi.org/.

Summary

Architects are expected to work with colleagues across an organization, including technology professionals as well as professionals from other areas of the business. Architects should have knowledge of business processes that affect their work. This includes stakeholder management, change management, team skill development, customer success management, and cost management. These are examples of "soft skills," which complement the technical skills that architects are expected to have.

Successful organizations often operate within a rational strategy. The business strategy maps to a portfolio of programs and projects that enable the business to execute that strategy. Architects can help their business-oriented colleagues by understanding stakeholders and their interests when working on a project. Architects also use their own influence to shape architecture and other technical decisions. They can also help organizations, teams, and individuals manage change, especially complicated changes like digital transformations. Architects should also understand other common management processes such as team skill management, customer success management, and cost management.

Exam Essentials

Know that stakeholder management involves the interests and influence of individuals and groups who are affected by a project or program.   There are different kinds of stakeholders with varying levels of influence. Know how to identify stakeholders, discover their interests, and understand how to communicate with them.

Understand that change management is particularly challenging.   Change can occur at the individual, team, department, and enterprise levels. Change may be initiated internally or prompted by external factors. One way to manage change is to treat it like a scientific experiment and follow a methodology such as Plan-Do-Study-Act.

Know that team skills are a resource that can be managed.   As an architect, you are in a position to understand the skills needed to execute the projects in the corporate portfolio. You are also able to identify gaps between needed skills and the skills of employees. Use this knowledge to develop training and to recruit additional team members.

Understand that customer success management is a key business process that may require some architecture consultations.   Early stages of customer success management, such as customer acquisition, marketing, and sales, are not likely to need architecture skills, but later stages, such as professional services engagements and technical support, may benefit from the advice of an architect.

Know the various aspects of cost management.   The main steps in cost management are resource planning, cost estimating, cost budgeting, and cost control. Architects may be especially helpful with resource planning and cost estimating, since these require knowledge of how projects serve business strategy and an understanding of the cost of developing services. Architects can use their influence to shape cost budgeting decisions. Architects are not often involved in cost controls, but they may be able to use their technical knowledge to help managers who are involved.

Review Questions

1. You have been asked to help with a new project kickoff. The project manager has invited engineers and managers from teams directly working on the project. They have also invited members of teams that might use the service to be built by the project. What is the motivation of the project manager for inviting these various participants?

    A. To communicate with stakeholders

    B. To meet compliance requirements

    C. To practice good cost control measures

    D. To solicit advice on building team skills

2. A junior engineer asks you to explain some terms often used in meetings. In particular, the engineer wants to know the difference between a project and a program. How would you explain the difference?

    A. There is no difference; the two terms are used interchangeably.

    B. A project is part of a program, and programs span multiple departments; both exist to execute organizational strategy.

    C. A program is part of a project, and projects span multiple departments; both exist to execute organizational strategy.

    D. A project is used only to describe software development efforts, while a program can refer to any company initiative.

3. An architect writes a post for an internal blog describing the pros and cons of two approaches to improving the reliability of a widely used service. This is an example of what stage of stakeholder management?

    A. Identifying stakeholders

    B. Determining their roles and scope of interests

    C. Developing a communications plan

    D. Communicating with and influencing stakeholders

4. Your company provides a SaaS product used by mobile app developers to capture and analyze log messages from mobile devices in real time. Another company begins to offer a similar service but includes alerting based on metrics as well as log messages. This prompts the executives to change strategy from developing additional log analysis features to developing alerting features. This is an example of a change prompted by which one of the following?

    A. Individual choice

    B. Competition

    C. Skills gap

    D. Unexpected economic factors

5. In May 2018, the EU began enforcement of a new privacy regulation known as the GDPR. This required many companies to change how they manage personal information about citizens of the EU. This is an example of what kind of change?

A. Individual choice

B. Competition

C. Skills gap

D. Regulation

6. A program manager asks for your advice on managing change in projects. The program manager is concerned that there are multiple changes underway simultaneously, and it is difficult to understand the impact of these changes. What would you suggest as an approach to managing this change?

A. Stop making changes until the program manager can understand their potential impacts.

B. Communicate more frequently with stakeholders.

C. Implement a Plan-Do-Study-Act methodology.

D. Implement cost control measures to limit the impact of simultaneous changes.

7. A company for whom you consult is concerned about the potential for startups to disrupt its industry. The company has asked for your help implementing new services using IoT, cloud computing, and AI. There is a high risk that this initiative will fail. This is an example of which one of the following?

A. Typical change management issues

B. A digital transformation initiative

C. A project in response to a competitor's product

D. A cost management initiative

8. You and another architect in your company are evaluating the skills possessed by members of several software development teams. This exercise was prompted by a new program to expand the ways that customers can interact with the company. This will require a significant amount of mobile development. This kind of evaluation is an example of which part of team skill management?

A. Defining skills needed to execute programs and projects defined by organizational strategy

B. Identifying skill gaps on a team or in an organization

C. Working with managers to develop plans to develop skills of individual contributors

D. Helping recruit and retain people with the skills needed by the team

9. You and an engineering manager in your company are creating a schedule of training courses for engineers to learn mobile development skills. This kind of planning is an example of which part of team skill management?

   A. Defining skills needed to execute programs and projects defined by organizational strategy

   B. Identifying skill gaps on a team or in an organization

   C. Working with managers to develop plans to develop skills of individual contributors

   D. Helping recruit and retain people with the skills needed by the team

10. After training engineers on the latest mobile development tools and techniques, managers determine that the teams do not have a sufficient number of engineers to complete software development projects in the time planned. The managers ask for your assistance in writing job advertisements reaching out to your social network. These activities are an example of which part of team skill management?

    A. Defining skills needed to execute programs and projects defined by organization strategy

    B. Identifying skill gaps on a team or in an organization

    C. Working with managers to develop plans to develop skills of individual contributors

    D. Helping recruit and retain people with the skills needed by the team

11. A team of consultants from your company is working with a customer to deploy a new offering that uses several services that your company provides. They are making design decisions about how to implement authentication and authorization and want to discuss options with an architect. This is an example of which aspect of customer success management?

    A. Customer acquisition

    B. Marketing and sales

    C. Professional services

    D. Training and support

12. Customers are noticing delays in receiving messages from an alerting service that your company provides. They call your company and provide details that are logged into a central database and reviewed by engineers who are troubleshooting the problem. This is an example of which aspect of customer success management?

    A. Customer acquisition

    B. Marketing and sales

    C. Professional services

    D. Training and support

13. As an architect, you have been invited to attend a trade conference in your field of expertise. In addition to presenting at the conference, you will spend time at your company's booth in the exhibit hall, where you will discuss your company's products with conference attendees. This is an example of what aspect of customer success management?

   A. Customer acquisition

   B. Marketing and sales

   C. Professional services

   D. Training and support

14. A group of executives has invited you to a meeting to represent architects in a discussion about identifying projects and programs that require funding and prioritizing those efforts based on the company's strategy and needs. This is an example of what aspect of cost management?

   A. Resource planning

   B. Cost estimating

   C. Cost budgeting

   D. Cost control

15. An engineer has been tasked with creating reports to help managers track spending. This is an example of what aspect of cost management?

   A. Resource planning

   B. Cost estimating

   C. Cost budgeting

   D. Cost control

Chapter

11

Development and Operations

PROFESSIONAL CLOUD ARCHITECT
CERTIFICATION EXAM OBJECTIVES
COVERED IN THIS CHAPTER INCLUDE
THE FOLLOWING:

✓ 5.1 Advising development/operation team(s) to ensure successful deployment of the solution

✓ 5.2 Interacting with Google Cloud using GCP SDK

Application Development Methodologies

Application development methodologies are principles for organizing and managing software development projects. *Methodologies* provide a set of practices that developers and stakeholders follow in order to produce operational software.

When a problem is well understood and the deliverable functionality is known in detail, you may find that a process that starts with requirements and analysis and then moves to design and coding in a linear fashion works well. For example, if you were trying to implement a tic-tac-toe game using only the ASCII characters available on a Linux terminal, this methodology may work. If you are planning to develop a tic-tac-toe game that will be played on mobile devices, support multiple mobile platforms, and include additional features such as leader boards and competitions, then it is unlikely that you will be able to use a strictly linear development methodology and succeed.

Software developers and other stakeholders have developed a variety of application development methodologies. Many of these methodologies are specific implementations of one of three paradigms or models of software development.

- Waterfall
- Spiral
- Agile

Waterfall methodologies are the oldest of the three. The practices advocated in spiral and agile methodologies are designed to avoid some of the drawbacks of waterfall methodologies.

Waterfall

The waterfall model of applications development is aptly named because with *waterfall methodologies*, once you complete a phase, there is no going back, much like going over a waterfall. The typical phases in a waterfall methodology are as follows:

- Requirements
- Design

- Implementation
- Testing and verification
- Maintenance

Advocates of the waterfall methodology argue that spending time in early stages of application development will result in lower overall costs. For example, if all functional requirements are known before design starts, then all of those requirements can be taken into account when designing. Similarly, if a design is detailed and comprehensive, then developers will save time coding because they will know exactly what needs to be implemented. In theory, waterfall methodologies should reduce the risk of investing time in developing code that will not be used or having to redesign a component because a requirement was missed.

Waterfall methodologies do not work well in situations where requirements cannot be completely known in the early stages or when requirements may change. Requirements may change for business reasons.

Gathering requirements for a new user interface, for example, can be difficult without understanding how users want to interact with a system. User interface designers could get some requirements by interviewing users about their needs and expectations, but users do not necessarily know what they will want until they interact with the system.

Business requirements can change over the course of a project. A sales team may ask developers to create a customer management application with specific functionality, such as assigning each salesperson to a geographic territory. Several weeks later, the sales team reorganizes and now assigns salespeople to products, not geographic territories. In this scenario, the developers cannot proceed with the original specifications without risking building an application that does not meet business requirements.

One way to allow for changes in requirements and design phases is to revisit these stages multiple times over the course of a development project.

Spiral

Spiral methodologies drop the strict requirement of not returning to an earlier stage in the process. Spiral methodologies use similar phases to waterfall methodologies, but instead of trying to complete each stage for the entire application, spiral approaches work on only a limited set of functionalities at a time. After all the stages have been completed for one set of functionalities, stakeholders determine what to work on next, and the process begins again.

Spiral models are designed to reduce risk in application development. They do this by specifying what should occur in each cycle, including the following:

- Understanding stakeholders' objectives
- Reviewing product and process alternatives
- Identifying risks and how to mitigate them
- Securing stakeholder commitment to the next iteration

An advantage of spiral approaches is that you can learn things in each iteration that can be applied in later iterations. Spiral approaches are adaptive, too. For example, if business requirements change after a component has been developed and deployed, it can be changed in a later iteration without disrupting the normal flow of the development process.

Agile

Agile methodologies are increasingly being used for software development. These methodologies are distinguished by their focus on close collaboration between developers and stakeholders and on frequent code deployments. Early advocates for agile methods summarized the principles of agile as follows:

- Individuals and interactions over processes and tools
- Working software over comprehensive documentation
- Customer collaboration over contract negotiation
- Responding to change over following a plan

See The Agile Manifesto (`https://agilmanifesto.org`) for more on the motivations for this methodology.

Like spiral methodologies, agile methodologies are iterative. However, they typically have shorter cycles and focus on smaller deliverables. Each iteration includes planning, design, development, testing, and deployment.

There is a focus on quality in agile methodologies. This includes meeting business requirements and producing functional, maintainable code. Testing is part of the development stage in agile and not limited to the post-development test phase found in waterfall methodologies.

Agile processes are transparent. There is close collaboration between developers and business stakeholders. This collaboration helps keep a focus on business value and allows developers to learn about changes in requirements quickly. These practices make agile more adaptive than either the waterfall or spiral methodology.

Architects can help application developers decide on the most appropriate methodology for their development efforts. In many cases, agile methods work well because of close collaboration and transparency. This reduces the risk that some critical functionality will be missed or that stakeholders are left uninformed about the status of a project. Agile is well suited to projects that must adapt to changing business and technical requirements.

When developing applications to support business processes that change slowly and have complex requirements, a spiral methodology may be appropriate. In such cases, there may be too many stakeholders and domain experts involved to work collaboratively. In such cases, detailed analysis and documentation may be required so that all stakeholders understand the objectives and risks and agree to them. The iterative nature of a spiral methodology provides opportunities to adapt to changing requirements.

A waterfall methodology may be appropriate for critical safety software, such as an application used with a medical device. In such a case, the requirements may be fairly narrow and fixed. Extensive testing and verification would be required so that it is appropriate to have a separate testing phase in addition to testing done during development. Other devices may interface with the medical device, so detailed technical documentation would be needed.

Another aspect of application development that architects should understand is the accumulation of technical debt.

Technical Debt

Application development involves trade-offs. To get a product to market fast enough to beat a competitor, developers may have to choose a design or coding method that can be implemented quickly but is not the option they would have chosen if they had more time. When this happens, an application has code or design features that should be changed in the future. If it is not, then the applications will continue to function with substandard code. More substandard code may be added in the future, leading to an accumulation of substandard code in an application.

This situation has been compared to incurring monetary debt. Ward Cunningham, one of the authors of the Agile Manifesto, coined the term *technical debt* to describe the process of making expedient choices in order to meet an objective, like releasing code by a particular date. Technical debt incurs something analogous to interest on the national debt, which is the loss of future productivity. Ideally, technical debt is paid down by refactoring code and implementing a better solution.

Projects incur technical debt for many reasons, including the following:

- Insufficient understanding of requirements
- Need to deliver some functional code by a set time or within a fixed budget
- Poor collaboration between teams developing in parallel
- Lack of coding standards
- Insufficient testing

Incurring technical debt is not necessarily a negative factor. Like monetary debt, technical debt can enable a project to move forward and realize more benefit than if the team had not incurred the technical debt. For example, a team may have a deadline to deliver a functioning module within 30 days. If the module is delivered on time and passes a suite of verification tests, then the next larger phase of the project will be funded.

To meet the 30-day deadline, the developers could decide to implement minimal error handling and perform only cursory code reviews. This allows the team to make the deadline and continue developing the larger application. One of the first things they should do in the next phase of the project is to revise the code in order to improve error handling and perform more thorough code reviews. If the team had not cut corners and had missed the deadline, then there would have been no follow-on development, and the project would have been terminated.

While incurring technical debt is not necessarily a negative factor, not paying it down is. In the previous example, minimal error handling may lead to a less reliable application that simply throws errors up the stack instead of responding to the error in a way that allows the application to continue to operate. Multiple bugs may have been missed because of cursory code reviews, and this could lead to problems in production that adversely impact users of the application.

Technical debt can come in several forms, including code technical debt, architecture design debt, and environment debt. The previous example is an example of code technical debt.

Architecture design debt is incurred when an architecture design choice is made for expedience but will require rework later. For example, an application may be designed to run on a single machine instance. If the application needs to scale up, it will have to run on a larger instance. This is known as *vertical scaling*. Once the application reaches the limits of vertical scaling, it would have to be rearchitected to work in a distributed environment. This could require changes at multiple levels, such as adding a load balancer and implementing a data partitioning scheme.

Environment debt occurs when expedient choices are made around tooling. For example, instead of implementing a CI/CD platform, a team may decide to build their application and run tests manually. This would save the time required to set up a CI/CD platform, but it leaves developers to perform manual deployments and test executions repeatedly.

Architects should be aware of the level of technical debt in a project. Paying down technical debt of all kinds is important and should be planned for accordingly.

API Best Practices

APIs provide programmatic access to services. APIs are often REST APIs or RPC APIs. *REST APIs* are resource oriented and use HTTP, while *RPC APIs* tend to be oriented around functions implemented using sockets and designed for high efficiency. For further details on API recommendations, see the Google Cloud API Design Guide (https://cloud .google.com/apis/design/), which specifies design principles for both REST APIs and RPC APIs.

The following are some Google-recommended API design practices, and these apply to both types of APIs.

Resources and Standard Methods

APIs should be designed around resources and operations that can be performed on those resources. Resources have a resource name and a set of methods. The standard set of methods is as follows:

List: Uses HTTP GET and returns a list of resources

Get: Uses HTTP GET to return a resource

Create: Uses HTTP POST to create an object

Update: Uses HTTP PUT or PATCH to update a resource

Delete: Uses HTTP DELETE to remove a resource

Custom methods are used to implement functionality that is not available in the standard methods. Standard methods are preferred over custom methods.

Resources may be simple resources or collections. *Simple resources* consist of a single entity. *Collections* are lists of resources of the same type. *List resources* often support pagination, sort ordering, and filtering.

Resources should be named using a hierarchical model. For example, consider an application that maintains customer contacts. Each customer is identified by their email address. A contact may be an outgoing email or an incoming email. Each email has a unique identifier. The following is an example of a message resource name:

```
//customers.example.com/contacts/somename@example.com/outgoing/message1
```

Note that a resource name is not the same as the REST URL. A REST URL should include an API version number. The following is the REST URL for the preceding example:

```
https://customers.example.com/v2/contacts/somename@example.com/outgoing/message1
```

When an API calls results in an error, a standard HTTP error should be returned. Additional detail about the error can be provided in the message payload. HTTP 200 is the standard return code for a successful call. The following are example HTTP error codes:

400: Bad request (for example, the call contained an invalid argument)

401: Request not authenticated

403: Permission denied

404: Resource not found

500: Unknown server error

501: Method not implemented by the API

503: Server unavailable

In addition to conventions around naming and error messages, there are recommended best practices for securing APIs.

API Security

APIs should enforce controls to protect the confidentiality and integrity of data and the availability of services. Confidentiality and integrity are protected in part by HTTPS-provided encryption. This protects data in transit between a client and an API endpoint. Persistently stored data is encrypted by default in all Google Cloud storage systems. Application designers are responsible for protecting the confidentiality and integrity of data when it is in use by an application.

Authentication

API functions execute operations on behalf of an entity with an identity. In the Google Cloud Platform, an identity may be a user or a service account. Identities should be managed by a centralized system, such as Cloud Identity and IAM. Identities should be assigned roles, which are collections of permissions. Predefined roles in IAM are designed to accommodate common requirements for different types of users of services.

One way to authenticate users of API functions is to require an API key. API keys are strings of alphanumeric characters that uniquely identify a user to a service. API keys are useful for tracking usage by user and performing basic authentication; however, anyone with access to an API key can access the APIs as if they were the intended user.

Authorization

When services share a common access management service, it can be used to enforce authorizations. In situations when a service has to call another service that does not share an authorization service, you can use secure tokens that make assertions or claims about what the holder of the token is allowed to do with a service.

JSON Web Tokens (JWT) are commonly used for authenticating when making API calls. When users log into services, they can receive a JWT, which they then pass to subsequent API calls. The JWT contains claims about what the holder of the token is allowed to do. JWTs are digitally signed and can be encrypted. A JWT is a JSON structure with three parts.

- Header
- Payload
- Signature

Headers contain a type attribute indicating that the token is a JWT type of token and the name of the algorithm used to sign the token.

The *payload* is a set of claims. *Claims* make statements about the issuer, subject, or token. They may include commonly used claims such as an expiration time or the name of the subject. They may also include private claims that are known to the parties that agree to use them. These might include application-specific claims, such as a permission to query a specific type of data.

The *signature* is the output of the signature algorithm generated using the header, the payload, and a secret.

The JWT is encoded in three Base64-encoded strings.

Resource Limiting

Maintaining the availability of a service is another aspect of security. If a service were to try to respond to all function calls from all users at all times, there would be a risk of overloading the system.

Users could intentionally or unintentionally send large volumes of function calls to a service. Eventually resources could be exhausted, and API calls will return with connection failures or other error messages. To prevent the unauthorized use of system resources, APIs should include resource-limiting mechanisms.

One way to limit resource consumption is to set a maximum threshold for using a service for a given period of time. For example, a user may be limited to 100 API calls a minute. Once a user has made 100 calls, no other calls from that user will be executed until the start of the next minute.

Another way to control resource usage is by rate limiting. In this case, you set a maximum rate, such as 100 API calls a minute, which would be an average of one call every 0.6 seconds. If a user invokes API functions at a rate faster than one every 0.6 seconds, some calls can be dropped until the rate falls below the rate limit.

For more on API security, see the Open Web Application Security Project's (OWASP's) API Security project at https://www.owasp.org/index.php/ OWASP_API_Security_Project.

Testing Frameworks

Testing is an important activity of software development, and it is part of all software development methodologies. Automated testing enables efficient continuous integration/ continuous deployment. Testing tools can employ a variety of approaches or models.

Testing Framework Models

Testing tools that enable automation may employ a number of different testing frameworks, including the following:

- Data-driven testing
- Modularity-driven testing
- Keyword-driven testing
- Model-based testing
- Test-driven development
- Hybrid testing

Data-driven testing uses structured data sets to drive testing. Tests are defined using a set of conditions or input values and expected output values. A test is executed by reading the test data source; then, for each condition or set of inputs, the tested function is executed, and the output is compared to the expected value. Data-driven testing is appropriate for testing APIs or functions executed from a command line.

Modularity-driven testing uses small scripts designed to test a limited set of functionalities. These scripts are combined to test higher-order abstractions. For example, a developer may create test scripts for creating, reading, updating, and deleting a customer record. Those four scripts may be combined into a customer management test script. Another script designed to search and sort customers may be combined with the customer management test script into a higher-level script that tests all customer data operations.

Keyword-driven testing separates test data from instructions for running a test. Each test is identified using a keyword or key term. A *test* is defined as a sequence of steps to execute. For example, the steps to enter a new customer into a database might start with the following:

1. Opening a customer form
2. Clicking the New Customer button
3. Waiting for a new window to appear with the data entry form
4. Clicking in the First Name field on the New Customer form
5. Entering a name in the first name field
6. And so on...

In addition to these instructions, data for each test is stored in another document or data source. For example, the test data may be in a spreadsheet. Each row in the spreadsheet contains example names, addresses, phone numbers, and email addresses.

The set of instructions can change as the software changes without needing to change the test data. For example, if the application is changed so that a new window is not opened, then this set of instructions can be updated without requiring any changes to the test data. This framework is well suited to manual testing, especially for testing graphical user interfaces. Keyword test frameworks can also be automated.

In *model-based testing*, instead of having a person generate test data, a simulation program is used to generate it. Typically, when model-based testing is used, the simulator is built in parallel with the system under test. Model-based testing uses several methods to simulate the system being tested, including describing the expected system behavior in a finite state machine model or defining logical predicates that describe the system.

Test-driven development incorporates testing into the development process. In this framework, requirements are mapped to tests. The tests are usually specific and narrowly scoped. This encourages developing small amounts of code and frequent testing. Once a piece of code passes its tests, it can be integrated into the baseline of code.

Hybrid testing is a testing framework that incorporates two or more distinct frameworks.

Automated Testing Tools

Developers have a choice of testing tools that range from functionally limited, language-specific tools to general-purpose testing platforms. Here are some examples of automated testing tools.

Developing unit tests can be done with language-specific tools. For example, pytest (`https://docs.pytest.org/en/latest/`) is a Python testing framework that makes it easy to write and execute unit tests for Python programs. JUnit (`https://junit.org/junit5/`) is a comparable framework for developers testing Java code.

Selenium (`https://www.seleniumhq.org/`) is a widely used open source browser automation tool that can be used as part of testing. The Selenium WebDriver API enables tests to function as if a user were interacting with a browser. Selenium scripts can be written in a programming language or by using the Selenium IDE.

Katalon Studio (`https://www.katalon.com/`) is an open source, interactive testing platform that builds on Selenium. It can be used to test web-based and mobile applications and APIs.

Data and System Migration Tooling

Data and system migration tools support the transition from on-premises or other clouds to GCP cloud-based infrastructure. For the purposes of the Google Cloud Professional Architect exam, it helps to understand the types of migrations that organizations can implement and the tools and services that can help with the migration.

Types of Cloud Migrations

Cloud migration projects typically fall into one of three categories.

Lift and shift: In lift-and-shift projects, infrastructure and data are moved from an on-premises data center to the cloud with minimal changes.

Move and improve: In move-and-improve projects, infrastructure and architecture are modified to take advantage of cloud infrastructure, for example moving to containers managed by the Kubernetes Engine.

Rebuild in the cloud: In rebuild-in-the-cloud projects, a legacy application is replaced by a new, native cloud application.

When implementing a lift-and-shift migration, you should perform an inventory of all applications, data sources, and infrastructure. Identify dependencies between applications because that will influence the order in which you migrate applications to the cloud. You should also review software license agreements. Some licenses may need to be revised to move applications to the cloud. For example, if an enterprise application is run under a site license for one data center and you plan to run that application in both the cloud and on-premises for some period of time, additional licensing would be required.

When migrating and changing applications and infrastructure, you will need a detailed plan identifying what systems will change, how those changes will impact other systems, and the order in which systems will be migrated and modified.

In addition to thinking about migration in terms of applications, it is important to think of how data will migrate to the cloud.

Migration Services and Tools

Migrations typically require the transfer of large volumes of data. How you will go about transferring that data is determined by a number of factors, including the following:

- Volume of data
- Network bandwidth

- Workflow time constraints on data transfer
- Location of data

The time required to transfer data is a function of the volume of data and the network bandwidth. For example, transferring 1 GB of data over a 100 Gbps network will take about 0.1 seconds; on a 1 Mbps network, that same data transfer will take about 3 hours. Transferring one petabyte of data will require 30 hours over a 100 Gbps network and more than 120 days over a 1 Gbps network.

You have several options for transferring data into Google Cloud, including the following:

- Google Transfer Service
- gsutil command-line utility
- Google Transfer Appliance
- Third-party vendors

The *Google Transfer Service* allows for the transfer of data from an HTTP/S location, an AWS S3 bucket, or a Cloud Storage bucket. The data is always transferred to a Cloud Storage bucket. Transfer operations are defined using transfer jobs that run in the Google Cloud. The Transfer Service is the recommended way of transferring data from AWS or other cloud providers to Google Cloud.

The *gsutil command-line utility* is the recommended way to transfer data from on-premises to the Google Cloud. Consider compressing and de-duplicating data before transferring data to save time on the transfer operation. Compressing data is CPU intensive, so there is a trade-off between reducing transfer time and incurring additional CPU load.

gsutil is multithreaded, which improves performance when transferring a large number of files. gsutil also supports parallel loading of chunks or subsets of data in large files. The chunks are reassembled at the destination. gsutil also supports restarts after failures. You can tune gsutil transfers with command-line parameters specifying the number of processes, number of threads per process, and other options.

If large volumes of data will be transferred and a transfer over the network would take too long, then it is recommended that you use the *Google Transfer Appliance*, which is a high-capacity storage device that is shipped to your site. Currently, 100 TB and 480 TB appliances are available. Those configurations may change in the future. The appliance is installed on your network, and data is transferred to the storage unit, which is then shipped back to Google. After Google receives the storage unit, it will make the unit accessible to you so that you can log into the console and transfer the data to a Cloud Storage bucket.

Another option is to use a third-party service, such as those offered by Zadara, Iron Mountain, and Prime Focus Technologies.

Google has a table of transfer times by network bandwidth and data size at https://cloud.google.com/solutions/transferring-big-data-sets-to-gcp. This is helpful for understanding the expected load times by network bandwidth and data size.

The GCP SDK is a set of command-line tools for managing Google Cloud resources. These commands allow you to manage infrastructure and perform operations from the command line instead of the console. The GCP SDK components are especially useful for automating routine tasks and for viewing information about the state of your infrastructure.

GCP SDK Components

The Cloud SDK includes the following:

gcloud: A command-line tool for interacting with most GCP services

gsutil: A command-line tool for working with Cloud Storage

bq: A command-line tool for working with BigQuery

gcloud, gsutil, and bq are installed by default when installing the GCP SDK. Additional components can be installed as needed using the gcloud components install command. The additional components include the following:

cbt: A command-line tool for Bigtable (Note: The current versions of gcloud include a gcloud bigtable component.)

kubectl: A command-line tool for managing Kubernetes clusters

pubsub emulator: A Cloud Pub/Sub emulator

The gcloud components list command generates a list of available components. The list contains the name of each component, an ID, the size of the component, and the status of the component on the local device, which is one of these: not installed, installed (and up to date), and update available (installed but not up to date).

Some components are in alpha or beta release. These are run using the gcloud alpha and gcloud beta commands, respectively.

In addition to accessing the SDK from the command line, you can also use client libraries developed for several languages, including Java, Go, Python, Ruby, PHP, C#, Node.js, and Go.

Additional libraries may be developed in the future. The gcloud alpha and gcloud beta commands may change over time. See the Google Cloud documentation for the current list of available GCP SDK utilities, commands, and client libraries.

GCP SDK supports both user account and service account authorization. User account authorization is recommended for use with scripts or automation tools. User account authorization is enabled using the gcloud init command. Service account authorization is enabled using the gcloud auth activate-service-account command.

Summary

Architects support application development and operations. For example, architects can help teams and organizations choose an application development methodology suitable for their needs. Options include waterfall, spiral, and agile methodologies. Agile methodologies work well in many cases, in part because of their focus on collaboration and rapid, incremental development. In addition to planning new feature work, application developers should invest time and resources to pay down technical debt.

Follow established recommended practices when designing APIs, such as orienting the API around entities, not functions performed on those entities. Include security considerations, such as authorizations and rate limiting, when designing APIs.

Testing should be automated. Developers can choose from a variety of testing frameworks to find one or more that fits well with their development processes.

When migrating applications and data to the cloud, consider data volumes and bandwidth when choosing a method to migrate data.

The GCP SDK is set of command-line tools and language-specific libraries for managing GPC resources. Most GPC services can be managed using the gcloud commands, but Cloud Storage and BigQuery have their own command-line utilities called gsutil and bq, respectively.

Exam Essentials

Know the defining characteristics of different application development methodologies.   Waterfall is a linear process that does not repeat a phase once it is completed. Waterfall was an early application development approach. The need to know all requirements early in the development process is particularly problematic. Spiral methodologies repeat the main phases of the application development process. At the beginning of each iteration, stakeholders define the scope of work and identify risks. Agile methodologies are highly collaborative, transparent, and drive to release code frequently.

Understand technical debt.   Application development requires trade-offs. Coding and design decisions have to be made in the broad business context, such as the need to deliver a functional product by a set date. When an application contains code that is intentionally suboptimal, that is a form of technical debt. Technical debt is repaid by refactoring code. Architects and developers should consider paying down technical debt as a necessary part of the software development process.

Know API best practices.   APIs should be designed around resources and operations that can be performed on those resources. Resources have a resource name and a set of methods. The standard set of methods is list, get, create, update, and delete. When an API calls results in an error, a standard HTTP error should be returned. Additional detail about the error can be provided in the message payload.

Understand ways of securing APIs.   APIs should enforce controls to protect the confidentiality and integrity of data and the availability of services. Confidentiality and integrity are protected in part by HTTPS-provided encryption. One way to authenticate users of API functions is to require an API key. API keys are strings of alphanumeric characters that uniquely identify a user to a service. JSON Web Tokens (JWTs) are commonly used for authenticating when making API calls. To prevent the unauthorized use of system resources, APIs should include resource-limiting mechanisms.

Understand that there are a variety of testing frameworks and test automation tools.   Testing frameworks include data-driven, keyword-driven, model-based, test-driven, and hybrid testing. Developers have a choice of testing tools that range from functionally limited, language-specific tools to general-purpose testing platforms.

Know the different kinds of migrations.   Cloud migration projects typically fall into one of three categories: lift and shift, move and improve, and rebuild in the cloud. There are several ways to transfer data during a migration. When deciding on a transfer method, consider volume of data, network bandwidth, workflow time constraints on data transfer, and location of data.

Understand how and when to use the GCP GDK.   The GCP SDK is a set of command-line tools for managing Google Cloud resources. These commands allow you to manage infrastructure and perform operations from the command line instead of the console. The GCP SDK components are especially useful for automating routine tasks and for viewing information about the state of your infrastructure.

Review Questions

1. A team of developers is tasked with developing an enterprise application. They have interviewed stakeholders and collected requirements. They are now designing the system and plan to begin implementation next. After implementation, they will verify that the application meets specifications. They will not revise the design once coding starts. What application development methodology is this team using?

   A. Extreme programming

   B. Agile methodology

   C. Waterfall methodology

   D. Spiral methodology

2. A team of developers is tasked with developing an enterprise application. They have interviewed stakeholders and set a scope of work that will deliver a subset of the functionality needed. Developers and stakeholders have identified risks and ways of mitigating them. They then proceed to gather requirements for the subset of functionalities to be implemented. That is followed by design, implementation, and testing. There is no collaboration between developers and stakeholders until after testing, when developers review results with stakeholders and plan the next iteration of development. What application development methodology is this team using?

   A. Extreme programming

   B. Agile methodology

   C. Waterfall methodology

   D. Spiral methodology

3. A team of developers is tasked with developing an enterprise application. They meet daily with stakeholders to discuss the state of the project. The developers and stakeholders have identified a set of functionalities to be implemented over the next two weeks. After some design work, coding begins. A new requirement is discovered, and developers and stakeholders agree to prioritize implementing a feature to address this newly discovered requirement. As developers complete small functional units of code, they test it. If the code passes the tests, the code unit is integrated with the version-controlled codebase. What application development methodology is this team using?

   A. Continuous integration

   B. Agile methodology

   C. Waterfall methodology

   D. Spiral methodology

4. You are a developer at a startup company that is planning to release its first version of a new mobile service. You have discovered a design flaw that generates and sends more data to mobile devices than is needed. This is increasing the latency of messages between mobile devices and backend services running in the cloud. Correcting the design flaw will delay the release of the service by at least two weeks. You decide to address the long latency problem by coding a workaround that does not send the unnecessary data. The design flaw is still there and is generating unnecessary data, but the service can ship under these conditions. This is an example of what?

   A. Incurring technical debt

   B. Paying down technical debt

   C. Shifting risk

   D. Improving security

5. You are a developer at a startup company that has just released a new service. During development, you made suboptimal coding choices to keep the project on schedule. You are now planning your next two weeks of work, which you decide will include implementing a feature the product manager wanted in the initial release but was postponed to a release occurring soon after the initial release. You also include time to refactor code that was introduced to correct a bug found immediately before the planned release date. That code blocks the worst impact of the bug, but it does not correct the flaw. Revising that suboptimal code is an example of what?

   A. Incurring technical debt

   B. Paying down technical debt

   C. Shifting risk

   D. Improving security

6. As a developer of a backend service for managing inventory, your manager has asked you to include a basic API for the inventory service. You plan to follow best practice recommendations. What is the minimal set of API functions that you would include?

   A. Create, read, update, and delete

   B. List, get, create, update, and delete

   C. Create, delete, and list

   D. Create and delete

7. A junior developer asks your advice about handling errors in API functions. The developer wants to know what kind of data and information should be in an API error message. What would you recommend?

   A. Return HTTP status 200 with additional error details in the payload.

   B. Return a status code form with the standard 400s and 500s HTTP status codes along with additional error details in the payload.

   C. Return error details in the payload, and do not return a code.

   D. Define your own set of application-specific error codes.

8. A junior developer asks your advice about performing authentication in API functions. The developer wants to know how they can allow users of the API to make assertions about what they are authorized to do. What would you recommend?

    A. Use JSON Web Tokens (JWTs)

    B. Use API keys

    C. Use encryption

    D. Use HTTPS instead of HTTP

9. Your startup has released a new online game that includes features that allow users to accumulate points by playing the game. Points can be used to make in-game purchases. You have discovered that some users are using bots to play the game programmatically much faster than humans can play the game. The use of bots is unauthorized in the game. You modify the game API to prevent more than 10 function calls per user, per minute. This is an example of what practice?

    A. Encryption

    B. Defense in depth

    C. Least privileges

    D. Resource limiting

10. A team of developers is creating a set of tests for a new service. The tests are defined using a set of conditions or input values and expected output values. The tests are then executed by reading the test data source, and for each test the software being tested is executed and the output is compared to the expected value. What kind of testing framework is this?

    A. Data-driven testing

    B. Hybrid testing

    C. Keyword-driven testing

    D. Model-based testing

11. Your company is moving an enterprise application to Google Cloud. The application runs on a cluster of virtual machines, and workloads are distributed by a load balancer. Your team considered revising the application to use containers and the Kubernetes Engine, but they decide not to make any unnecessary changes before moving the application to the cloud. This is an example of what migration strategy?

    A. Lift and shift

    B. Move and improve

    C. Rebuild in the cloud

    D. End of life

12. As a consultant to an insurance company migrating to the Google Cloud, you have been asked to lead the effort to migrate data from AWS S3 to Cloud Storage. Which transfer method would you consider first?

    A. Google Transfer Service

    B. `gsutil` command line

    C. Google Transfer Appliance

    D. Cloud Dataproc

13. You are a consultant to an insurance company migrating to GCP. Five petabytes of business-sensitive data need to be transferred from the on-premises data center to Cloud Storage. You have a 10 GB network between the on-premises data center and Google Cloud. What transfer option would you recommend?

   A. gsutil

   B. gcloud

   C. Cloud Transfer Appliance

   D. Cloud Transfer Service

14. You are migrating a data warehouse from an on-premises database to BigQuery. You would like to write a script to perform some of the migration steps. What component of the GCP SDK will you likely need to use to create the new data warehouse in BigQuery?

   A. cbt

   B. bq

   C. gsutil

   D. kubectl

15. You are setting up a new laptop that is configured with a standard set of tools for developers and architects, including some GCP SDK components. You will be working extensively with the GCP SDK and want to know specifically which components are installed and up to date. What command would you run on the laptop?

   A. gsutil component list

   B. cbt component list

   C. gcloud component list

   D. bq component list

Chapter

12

Migration Planning

PROFESSIONAL CLOUD ARCHITECT CERTIFICATION EXAM OBJECTIVES COVERED IN THIS CHAPTER INCLUDE THE FOLLOWING:

✓ 1.4 Creating a migration plan (i.e. documents and architectural diagrams)

For many organizations, cloud computing is a new approach to delivering information services. These organizations may have built large, complex infrastructures running a wide array of applications using on-premises data centers. Now those same organizations want to realize the advantages of cloud computing. They can start by building new systems in the cloud. That will bring some benefits, but there are likely further advantages to migrating existing applications from on-premises data centers to the cloud. This requires methodical planning that includes the following:

- Integrating cloud services with existing systems
- Migrating systems and data
- License mapping
- Network management planning
- Testing and proof-of-concept development

Each of these is covered individually in this chapter.

Integrating Cloud Services with Existing Systems

Cloud migrations are inherently about incrementally changing existing infrastructure in order to use cloud services to deliver information services. During migrations, some applications will move to the cloud, but those migrated applications may be integrated with other applications still running on-premises. You will need to plan a migration carefully to minimize the risk of disrupting services while maximizing the likelihood of successfully moving applications and data to the cloud.

It helps to think of these tasks as part of a five-step migration.

1. Assessment
2. Pilot
3. Data migration
4. Application migration
5. Optimization

During the *assessment phase*, take inventory of applications and infrastructure. Document considerations for moving each application to the cloud, including issues such as compliance, licensing, and dependencies. Not all applications are suitable for the cloud; some will be better suited for staying in the current environment. For example, a legacy application running on a mainframe that is scheduled to be removed from service within the next two years is not a good candidate for migrating to the cloud. Identify each application's dependencies on other applications and data.

The next step is the *pilot phase*. During this stage, you will migrate one or two applications in an effort to learn about the cloud, develop experience running applications in the cloud, and get a sense of the level of effort required to set up networking and security.

Next, in the *data migration phase*, you will begin to move data to the cloud. Consider which applications are dependent on specific data sources. Also understand the level of security required for each data source. Confidential and sensitive data will require more attention to security than public information. At this stage, you can decide how you will migrate data, for example, by using `gsutil` or the Google Cloud Transfer Appliance. Also, if data is being updated during the migration, you will need to develop a way to synchronize the on-premises data with the cloud data after the data has been largely migrated.

After the data has been migrated, you can move applications. If you are using a lift-and-shift model for the *application migration phase*, then virtual machines can be migrated from on-premises to the cloud. If you want to migrate applications running on VMs to containers running on Kubernetes clusters, you will need to plan for that transition.

Finally, once data and applications are in the cloud, you can shift your focus to optimizing the cloud implementation. For example, during the *optimization phase*, you may add Stackdriver monitoring and logging to applications. You may improve reliability by using multiregional features such as global load balancing. Some third-party tools, such as ETL tools, can be replaced by GCP services, such as Cloud Dataflow. You can also consider using managed database services instead of managing your own databases.

Migrating Systems and Data

Part of migration planning is determining which applications should be migrated and in what order. You also need to consider how to migrate data.

Planning for Systems Migrations

A significant amount of effort can go into understanding applications and their dependencies. During the assessment phase, document the characteristics of each application that may be migrated to the cloud. Include at least the following:

- Consider the criticality of the system. Systems that must be available 24 hours a day 7 days a week or risk significant adverse impact on the business are highly critical and considered Tier 1. Moderately important applications, such as batch processing jobs that can tolerate some delay or degradation in service, are Tier 2. Tier 3 applications include all others.

- Document the production level of each application. Typical levels are production, staging, test, and development.

- Also note whether the application is developed by a third party or in-house and the level of support available. If the third-party vendor that developed the application is out of business or if a custom application has been minimally maintained for extended periods and there is relatively little in-house expertise with the application, document that risk.

- Consider the service-level agreements (SLAs) that the application has in place. Can this application tolerate downtime without missing SLA commitments? What compliance issues should be considered with moving this application?

- How well documented is the application? Is there design, runtime, and architecture documentation? What troubleshooting guides are available?

- If the application were moved to the cloud, what level of effort would be required to make it functional in the cloud? An application running on-premises in a Docker container will require minimal changes, while an application running on an operating system not available in the cloud will likely be more problematic.

- What databases are read from by this application? What databases are written to by this application? Are these high availability databases? If so, where are failover databases located? What is the recovery time objective in the event of a failover?

- On what other systems is the application dependent, such as identity management, messaging, monitoring, and log collection? How is the application backed up?

- How well automated are the deployment and maintenance of the application? Are manual operations needed for normal operations?

The answers to these questions will help you determine the level of risk involved with migrating an application and the level of effort required to perform the migration. The information is also useful for understanding the dependencies between applications. If an application is moved to the cloud, it must be able to access all other systems and data upon which it depends; similarly, systems that depend on the migrated application must be able to continue to access it.

The details collected here can also inform you about tolerable downtime to perform a switchover that stops sending traffic to the on-premises solution and starts sending it to the cloud implementation of the system. If no downtime is acceptable, you will need to have two systems running in parallel: one in the cloud and one on-premises before switching over. You should also carefully consider how to manage any state information that is maintained by the system. Maintaining consistency in distributed systems is not trivial. If systems have scheduled maintenance windows, those could be used to perform a switchover without risking missing SLA commitments. For Tier 3 applications, a switchover may only require notifying users that the system will be unavailable for a time.

You should understand how to deploy a migrated system in the cloud. If the system's deployment is already automated, then the same processes may be used in the cloud. For example, code could be copied from an on-premises version control repository to one in the cloud. The build, test, and deployment scripts could be copied as well. If a CI/CD system like Jenkins is used, then it will need to be in place in the cloud as well. Alternatively, you could modify the deployment process to use GCP services such as Cloud Build.

Determine how you will monitor the performance of the system after migration. If an application depends on an on-premises log collection service, for example, a comparable service will be needed in the cloud. Stackdriver Logging would be a good option if you are open to some modification to the system.

Finally, consider any business factors that may influence the ROI of running the application in the cloud. For example, if a hardware refresh required to continue to support the application or business is lost because the application cannot scale sufficiently in the current environment, then stakeholders may want to prioritize moving that application.

In addition to considering risks and level of effort required to migrate an application, it is important to understand how data will be moved.

Planning for Data Migration

As you plan for data migrations, you will need to consider factors related to data governance and the way that data is stored. Different types of storage require different procedures to migrate data. This section covers two scenarios: migrating object storage and migrating relational data. These are not the only ways that you might need to migrate data, but they demonstrate some of the factors that you'll need to keep in mind as you plan a data migration.

Data Governance and Data Migration

Before migrating data, you should understand any regulations that cover that data. For example, in the United States, the privacy of personal healthcare data is governed by HIPAA regulations, while in the European Union, the GDPR restricts where data on EU citizens may be stored. Businesses and organizations may have their own data classifications and data governance policies. These should be investigated, and if they exist, considered when planning data migrations.

Migrating Object Storage

Archived data, large object data, and other data that is stored on-premises in an object store or filesystem storage may be migrated to Cloud Storage. In these cases, you should do the following:

- Plan the structure of buckets
- Determine roles and access controls

- Understand the time and cost of migrating data to Cloud Storage
- Plan the order in which data will be transferred
- Determine the method to transfer the data

When transferring data from an on-premises data center, transferring with gsutil is a good option when the data volume is less than 10 TB of data and network bandwidth is at least 100 Mbps. If the volume of data is over 20 TB, the Google Transfer Appliance is recommended. When the volume of data is between 10 TB and 20TB, consider the time needed to transfer the data at your available bandwidth. If the cost and time requirements are acceptable, use gsutil; otherwise, use the Google Transfer Appliance.

Google has a table of transfer times by network bandwidth and data size at https://cloud.google.com/solutions/transferring-big-data-sets-to-gcp. This is helpful for understanding the expected load times by network bandwidth and data size.

Migrating Relational Data

When migrating relational databases to the cloud, you should consider the volume of data to migrate, but you should also understand how the database is used and any existing SLAs that may constrain your migration options.

One way to migrate a relational database is to export data from the database, transfer the data to the cloud, and then import the data into the cloud instance of the database. This option requires the database to be unavailable to users during the migration. To ensure a consistent export, the database should be locked for writes during the export operation. It can be available for read operations during the export. Once the data is available in the cloud database, database applications can be configured to point to the new database.

If a database SLA or other requirements do not allow for an export-based migration, you should consider creating a replica of the database in which the replica database is in the Google cloud. This configuration is referred to as *primary/replica* or *leader/follower*, and in general it is the preferred migration method. Whenever there is a change to the primary or leader, the same change is made to the replica or follower instance. Once the database has synchronized the data, database applications can be configured to point to the cloud database.

Licensing Mapping

Another task in migration planning is understanding the licenses for the software you plan to use in the cloud. Operating system, application, middleware services, and third-party tools may all have licenses.

There are few a different ways to pay for software running in the cloud. In some cases, the cost of licensing is included with cloud service charges. For example, the cost of licensing a Windows server operating system may be included in the hourly charge.

In other cases, you may have to pay for the software directly in one of two ways. You may have an existing license that can be used in the cloud, or you may purchase a license from the vendor specifically for use in the cloud. This is sometimes referred to as the *bring-your-own-license (BYOL) model*.

In other cases, software vendors will charge based on usage, much like cloud service pricing. For example, you may be charged for each hour the software is in use on an instance. This is called the *pay-as-you-go model* or *metered model*.

Even though you have a license to run software on-premises, do not assume that the license applies to cloud use. Vendors may have restrictions that limit the use of a license to on-premises infrastructures. It is important to verify if the license can be moved to the cloud or converted to a cloud license.

Also consider the fact that licenses for software that you have may be used in the cloud but may not map neatly to new usage patterns. For example, a single site license for an on-premises application may not be appropriate for an application that will run in multiple regions in the cloud.

As you analyze your licenses, you may find that you have more than one option when moving applications to the cloud. For example, you may have the option to bring your own license or pay as you go. You should consider how the application will be used and assess which of the options is better for your organization.

Network and Management Planning

While much of this chapter has focused on application and data migration, it is important to consider networking as well. If you are planning to migrate completely to the cloud and eventually stop using on-premises solutions, you will need to plan to configure your GCP network as well as plan for the transition period when you will have both on-premises and cloud-based infrastructure. If you intend to continue to use on-premises infrastructure along with cloud infrastructure in a hybrid cloud scenario, you will also need to have a plan for your GCP network as well as long-term connectivity between the cloud and your on-premises network.

Network migration planning can be broken down into four broad categories of planning tasks.

- Virtual private clouds (VPCs)
- Access controls
- Scaling
- Connectivity

Planning for each of these will help identify potential risks and highlight architecture decisions that need to be made.

This chapter briefly describes networking considerations that you should address when planning a migration. For more details on GCP networking, see Chapter 6, "Designing Networks."

Virtual Private Clouds

Virtual private clouds are collections of networking components and configurations that organize your infrastructure in the Google Cloud. The components of VPCs include the following:

- Networks
- Subnets
- IP addresses
- Routes
- Virtual private networks (VPNs)

VPC infrastructure is built on Google's software-defined networking platform. Google manages the underlying software and hardware that implement VPCs.

Networks are private RFC 1918 address spaces. These are networks that use one of three ranges.

10.0.0.0 to 10.255.255.255, with 16,777, 216 available addresses

72.16.0.0 to 172.31.255.255, with 1,048,576 available addresses

192.168.0.0 to 192.168.255.255, with 65,546 available addresses

Within networks, you can create subnets to group resources by region or zone. Google networking can manage subnets automatically, or you can manage your own subnets. Automatically managed subnets are useful when you want a subnet in each region and the predefined address space used in each region does not overlap with other uses, such as VPN connections. In general, it is recommended that you manage your own subnets, which are called *custom mode networks*. These provide you with complete control over which regions have subnets and the address ranges of each subnet.

VM instances support up to two IP addresses: one internal and one external. The internal IP address is used for traffic within the VPC network. The external IP address is optional, and it is used to communicate with external networks. External addresses may be ephemeral or static. As part of your planning process, you should map out the use of external IP addresses and if they should be ephemeral or static. Static IP addresses are used when you need a consistent long-term IP address, for example, for a public website or API endpoint.

Routes are rules for forwarding traffic. Some routes are generated automatically when VPCs are created, but you can also create custom routes. Routes between subnets are created by default. You may want to create custom routes if you need to implement *many-to-one NAT* or *transparent proxies*.

VPNs are provided by the Cloud VPN service that links your Google Cloud VPC to an on-premises network. VPCs use IPSec tunnel to secure transmission. A single VPN gateway can sustain up to 3 Gbps. If this is not sufficient, you may need to plan for additional VPN gateways or use a Cloud Interconnect connection instead.

Network Access Controls

You should plan how you will control access to network management functions using IAM roles. Some networking-specific roles that you may want to consider assigning are as follows:

Network Admin: For full permissions to manage network resources

Network Viewer: For read-only access to network resources

Security Admin: For managing firewall rules and SSL certificates

Compute Instance Admin: For managing VM instances

Firewalls are used to control the flow of traffic between subnets and networks. You should plan what types of traffic will be allowed to enter and leave each subnet. For firewall rule purposes, you will need to define the traffic protocol, such as TCP or IP, whether it applies to incoming (ingress) or outgoing (egress) traffic, and the priority of the rule. Higher-priority rules take precedence over lower-priority rules.

Scaling

Planning for network scalability may entail the use of load balancing and, if you have large static objects that are referenced from around the globe, the use of a content distribution network.

Cloud load balancing can distribute traffic and workloads globally using a single *anycast IP address*.

Application layer load balancing can be done using HTTP(S) layer 7 load balancing, which can distribute traffic across regions routing traffic to the nearest healthy node. Traffic can also be routed based on content type. For example, video may be distributed globally using Cloud CDN, Google Cloud's *content distribution network*.

Network load balancing occurs at Layer 4. This type of load balancing is useful for dealing with spikes in TCP and IP traffic, load balancing additional protocols, or supporting session affinity.

Also consider how you will manage DNS records for services. Cloud DNS is a Google-managed DNS service that can be used to make your services globally available. Cloud DNS is designed to provide high availability and low-latency DNS services.

Connectivity

If you are maintaining a hybrid cloud, you will want to plan for networking between the Google Cloud and your on-premises data center.

You may want to consider using Cloud Interconnect, which routes traffic directly to Google Cloud without going over internet networks. Cloud Interconnect is available in three forms.

Carrier peering: Provided by network service providers

Direct peering: A peering service to a Google peering location

CDN interconnect: Provides direct access to Google's edge network

See the Google documentation (https://cloud.google.com/interconnect/pricing) for details on the capacities and costs of each of these options.

Summary

Migration planning requires broad scope planning that ranges from business service considerations to network design planning. It should include planning for integration with existing systems. This itself is a broad topic within migration planning and is best addressed using a five-step plan that includes assessment, pilot, data migration, application migration, and optimization. Before migrating systems and data, it is important to understand dependencies between systems, service level commitments, and other factors that contribute to the risk of migrating a service. Generally, it is recommended to migrate data first and then migrate applications. Migrating databases takes additional planning to avoid data loss or disruption in services during the migration. Review software licenses during migration planning and determine how you will license software in the cloud. Options include bring your own license, pay as you go, or including the license with other cloud charges. Network planning includes planning virtual private clouds, network access controls, scalability, and connectivity.

Exam Essentials

Cloud migrations are inherently about incrementally changing existing infrastructure in order to use cloud services to deliver information services. You will need to plan a migration carefully to minimize the risk of disrupting services while maximizing the likelihood of successfully moving applications and data to the cloud. For many organizations, cloud computing is a new approach to delivering information services. These organizations may have built large, complex infrastructures running a wide array of applications using on-premises data centers. Now those same organizations want to realize the advantages of cloud computing.

Know the five stages of migration planning: assessment, pilot, data migration, application migration, and optimization. During the assessment phase, take inventory of applications and infrastructure. During the pilot stage, you will migrate one or two applications in an effort to learn about the cloud and develop experience running applications in the cloud. In the data migration and application migration phases, data and applications are moved in a logical order that minimizes the risk of service disruption. Finally, once data and applications are in the cloud, you can shift your focus to optimizing the cloud implementation.

Understand how to assess the risk of migrating an application.   Considerations include service-level agreements, criticality of the system, availability of support, and quality of documentation. Consider other systems on which the migrating system depends. Consider other applications that depend on the migrating system. Watch for challenging migration operations, such as performing a database replication and then switching to a cloud instance of a database.

Understand how to map licensing to the way you will use the licensed software in the cloud.   Operating system, application, middleware services, and third-party tools may all have licenses. There are a few different ways to pay for software running in the cloud. In some cases, the cost of licensing is included with cloud service charges. In other cases, you may have to pay for the software directly in one of two ways. You may have an existing license that can be used in the cloud, or you may purchase a license from the vendor specifically for use in the cloud. This is sometimes referred to as the a BYOL model. In other cases, software vendors will charge based on usage, much like cloud service pricing.

Know the steps involved in planning a network migration.   Network migration planning can be broken down into four broad categories of planning tasks: VPCs, access controls, scaling, and connectivity. Planning for each of these will help identify potential risks and highlight architecture decisions that need to be made. Consider how you will use networks, subnets, IP addresses, routes, and VPNs. Plan for linking on-premises networks to the Google Cloud using either VPNs or Cloud Interconnect.

Review Questions

1. Your midsize company has decided to assess the possibility of moving some or all of its enterprise applications to the cloud. As the CTO, you have been tasked with determining how much it would cost and what the benefits of a cloud migration would be. What would you do first?

    A. Take inventory of applications and infrastructure, document dependencies, and identify compliance and licensing issues.

    B. Create a request for proposal from cloud vendors.

    C. Discuss cloud licensing issues with enterprise software vendors.

    D. Interview department leaders to identify their top business pain points.

2. You are working with a colleague on a cloud migration plan. Your colleague would like to start migrating data. You have completed an assessment but no other preparation work. What would you recommend before migrating data?

    A. Migrating applications

    B. Conducting a pilot project

    C. Migrating all identities and access controls

    D. Redesigning relational data models for optimal performance

3. As the CTO of your company, you are responsible for approving a cloud migration plan for services that include a wide range of data. You are reviewing a proposed plan than includes an assessment, pilot project, data migration, application migration, and optimization. What should you look for as part of the data migration plan?

    A. Database reconfiguration data

    B. Firewall rules to protect databases

    C. An assessment of data classification and regulations relevant to the data to be migrated

    D. A detailed description of current backup operations

4. A client of yours is prioritizing applications to move to the cloud. One system written in Java is a Tier 1 production system that must be available 24/7; it depends on three Tier 2 services that are running on-premises, and two other Tier 1 applications depend on it. Which of these factors is least important from a risk assessment perspective?

    A. The application is written in Java.

    B. The application must be available 24/7.

    C. The application depends on three Tier 2 services.

    D. Two other Tier 1 applications depend on it.

5. As part of a cloud migration, you will be migrating a relational database to the cloud. The database has strict SLAs, and it should not be down for more than a few seconds a month. The data stores approximately 500 GB of data, and your network has 100 Gbps bandwidth. What method would you consider first to migrate this database to the cloud?

    A. Use a third-party backup and restore application.

    B. Use the MySQL data export program, and copy the export file to the cloud.

C. Set up a replica of the database in the cloud, synchronize the data, and then switch traffic to the instance in the cloud.

D. Transfer the data using the Google Transfer Appliance.

6. Your company is running several third-party enterprise applications. You are reviewing the licenses and find that they are transferrable to the cloud, so you plan to take advantage of that option. This form of licensing is known as which one of the following?

A. Compliant licensing

B. Bring-your-own license

C. Pay-as-you-go license

D. Metered pricing

7. Your company is running several third-party enterprise applications. You are reviewing the licenses and find that they are not transferrable to the cloud. You research your options and see that the vendor offers an option to pay a licensing fee based on how long you use the application in the cloud. What is this option called?

A. Compliant licensing

B. Bring-your-own license

C. Pay-as-you-go license

D. Incremental payment licensing

8. You have been asked to brief executives on the networking aspects of the cloud migration. You want to begin at the highest level of abstraction and then drill down into lower-level components. What topic would you start with?

A. Routes

B. Firewalls

C. VPCs

D. VPNs

9. You have created a VPC in Google Cloud, and subnets were created automatically. What range of IP addresses would you not expect to see in use with the subnets?

A. 10.0.0.0 to 10.255.255.255

B. 72.16.0.0 to 172.31.255.255

C. 192.168.0.0 to 192.168.255.255

D. 201.1.1.0 to 201.2.1.0

10. A network engineer is helping you plan connectivity between your on-premises network and Google Cloud. The engineer estimates that you will need 6 Gbps of bandwidth in total between the on-premises data center and Google Cloud. The traffic may be split between multiple connections. How many VPN endpoints will you need?

A. 1

B. 2

C. 3

D. 6

11. During migration planning, you learn that traffic to the subnet containing a set of databases must be restricted. What mechanism would you plan to use to control the flow of traffic to a subnet?

   A. IAM roles

   B. Firewall rules

   C. VPNs

   D. VPCs

12. During migration planning, you learn that some members of the network management team will need the ability to manage all network components, but others on the team will only need read access to the state of the network. What mechanism would you plan to use to control the user access?

   A. IAM roles

   B. Firewall rules

   C. VPNs

   D. VPCs

13. Executives in your company have decided that the company should not route its GCP-only traffic over public internet networks. What Google Cloud service would you plan to use to distribute the workload of an enterprise application?

   A. Global load balancing

   B. Simple network management protocol

   C. Content delivery network

   D. VPNs

14. Executives in your company have decided to expand operations from just North America to Europe as well. Applications will be run in several regions. All users should be routed to the nearest healthy server running the application they need. What Google Cloud service would you plan to use to meet this requirement?

   A. Global load balancing

   B. Cloud Interconnect

   C. Content delivery network

   D. VPNs

15. Executives in your company have decided that the company should expand its service offerings to a global market. You company distributes education content online. Maintaining low latency is a top concern. What type of network service would you expect to use to ensure low-latency access to content from around the globe?

   A. Routes

   B. Firewall rules

   C. Content delivery network

   D. VPNs

Appendix

Answers to Review Questions

Chapter 1: Introduction to the Google Professional Cloud Architect Exam

1. B. The correct answer is B. Business requirements are high-level, business-oriented requirements that are rarely satisfied by meeting a single technical requirement. Option A is incorrect because business sponsors rarely have sufficient understanding of technical requirements in order to provide a comprehensive list. Option C is incorrect, because business requirements constrain technical options but should not be in conflict. Option D is incorrect because there is rarely a clear consensus on all requirements. Part of an architect's job is to help stakeholders reach a consensus.

2. B. The correct answer is B. Managed services relieve DevOps work, preemptible machines cost significantly less than standard VMs, and autoscaling reduces the chances of running unnecessary resources. Options A and D are incorrect because access controls will not help reduce costs, but they should be used anyway. Options C and D are incorrect because there is no indication that a NoSQL database should be used.

3. A. The correct answer is A. CI/CD supports small releases, which are easier to debug and enable faster feedback. Option B is incorrect, as CI/CD does not only use preemptible machines. Option C is incorrect because CI/CD works well with agile methodologies. Option D is incorrect, as there is no limit to the number of times new versions of code can be released.

4. B. The correct answer is B. The finance director needs to have access to documents for seven years. This requires durable storage. Option A is incorrect because the access does not have to be highly available; as long as the finance director can access the document in a reasonable period of time, the requirement can be met. Option C is incorrect because reliability is a measure of being available to meet workload demands successfully. Option D is incorrect because the requirement does not specify the need for increasing and decreasing storage to meet the requirement.

5. C. The correct answer is C. An incident in the context of IT operations and service reliability is a disruption that degrades or stops a service from functioning. Options A and B are incorrect—incidents are not related to scheduling. Option D is incorrect; in this context, incidents are about IT services, not personnel.

6. D. The correct answer is D. HIPAA governs, among other things, privacy and data protections for private medical information. Option A is incorrect, as GDPR is a European Union regulation. Option B is incorrect, as SOX is a U.S. financial reporting regulation. Option C is incorrect, as PCI DSS is a payment card industry regulation.

7. C. The correct answer is C. Cloud Spanner is a globally consistent, horizontally scalable relational database. Option A is incorrect. Cloud Storage is not a database; rather, it is an object storage system. Option B is incorrect because BigQuery is an analytics database. Option D is incorrect, as Microsoft SQL Server is not a managed database in Google Cloud.

8. A. The correct answer is A. Cloud Datastore is a managed document database and a good fit for storing documents. Option B is incorrect because Cloud Spanner is a relational database and globally scalable. There is no indication that the developer needs a globally scalable solution. Option C is incorrect, as Cloud Storage is an object storage system, not a managed database. Option D is incorrect because BigQuery is an analytic database designed for data warehousing and similar applications.

9. C. The correct answer is C. VPCs isolate cloud resources from resources in other VPCs, unless VPCs are intentionally linked. Option A is incorrect because a CIDR block has to do with subnet IP addresses. Option B is incorrect, as direct connections are for transmitting data between a data center and Google Cloud—it does not protect resources in the cloud. Option D is incorrect because Cloud Pub/Sub is a messaging service, not a networking service.

10. A. The correct answer is A. Dress4Win is at capacity with its existing infrastructure and wants to innovate faster. Options B and C are incorrect because the decision is not influenced by competitors moving to the cloud. Option D is incorrect because short-term cost savings are not a consideration.

11. C. The correct answer is C. Cloud SQL offers a managed MySQL service. Options A and B are incorrect, as neither is a database. Cloud Dataproc is a managed Hadoop and Spark service. Cloud Dataflow is a stream and batch processing service. Option D is incorrect, because PostgreSQL is another relational database, but it is not a managed service. PostgreSQL is an option in Cloud SQL, however.

12. C. The correct answer is C. In Compute Engine, you create virtual machines and choose which operating system to run. All other requirements can be realized in App Engine.

13. B. The correct answer is B. A significant increase in the use of streaming input will require changes to how data is ingested and require scalable ingestion services. An increase of almost two orders of magnitude in the number of pieces of equipment transmitting data will likely require architectural changes. Option A is incorrect, as additional reporting is easily accommodated. Option C is incorrect because the initial design will take into account that TerramEarth is in a competitive industry. Option D is incorrect, as collaborating with other companies will not require significant changes in systems design.

14. A. The correct answer is A. Cloud Bigtable is a scalable, wide-column database designed for low-latency writes, making it a good choice for time-series data. Option B is incorrect because BigQuery is an analytic database not designed for the high volume of low-latency writes that will need to be supported. Options C and D are not managed databases.

15. B. The correct answer is B. This is a typical use case for BigQuery, and it fits well with its capabilities as an analytic database. Option A is incorrect, as Cloud Spanner is best used for transaction processing on a global scale. Options C and D are not managed databases. Cloud Storage is an object storage service; Cloud Dataprep is a tool for preparing data for analysis.

Chapter 2: Designing for Business Requirements

1. A. Option A is correct. Dress4Win is a consumer, e-commerce service that will grow with respect to the number of customers. Also, the number of designers and retailers will influence the growth in demand for compute and storage resources. Option B is incorrect because the length of run time is not relevant to compute or storage requirements. The type of storage used does not influence the amount of data the application needs to manage, or the amount of computing resources needed. Compliance and regulations may have some effect on security controls and monitoring, but it will not influence compute and storage resources in a significant way.

2. A, C. Options A and C are correct. Both multiregional cloud storage and CDNs distribute data across a geographic area. Option B is incorrect because Coldline storage is used for archiving. Option D is incorrect because Cloud Pub/Sub is a messaging queue, not a storage system. Option E is a managed service for batch and stream processing.

3. B. Option B is correct. High volumes of time-series data need low-latency writes and scalable storage. Time-series data is not updated after it is collected. This makes Bigtable, a wide-column data store with low-latency writes, the best option. Option A is wrong because BigQuery is an analytic database designed for data warehousing. Option C is wrong because Cloud Spanner is a global relational database. Write times would not be as fast as they would be using Bigtable, and the use case does not take advantage of Cloud Spanner's strong consistency in a horizontally scalable relational database. Option D is not a good option because it is an object store, and it is not designed for large volumes of individual time-series data points.

4. A. Option A is correct. Cloud Dataflow is a batch and stream processing service that can be used for transforming data before it is loaded into a data warehouse. Option C is incorrect, Cloud Dataprep is used to prepare data for analysis and machine learning. Option B, Cloud Dataproc, is a managed Hadoop and Spark service, not a data cleaning and preparing service. Option D, Cloud Datastore, is a document database, not a data processing service.

5. C. The correct answer is C, write data to a Cloud Pub/Sub topic. The data can accumulate there as the application processes the data. No data is lost because Pub/Sub will scale as needed. Option A is not a good option because local storage does not scale. Option B is not a good choice because caches are used to provide low-latency access to data that is frequently accessed. Cloud Memorystore does not scale as well as Cloud Pub/Sub, and it may run out of space. Option D is not a good choice because tuning will require developers to invest potentially significant amounts of time without any guarantee of solving the problem. Also, even with optimizations, even larger spikes in data ingestion could result in the same problem of the processing application not being able to keep up with the rate at which data is arriving.

6. B. Option B is correct. Using Cloud Dataproc will reduce the costs of managing the Spark cluster, while using preemptible VMs will reduce the compute charges. Option A is not the best option because you will have to manage the Spark cluster yourself, which will increase the total cost of ownership. Option C is incorrect as Cloud Dataflow is not a

managed Spark service. Option D is incorrect because Cloud Memorystore does not reduce the cost of running Apache Spark and managing a cluster in Compute Engine is not the most cost-effective.

7. C. The relevant health regulation is HIPAA, which regulates healthcare data in the United States. Option A is incorrect, as GDPR is a European Union privacy regulation. Option B is incorrect, as SOX is a regulation that applies to the financial industry. Option D is incorrect, because the Payment Card Industry Data Security Standard does not apply to healthcare data.

8. B. Option B is correct. Message digests are used to detect changes in files. Option A is incorrect because firewall rules block network traffic and are not related to detecting changes to data. Options C and D are important for controlling access to data, but they are not directly related to detecting changes to data.

9. B. B is correct. Cloud KMS allows the customer to manage keys used to encrypt secret data. The requirements for the other categories are met by GCP's default encryption-at-rest practice. Public data does not need to be encrypted, but there is no additional cost or overhead for having it encrypted at rest. Option A would meet the security requirements, but it would involve managing keys for more data than is necessary, and that would increase administrative overhead. Option C does not meet the requirements of secret data. Option D is a terrible choice. Encryption algorithms are difficult to develop and potentially vulnerable to cryptanalysis attacks. It would cost far more to develop a strong encryption algorithm than to use Cloud KMS and default encryption.

10. C. The correct answer is C. Data that is not queried does not need to be in the database to meet business requirements. If the data is needed, it can be retrieved from other storage systems, such as Cloud Storage. Exporting and deleting data will reduce the amount of data in tables and improve performance. Since the data is rarely accessed, it is a good candidate for archival, Coldline storage. Answers A and B are incorrect because scaling either vertically or horizontally will increase costs more than the cost of storing the data in archival storage. Option D is incorrect because multiregional storage is more expensive than Coldline storage and multiregion access is not needed.

11. B. Option B is correct. The manager does not have an accurate cost estimate of supporting the applications if operational support costs are not considered. The manager should have an accurate estimate of TCO before proceeding. Option A is incorrect because the manager does not have an accurate estimate of all costs. Option C is incorrect because it does not address the reliability issues with the applications. Option D may be a reasonable option, but if managed services meet the requirements, using them will solve the reliability issues faster than developing new applications.

12. B. Option B is the best answer because it is a measure of how much customers are engaged in the game and playing. If average time played goes down, this is an indicator that customers are losing interest in the game. If the average time played goes up, they are more engaged and interested in the game. Options A and D are incorrect because revenue does not necessarily correlate with customer satisfaction. Also, it may not correlate with how much customers played the game if revenue is based on monthly subscriptions, for example. Option C is wrong because a year is too long a time frame for detecting changes as rapidly as one can with a weekly measure.

13. C. Option C is correct. In stream processing applications that collect data for a time and then produce summary or aggregated data, there needs to be a limit on how long the processor waits for late-arriving data before producing results. Options A and B are incorrect because you do not need to know requirements for data lifecycle management or access controls to the database at this point, since your focus is on ingesting raw data and writing statistics to the database. Option D is incorrect. An architect should provide that list to a project manager, not the other way around.

14. A. The correct option is A. Data Catalog is a managed service for metadata. Option B is incorrect, as Dataprep is a tool for preparing data for analysis and machine learning. Option C is incorrect, as Dataproc is a managed Hadoop and Spark service. Option D is incorrect because BigQuery is a database service designed for analytic databases and data warehousing.

15. B. The correct option is B. Cloud Spanner is a horizontally scalable relational database that provides strong consistency, SQL, and scales to a global level. Options A and C are incorrect because they do not support SQL. Option D is incorrect because an inventory system is a transaction processing system, and BigQuery is designed for analytic, not transaction processing systems.

16. B. Option B is correct. An API would allow dealers to access up-to-date information and allow them to query only for the data that they need. Dealers do not need to know implementation details of TerramEarth's database. Options A and C are incorrect because nightly extracts or exports would not give access to up-to-date data, which could change during the day. Option D is incorrect because it requires the dealers to understand how to query a relational database. Also, it is not a good practice to grant direct access to important business databases to people or services outside the company.

17. B. The correct option is B. Cloud Storage is an object storage system well suited to storing unstructured data. Option A is incorrect because Cloud SQL provides relational databases that are used for structured data. Option C is incorrect because Cloud Datastore is a NoSQL document database used with flexible schema data. Option D is incorrect, as Bigtable is a wide-column database that is not suitable for unstructured data.

18. A. Option A is correct. Cloud Pub/Sub is designed to provide messaging services and fits this use case well. Options B and D are incorrect because, although you may be able to implement asynchronous message exchange using those storage systems, it would be inefficient and require more code than using Cloud Pub/Sub. Option C is incorrect because this would require both the sending and receiving services to run on the same VM.

19. C. The correct answer is C. Cloud AutoML is a managed service for building machine learning models. TerramEarth's data could be used to build a predictive model using AutoML. Options A and D are incorrect—they are databases and do not have the tools for building predictive models. Option B is wrong because Cloud Dataflow is a stream and batch processing service.

Chapter 3: Designing for Technical Requirements

1. A. The correct answer is A. Redundancy is a general strategy for improving availability. Option B is incorrect because lowering network latency will not improve availability of the data storage system. Options C and D are incorrect because there is no indication that either a NoSQL or a relational database will meet the overall storage requirements of the system being discussed.

2. C. The minimum percentage availability that meets the requirements is option C, which allows for up to 14.4 minutes of downtime per day. All other options would allow for less downtime, but that is not called for by the requirements.

3. B. The correct answer is B. A code review is a software engineering practice that requires an engineer to review code with another engineer before deploying it. Option A would not solve the problem, as continuous integration reduces the amount of effort required to deploy new versions of software. Options C and D are both security controls, which would not help identify misconfigurations.

4. B. The correct answer is B, Live Migration, which moves running VMs to different physical servers without interrupting the state of the VM. Option A is incorrect because preemptible VMs are low-cost VMs that may be taken back by Google at any time. Option C is incorrect, as canary deployments are a type of deployment—not a feature of Compute Engine. Option D is incorrect, as arrays of disks are not directly involved in preserving the state of a VM and moving the VM to a functioning physical server.

5. D. Option D is correct. When a health check fails, the failing VM is replaced by a new VM that is created using the instance group template to configure the new VM. Options A and C are incorrect, as TTL is not used to detect problems with application functioning. Option B is incorrect because the application is not shut down when a health check fails.

6. B. The correct answer is B. Creating instance groups in multiple regions and routing workload to the closest region using global load balancing will provide the most consistent experience for users in different geographic regions. Option A is incorrect because Cloud Spanner is a relational database and does not affect how game backend services are run except for database operations. Option C is incorrect, as routing traffic over the public Internet means traffic will experience the variance of public Internet routes between regions. Option D is incorrect. A cache will reduce the time needed to read data, but it will not affect network latency when that data is transmitted from a game backend to the player's device.

7.   D. The correct answer is D. Users do not need to make any configuration changes when using Cloud Storage or Cloud Filestore. Both are fully managed services. Options A and C are incorrect because TTLs do not need to be set to ensure high availability. Options B and C are incorrect because users do not need to specify a health check for managed storage services.

8.   B. The best answer is B. BigQuery is a serverless, fully managed analytic database that uses SQL for querying. Options A and C are incorrect because both Bigtable and Cloud Datastore are NoSQL databases. Option D, Cloud Storage, is not a database, and it does not meet most of the requirements listed.

9.   C. The correct answer is C. Primary-primary replication keeps both clusters synchronized with write operations so that both clusters can respond to queries. Options A, B, and D are not actual replication options.

10.   B. Option B is correct. A redundant network connection would mitigate the risk of losing connectivity if a single network connection went down. Option A is incorrect, as firewall rules are a security control and would not mitigate the risk of network connectivity failures. Option C may help with compute availability, but it does not improve network availability. Option D does not improve availability, and additional bandwidth is not needed.

11.   C. The correct answer is C. Stackdriver should be used to monitor applications and infrastructure to detect early warning signs of potential problems with applications or infrastructure. Option A is incorrect because access controls are a security control and not related to directly improving availability. Option B is incorrect because managed services may not meet all requirements and so should not be required in a company's standards. Option D is incorrect because collecting and storing performance monitoring data does not improve availability.

12.   C. The correct answer is C. The two applications have different scaling requirements. The compute-intensive backend may benefit from VMs with a large number of CPUs that would not be needed for web serving. Also, the frontend may be able to reduce the number of instances when users are not actively using the user interface, but long compute jobs may still be running in the background. Options A and B are false statements. Option D is incorrect for the reasons explained in reference to Option C.

13.   C. The correct answer is C. The autoscaler may be adding VMs because it has not waited long enough for recently added VMs to start and begin to take on load. Options A and B are incorrect because changing the minimum and maximum number of VMs in the group does not affect the rate at which VMs are added or removed. Option D is incorrect because it reduces the time available for new instances to start taking on workload, so it may actually make the problem worse.

14.   C. The correct answer is C. If the server is shut down without a cleanup script, then data that would otherwise be copied to Cloud Storage could be lost when the VM shuts down. Option A is incorrect because buckets do not have a fixed amount of storage. Option B is incorrect because, if it were true, the service would not function for all users—not just several of them. Option D is incorrect because if there was a connectivity failure between the VM and Cloud Storage, there would be more symptoms of such a failure.

15. A. The correct answer is A. Pods are the lowest level of the computation abstractions. Deployments are collections of pods running a version of an application. Services are sets of deployments running an application, possibly with multiple versions running in different deployments. Options B, C, and D are all incorrect in the order of progression from lowest to highest level of abstraction.

16. B. The correct answer is B. The requirements are satisfied by the Kubernetes container orchestration capabilities. Option A is incorrect, as Cloud Functions do not run containers. Option C is incorrect because Cloud Dataproc is a managed service for Hadoop and Spark. Option D is incorrect, as Cloud Dataflow is a managed service for stream and batch processing using the Apache Beam model.

17. A. The correct answer is A. BigQuery should be used for an analytics database. Partitioning allows the query processor to limit scans to partitions that might have the data selected in a query. Options B and D are incorrect because Bigtable does not support SQL. Options C and D are incorrect because federation is a way of making data from other sources available within a database—it does not limit the data scanned in the way that partitioning does.

18. B. The correct answer is B. Mean time between failures is a measure of reliability. Option A is a measure of how long it takes to recover from a disruption. Options C and D are incorrect because the time between deployments or errors is not directly related to reliability.

19. A. The correct answer is A. Request success rate is a measure of how many requests were successfully satisfied. Option B is incorrect because at least some instances of an application may be up at any time, so it does not reflect the capacity available. Options C and D are not relevant measures of risk.

20. A. The correct answer is A. The persistent storage may be increased in size, but the operating system may need to be configured to use that additional storage. Option B is incorrect because while backing up a disk before operating on it is a good practice, it is not required. Option C is incorrect because changing storage size does not change access control rules. Option D is incorrect because any disk metadata that needs to change when the size changes is updated by the resize process.

Chapter 4: Designing Compute Systems

1. A. The correct answer is A. Compute Engine instances meet all of the requirements: they can run VMs with minimal changes, and application administrators can have root access. Option B would require the VMs to be deployed as containers. Option C is incorrect because App Engine Standard is limited to applications that can execute in a language-specific runtime. Option D is incorrect, as App Engine Flexible runs containers, not VMs.

2. B. The best option is B. It meets the requirement of creating and managing the keys without requiring your company to deploy and manage a secure key store. Option A is incorrect because it does not meet the requirements. Option C requires more setup and maintenance than Option B. Option D does not exist, at least for any strong encryption algorithm.

3. C. Option C is correct. The description of symptoms matches the behavior of preemptible instances. Option A is wrong because collecting performance metrics will not prevent shutdowns. Option B is incorrect, because shutdowns are not triggered by insufficient storage. Option D is incorrect, as the presence or absence of an external IP address would not affect shutdown behavior.

4. B. Option B is correct. Shielded VMs include the vTPM along with Secure Boot and Integrity Monitoring. Option A is incorrect—there is no such option. Options C and D are not related to vTPM functionality.

5. B. The correct answer is B. Unmanaged instance groups can have nonidentical instances. Option A is incorrect, as all instances are the same in managed instance groups. Option C is incorrect because there is no such thing as a flexible instance group. Option D is incorrect because Kubernetes clusters run containers and would require changes that are not required if the cluster is migrated to an unmanaged instance group.

6. B. The correct answer is B. The requirements call for a PaaS. Second-generation App Engine Standard supports Python 3.7, and it does not require users to manage VMs or containers. Option A is incorrect because you would have to manage VMs if you used Compute Engine. Option C is incorrect, as you would have to create containers to run in Kubernetes Engine. Option D is incorrect because Cloud Dataproc is a managed Hadoop and Spark service, and it is not designed to run Python web applications.

7. B. The correct answer is B. This solution notifies users immediately of any problem and does not require any servers. Option A does not solve the problem of reducing time to notify users when there is a problem. Options C and D solve the problem but do not notify users immediately. Option C also requires you to manage a server.

8. C. The correct answer is C. App Engine Flexible requires the least effort. App Engine Flexible will run the container and perform health checks and collect performance metrics. Options A and B are incorrect because provisioning and managing Compute Engine instances is more effort than using App Engine Flexible. Option D is incorrect because you cannot run a custom container in App Engine Standard.

9. A. The correct answer is A. Cluster masters run core services for the cluster, and nodes run workload. Options B and C are incorrect, as the cluster manager is not just an endpoint for APIs. Also, there is no runner node type. Option D is incorrect because nodes do not monitor cluster masters.

10. C. Option C is correct. Ingress Controllers are needed by Ingress objects, which are objects that control external access to services running in a Kubernetes cluster. Option A is incorrect, as Pods are the lowest level of computational unit, and they run one or more containers. Option B is incorrect, as Deployments are versions of a service that run in a cluster. Option D is incorrect, as Services do not control access from external services.

11. C. The correct answer is C. StatefulSets deploy pods with unique IDs, which allows Kubernetes to support stateful applications by ensuring that clients can always use the same pod. Answer A is incorrect, as pods are always used for both stateful and stateless applications. Options B and D are incorrect because they are not actually components in Kubernetes.

12. C. Option C is correct because Cloud Functions can detect authentications to Firebase and run code in response. Sending a message would require a small amount of code, and this can run in Cloud Functions. Options A and B would require more work to set up a service to watch for a login and then send a message. Option D is incorrect, as Cloud Dataflow is a stream and batch processing platform not suitable for responding to events in Firebase.

13. B. The correct answer is B. Deployment Manager is Google Cloud's IaaS manager. Option A is incorrect because Cloud Dataflow is a stream and batch processing service. Option C, Identity and Access Management, is an authentication and authorization service. Option D, App Engine Flexible, is a PaaS offering that allows users to customize their own runtimes using containers.

14. A. The correct answer is A. This application is stateful. It collects and maintains data about sensors in servers and evaluates that data. Option B is incorrect because the application stores data about a stream, so it is stateful. Option C is incorrect because there *is* enough information. Option D is incorrect because the application stores data about the stream, so it is stateful.

15. B. The correct answer is B. Of the four options, a cache is most likely used to store state data. If instances are lost, state information is not lost as well. Option A is incorrect; Memorystore is not a SQL database. Option C is incorrect because Memorystore does not provide extraction, transformation, and load services. Option D is incorrect because Memorystore is not a persistent object store.

16. C. Option C is the correct answer. Using a queue between the services allows the first service to write data as fast as needed, while the second service reads data as fast as it can. The second service can catch up after peak load subsides. Options A, B, and D do not decouple the services.

17. B. Option B is the correct answer. Cloud Dataflow is Google Cloud's implementation on Apache Beam. Option A, Cloud Dataproc, is a managed Hadoop and Spark service. Option C, Cloud Dataprep, is a data preparation tool for analysis and machine learning. Option D, Cloud Memorystore, is a managed cache service.

18. B. Option B is the correct answer. Stackdriver is Google Cloud's monitoring and logging service. Option A, Cloud Dataprep, is data preperation tool for analysis and machine learning. Option C, Cloud Dataproc, is a managed Hadoop and Spark service. Option D, Cloud Memorystore, is a managed cache service.

19. B. The correct answer is B. Managed instances groups can autoscale, so this option would automatically add or remove instances as needed. Options A and D are not as cost efficient as Option B. Option C is incorrect because App Engine Standard does not provide a C++ runtime.

20. B. Option B is correct. Cloud Dataflow is designed to support stream and batch processing, and it can write data to BigQuery. Options A is incorrect, as Firebase is GCP's mobile development platform. Option D is incorrect, Datastore is a NoSQL database. Option C is incorrect because Cloud Memorystore is a managed cache service.

Chapter 5: Designing Storage Systems

1. **A.** The correct answer is A. The Cloud Storage Coldline service is designed for long-term storage of infrequently accessed objects. Option B is not the best answer because Nearline should be used with objects that are not accessed up to once a month. Coldline storage is more cost effective and still meets the requirements. Option C is incorrect. Cloud Filestore is a network filesystem, and it is used to store data that is actively used by applications running on Compute Engine VM and Kubernetes Engine clusters.

2. **B.** The correct answer is B. Do not use sequential names or timestamps if uploading files in parallel. Files with sequentially close names will likely be assigned to the same server. This can create a hotspot when writing files to Cloud Storage. Option A is incorrect, as this could cause hotspots. Options C and D affect the lifecycle of files once they are written and do not impact upload efficiency.

3. **C.** The correct answer is C. Multiregional Cloud Storage replicates data to multiple regions. In the event of a failure in one region, the data could be retrieved from another region. Options A and B are incorrect because those are databases, not file storage systems. Option D is incorrect because it does not meet the requirement of providing availability in the event of a single region failure.

4. **B.** The correct answer is B. Cloud Filestore is a network-attached storage service that provides a filesystem that is accessible from Compute Engine. Filesystems in Cloud Filestore can be mounted using standard operating system commands. Option A, Cloud Storage, is incorrect because it does not provide a filesystem. Options C and D are incorrect because databases do not provide filesystems.

5. **C.** The correct answer is C. Cloud SQL is a managed database service that supports MySQL and PostgreSQL. Option A is incorrect because Bigtable is a wide-column NoSQL database, and it is not a suitable substitute for MySQL. Option B is incorrect because BigQuery is optimized for data warehouse and analytic databases, not transactional databases. Option D is incorrect, as Cloud Filestore is not a database.

6. **A.** The correct answer is A. Cloud Spanner is a managed database service that supports horizontal scalability across regions. It supports strong consistency so that there is no risk of data anomalies caused by eventual consistency. Option B is incorrect because Cloud SQL cannot scale globally. Option C is incorrect, as Cloud Storage does not meet the database requirements. Option D is incorrect because BigQuery is not designed for transaction processing systems.

7. **D.** The correct answer is D. All data in GCP is encrypted when at rest. The other options are incorrect because they do not include all GCP storage services.

8. **C.** The correct answer is C. The `bq` command-line tool is used to work with BigQuery. Option A, `gsutil`, is the command-line tool for working with Cloud Storage, and Option D, `cbt`, is the command-line tool for working with Bigtable. Option B, `gcloud`, is the command-line tool for most other GCP services.

9. A. The correct answer is A. dataViewer allows a user to list projects and tables and get table data and metadata. Options B and D would enable the user to view data but would grant more permissions than needed. Option C does not grant permission to view data in tables.

10. C. The correct answer is C. --dry-run returns an estimate of the number of bytes that would be returned if the query were executed. The other choices are not actually bq command-line options.

11. D. The correct answer is D. NoSQL data has flexible schemas. The other options specify features that are found in relational databases. ACID transactions and indexes are found in some NoSQL databases as well.

12. D. The correct answer is D. Bigtable is the best option for storing streaming data because it provides low-latency writes and can store petabytes of data. The database would need to store petabytes of data if the number of users scales as planned. Option A is a poor choice because a managed database would meet requirements and require less administration support. Option B will not scale to the volume of data expected. Option C, Cloud Spanner, could scale to store the volumes of data, but it is not optimized for low-latency writes of streaming data.

13. B. The correct answer is B—create multiple clusters in the instance and use Bigtable replication. Options A and C are not correct, as they require developing custom applications to partition data or keep replicas synchronized. Option D is incorrect because the requirements can be met.

14. B. The correct answer is B. Cloud Datastore is a managed document database, which is a kind of NoSQL database that uses a flexible JSON-like data structure. Option A is incorrect—it is not a database. Options C and D are not good fits because the JSON data would have to be mapped to relational structures to take advantage of the full range of relational features. There is no indication that additional relational features are required.

15. C. The correct answer is C. You could try to cache results to reduce the number of reads on the database. Option A is not a good choice because it does not reduce the number of reads, and there is no indication that the scale of Cloud Spanner is needed. Option B is not a good choice because Bigtable is a NoSQL database and may not meet the database needs of the application. Option D is incorrect because caching is an option.

16. B. Option B is correct. Lifecycle policies allow you to specify an action, like changing storage class, after an object reaches a specified age. Option A is incorrect, as retention policies prevent premature deleting of an object. Option C is incorrect. This is a feature used to implement retention policies.

17. A. The correct answer is A. Cloud CDN distributes copies of static data to points of presence around the globe so that it can be closer to users. Option B is incorrect. Premium Network routes data over the internal Google network, but it does not extend to client devices. Option C will not help with latency. Option D is incorrect because moving the location of the server might reduce the latency for some users, but it would likely increase latency for other users, as they could be located anywhere around the globe.

Chapter 6: Designing Networks

1. B. The correct answer is B. Default subnets are each assigned a distinct, nonoverlapping IP address range. Option A is incorrect, as default subnets use private addresses. Option C is incorrect because increasing the size of the subnet mask does not necessarily prevent overlaps. Option D is an option that would also ensure nonoverlapping addresses, but it is not necessary given the stated requirements.

2. A. The correct answer is A. A Shared VPC allows resources in one project to access the resources in another project. Option B is incorrect, as load balancing does not help with network access. Options C and D are incorrect because those are mechanisms for hybrid cloud computing. In this case, all resources are in GCP, so hybrid networking is not needed.

3. B. The correct answer is B. The `default-allow-internal` rule allows ingress connections for all protocols and ports among instances in the network. Option A is incorrect because implied rules cannot be deleted, and the implied rules alone would not be enough to enable all instances to connect to all other instances. Option C is incorrect because that rule governs the ICMP protocol for management services, like ping. Option D is incorrect because 65535 is the largest number/lowest priority allowed for firewall rules.

4. A. The correct answer is A. 0 is the highest priority for firewall rules. All the other options are incorrect because they have priorities that are not guaranteed to enable the rule to take precedence.

5. B. The correct answer is B. 8 is the number of bits used to specify the subnet mask. Option A is wrong because 24 is the number of bits available to specify a host address. Options C and D are wrong, as the integer does not indicate an octet.

6. C. The correct answer is C. Disabling a firewall rule allows you to turn off the effect of a rule quickly without deleting it. Option A is incorrect because it does not help isolate the rule or rules causing the problem, and it may introduce new problems because the new rules may take precedence in cases they did not before. Option B is not helpful because alone it would not help isolate the problematic rule or rules. Option D is incorrect because it will leave the VPC with only implied rules. Adding back all rules could be time-consuming, and having no rules could cause additional problems.

7. C. The correct answer is C. Hybrid networking is needed to enable the transfer of data to the cloud to build models and then transfer models back to the on-premises servers. Option A is incorrect because firewall rules restrict or allow traffic on a network—they do not link networks. Options B and D are incorrect because load balancing does not link networks.

8. D. The correct answer is D. With mirrored topology, public cloud and private on-premise environments mirror each other. Options A and B are not correct because gated topologies are used to allow access to APIs in other networks without exposing them to the public Internet. Option C is incorrect because that topology is used to exchange data and have different processing done in different environments.

9. B. The correct answer is B. Cloud VPN implements IPsec VPNs. All other options are incorrect because they are not names of actual services available in GCP.

10. B. The correct answer is B. Partner Interconnect provides between 50 Mbps and 10 Gbps connections. Option A, Cloud VPN, provides up to 3 Gbps connections. Option C, Direct Interconnect, provides 10 or 100 Gbps connections. Option D is not an actual GCP service name.

11. C. The correct answer is C. Both direct interconnect and partner interconnect can be configured to support between 60 Gbps and 80 Gbps. All other options are wrong because Cloud VPN supports a maximum of 3 Gbps.

12. A. The correct answer is A. Direct peering allows customers to connect their networks to a Google network point of access and exchange Border Gateway Protocol (BGP) routes, which define paths for transmitting data between networks. Options B and D are not the names of GCP services. Option C is not correct because global load balancing does not link networks.

13. A. The correct answer is A. HTTP(S) load balancers are global and will route HTTP traffic to the region closest to the user making a request. Option B is incorrect, as SSL Proxy is used for non-HTTPS SSL traffic. Option C is incorrect because it does not support external traffic from the public Internet. Option D is incorrect, as TCP Proxy is used for non-HTTP(S) traffic.

14. A. The correct answer is A. Only Internal TCP/UDP supports load balancing using private IP addressing. The other options are all incorrect because they cannot load balance using private IP addresses.

15. C. The correct answer is C. All global load balancers require the Premium Tier network, which routes all data over the Google global network and not the public Internet. Option A is incorrect, as object storage is not needed. Option C is incorrect because a VPN is not required. Option D is incorrect, as that is another kind of global load balancer that would require Premium Tier networking.

Chapter 7: Designing for Security and Legal Compliance

1. C. Option C, a service account, is the best choice for an account that will be associated with an application or resource, such as a VM. Both options A and B should be used with actual users. Option D is not a valid type of identity in GCP.

2. A. The correct answer is A. The identities should be assigned to groups and predefined roles assigned to those groups. Assigning roles to groups eases administrative overhead because users receive permissions when they are added to a group. Removing a user from a group removes permissions from the user, unless the user receives that permission in another way. Options B, C, and D are incorrect because you cannot assign permissions directly to a user.

3. B. The correct answer is option B. Fine-grained permission and predefined roles help implement least privilege because each predefined role has only the permissions needed to carry out a specific set of responsibilities. Option A is incorrect. Primitive roles are coarse grained and grant more permissions than often needed. Option C is incorrect. Simply creating a particular type of identity does not by itself associate permissions with users. Option D is not the best option because it requires more administrative overhead than Option B, and it is a best practice to use predefined roles as much as possible and only create custom roles when a suitable predefined role does not exist.

4. C. The correct option is C—three trust domains. The frontend, backend, and database are all logically separated. They run on three different platforms. Each should be in its own trust domain. Options A and B are incorrect, as they are too few. Option D is incorrect because all services should be considered within a trust domain.

5. A. The correct answer is A. A group should be created for administrators and granted the necessary roles, which in this case is roles/logging.admin. The identity of the person responsible for a period should be added at the start of the period, and the person who was previously responsible should be removed from the group. Option B is not the best option because it assigns roles to an identity, which is allowed but not recommended. If the team changes strategy and wants to have three administrators at a time, roles would have to be granted and revoked to multiple identities rather than a single group. Options C and D are incorrect because roles/logging.privateLogViewer does not grant administrative access.

6. D. The correct answer is D. You do not need to configure any settings to have data encrypted at rest in GCP. Options B, C, and D are all incorrect because no configuration is required.

7. A. The correct answer is A. Option B is incorrect, but it is a strong encryption algorithm and could be used to encrypt data. Option C is incorrect. DES is a weak encryption algorithm that is easily broken by today's methods. Option D is incorrect. Blowfish is a strong encryption algorithm designed as a replacement for DES and other weak encryption algorithms but it is not used in GCP.

8. B. The correct answer is B. The data encryption key is encrypted using a key encryption key. Option A is incorrect. There are no hidden locations on disk that are inaccessible from a hardware perspective. Option C is incorrect. Keys are not stored in a relational database. Option D is incorrect. An elliptic curve encryption algorithm is not used.

9. C. The correct answer is C. Layer 7 is the application layer, and Google uses ALTS at that level. Options A and B are incorrect. IPSec and TLS are used by Google but not at layer 7. Option D is incorrect. ARP is an address resolution protocol, not a security protocol.

10. C. The correct answer is C. Cloud KMS is the key management service in GCP. It is designed specifically to store keys securely and manage the lifecycle of keys. Options A and C are incorrect. They are both document databases and are not suitable for low-latency, highly secure key storage. Option D is incorrect. Bigtable is designed for low-latency, high-write volume operations over variable structured data. It is not designed for secure key management.

11. B. The correct answer is B. Cloud Storage is the best option for maintaining archived data such as log data. Also, since the data is not likely to be accessed, Coldline storage would be the most cost-effective option. Option A is incorrect because Stackdriver does not retain log

data for five years. Option C is not the best option since the data does not need to be queried, and it is likely not structured sufficiently to be stored efficiently in BigQuery. Option D is incorrect. Cloud Pub/Sub is a messaging service, not a long-term data store.

12. B. The correct answer is B. The duties of the development team are separated so that no one person can both approve a deployment and execute a deployment. Option A is incorrect. Defense in depth is the use of multiple security controls to mitigate the same risk. Option C is incorrect because least privilege applies to a set of permissions granted for a single task, such as deploying to production. Option D is incorrect. Encryption at rest is not related to the scenario described in the question.

13. C. The correct answer is C. The service will collect personal information of children under 13 in the United States, so COPPA applies. Option A is incorrect because HIPAA and HITECH apply to protected healthcare data. Option B is incorrect because SOX applies to financial data. Option D is incorrect because GDPR applies to citizens of the European Union, not the United States.

14. D. The correct answer is D. The service will collect personal information from citizens of the European Union, so GDPR applies. Option A is incorrect because HIPAA and HITECH apply to protected healthcare data. Option B is incorrect because SOX applies to financial data. Option C is incorrect, as it applies to children in the United States.

15. A. The correct answer is A. ITIL is a framework for aligning business and IT strategies and practices. Option B is incorrect because TOGAF is an enterprise architecture framework. Option C is incorrect because the Porters Five Forces Model is used to assess competitiveness. Option D is incorrect because the Ansoff Matrix is used to summarize growth strategies.

Chapter 8: Designing for Reliability

1. A. The correct answer is A. If the goal is to understand performance characteristics, then metrics, particularly time-series data, will show the values of key measurements associated with performance, such as utilization of key resources. Option B is incorrect because detailed log data describes significant events but does not necessarily convey resource utilization or other performance-related data. Option C is incorrect because errors are types of events that indicate a problem but are not helpful for understanding normal, baseline operations. Option D is incorrect because acceptance tests measure how well a system meets business requirements but does not provide point-in-time performance information.

2. B. The correct answer is B. Alerting policies are sets of conditions, notification specifications, and selection criteria for determining resources to monitor. Option A is incorrect because one or more conditions are necessary but not sufficient. Option C is incorrect because a log message specification describes the content written to a log when an event occurs. Option D is incorrect because acceptance tests are used to assess how well a system meets business requirements; it is not related to alerting.

3. C. The correct answer is C. Audit logs would contain information about changes to user privileges, especially privilege escalations such as granting root or administrative access.

Option A and Option B are incorrect, as neither records detailed information about access control changes. Option D may have some information about user privilege changes, but notes may be changed and otherwise tampered with, so on their own they are insufficient sources of information for compliance review purposes.

4.   C. The correct option is C. Release management practices reduce manual effort to deploy code. This allows developers to roll out code more frequently and in smaller units and, if necessary, quickly roll back problematic releases. Option A is incorrect because release management is not related to programming paradigms. Option B is incorrect because release management does not require waterfall methodologies. Option D is incorrect. Release management does not influence the use of stateful or stateless services.

5.   A. The correct answer is A. These are tests that check the smallest testable unit of code. These tests should be run before any attempt to build a new version of an application. Option B is incorrect because a stress test could be run on the unit of code, but it is more than what is necessary to test if the application should be built. Option C is incorrect because acceptance tests are used to confirm that business requirements are met; a build that only partially meets business requirements is still useful for developers to create. Option D is incorrect because *compliance tests* is a fictitious term and not an actual class of tests used in release management.

6.   C. The correct answer is C. This is a canary deployment. Option A is incorrect because Blue/Green deployment uses two fully functional environments and all traffic is routed to one of those environments at a time. Option B and Option D are incorrect because they are not actual names of deployment types.

7.   D. The correct answer is D. GitHub and Cloud Source Repositories are version control systems. Option A is incorrect because Jenkins is a CI/CD tool, not a version control system. Option B is incorrect because neither Syslog nor Cloud Build is a version control system. Option C is incorrect because Cloud Build is not a version control system.

8.   D. The correct answer is D. A Blue/Green deployment is the kind of deployment that allows developers to deploy new code to an entire environment before switching traffic to it. Option A and Option B are incorrect because they are incremental deployment strategies. Option C is not an actual deployment strategy.

9.   A. The correct option is A. The developers should create a patch to shed load. Option B would not solve the problem, since more connections would allow more clients to connect to the database, but CPU and memory are saturated, so no additional work can be done. Option C could be part of a long-term architecture change, but it could not be implemented quickly. Option D could also be part of a longer-term solution to allow a database to buffer requests and process them at a rate allowed by available database resources.

10.   B. The correct answer is B. This is an example of upstream or client throttling. Option A is incorrect because load is not shed; rather, it is just delayed. Option C is incorrect. There is no rebalancing of load, such as might be done on a Kafka topic. Option D is incorrect. There is no mention of partitioning data.

Chapter 9: Analyzing and Defining Technical Processes

1. B. The correct answer is B. Analysis defines the scope of the problem and assessing options for solving the problem. Design produces high-level and detailed plans that guide development. Option A is incorrect, as business continuity planning is not required before development, though it can occur alongside development. Option C is incorrect because testing occurs after software is developed. Similarly, option D is incorrect because documentation comes after development as well.

2. A. The correct answer is A. COTS stands for commercial off-the-shelf software, so the question is about research related to the question of buy versus build. Option B is incorrect, as COTS is not an ORM. Options C and D are both incorrect. COTS is not about business continuity or disaster recovery.

3. C. Option C is correct. ROI is a measure used to compare the relative value of different investments. Option A is a measure of reliability and availability. Option B is a requirement related to disaster recovery. Option D is a fictitious measure.

4. C. The correct answer is C because questions of data structure are not usually addressed until the detail design stage. Option A is incorrect, as analysis is about scoping a problem and choosing a solution approach. Option B is incorrect because high-level design is dedicated to identifying subcomponents and how they function together. Option D is incorrect because the maintenance phase is about keeping software functioning.

5. C. The correct answer is C. In the middle of the night the primary goal is to get the service functioning properly. Operations documentation, like runbooks, provide guidance on how to start services and correct problems. Option A is incorrect because design documentation may describe why design decisions were made—it does not contain distilled information about running the service. Option B is incorrect, as user documentation is for customers of the service. Option D is incorrect because, although developer documentation may eventually help the engineer understand the reason why the service failed, it is not the best option for finding specific guidance on getting the service to function normally.

6. B. The correct answer is B. This is an example of continuous integration because code is automatically merged with the baseline application code. Option A is not an actual process. Option C is not an actual process, and it should not be confused with continual deployment. Option D is incorrect because the software development lifecycle includes continuous integration and much more.

7. D. The correct answer is D. This is an example of chaos engineering. Netflix's Simian Army is a collection of tools that support chaos engineering. Option A is incorrect because this is a reasonable approach to improving reliability, assuming that the practice is transparent and coordinated with others responsible for the system. Option B is incorrect. This is not a test to ensure that components work together. It is an experiment to see what happens when some components do not work. Option C is incorrect. This does test the ability of the system to process increasingly demanding workloads.

8. D. The correct answer is D. The goal of the post-mortem is to learn how to prevent this kind of incident again. Options A, B, and C are all wrong because they focus on blaming a single individual for an incident that occurred because of multiple factors. Also, laying blame does not contribute to finding a solution. In cases where an individual's negligence or lack of knowledge is a significant contributing factor, then other management processes should be used to address the problem. Post-mortems exist to learn and to correct technical processes.

9. C. The correct answer is C. ITIL is a set of enterprise IT practices for managing the full range of IT processes, from planning and development to security and support. Options A and B are likely to be found in all well-run software development teams. Option D may not be used at many startups, but it should be.

10. C. The correct answer is C. Disaster recovery is a part of business continuity planning. Options A and B are wrong. They are neither the same nor are they unrelated. Option D is incorrect because it has the relationship backward.

11. A. The correct answer is A. ISO/IEC 20000 is a service management standard. Options B and C are incorrect. They are programming language–specific standards for Java and Python, respectively. Option D is incorrect. ISO/IEC 27002 is a security standard, although you may reference it for security-related practices.

12. D. The correct answer is D. There may be an underlying bug in code or weakness in the design that should be corrected. Options A and B are incorrect because it should be addressed, since it adversely impacts customers. Option C is incorrect because software engineers and architects can recognize a customer-impacting flaw and correct it.

13. C. The correct answer is C. A disaster plan documents a strategy for responding to a disaster. It includes information such as where operations will be established, which services are the highest priority, what personnel are considered vital to recovery operations, as well as plans for dealing with insurance carriers and maintaining relations with suppliers and customers. Option A is incorrect. Recovery time objectives cannot be set until the details of the recovery plan are determined. Option B is incorrect because you cannot decide what risk to transfer to an insurance company before understanding what the risks and recovery objectives are. Option D is incorrect. A service management plan is part of an enterprise IT process structure.

14. C. The correct answer is C. Option A is not correct because blaming engineers and immediately imposing severe consequences is counterproductive. It will tend to foster an environment that is not compatible with agile development practices. Option B is incorrect because this could be highly costly in terms of engineers' time, and it is unlikely to find subtle bugs related to the complex interaction of multiple components in a distributed system. Option D is incorrect because, while additional training may be part of the solution, that is for the manager to decide. Post-mortems should be blameless, and suggesting that someone be specifically targeted for additional training in a post-mortem implies some level of blame.

15. C. The correct answer is C. The criteria for determining when to invoke the disaster recovery plan should be defined before a team might have to deal with a disaster. Options A, B, and C are all incorrect because the decision should not be left to the sole discretion of an individual manager, service owner, or engineer. A company policy should be in place for determining when to invoke a DR plan.

Chapter 10: Analyzing and Defining Business Processes

1. A. The correct answer is A. Each of the individuals invited to the meeting have an interest in the project. Option B is incorrect since there is no mention of compliance requirements and regulations do not typically dictate meeting structures. Options C and D are incorrect, as there is no discussion of cost or skill building.

2. B. Option B is correct. A project is part of a program, and programs span multiple departments; both exist to execute organizational strategy. Option A is incorrect because the words do mean different things. Option C is incorrect because programs are not part of projects. Option D is incorrect because projects do not refer only to software engineering efforts.

3. D. The correct answer is D. This is an example of communicating with stakeholders and influencing their opinions about options. Option A is incorrect, as the stakeholders are not identified here. Option B is incorrect because there is no discussion of individuals' roles and scope of interest. Option C is incorrect because the architect did not publish a plan.

4. B. The correct answer is B. This is a change because of the introduction of a competitive product with more features. Option A is incorrect. This is not a change prompted by the actions of an individual, such as someone leaving the company. Option C is incorrect because a skills gap did not trigger the change, although there may be a skills gap on the team that now has to implement alerting. Option D is incorrect. There is no mention of economic factors, such as a recession.

5. D. The correct answer is D. The changes were prompted by a new regulation. Option A is incorrect. This is not a change prompted by the actions of an individual, such as someone leaving the company. Option B is incorrect, as there is no mention of competitive pressures. Option C is incorrect. A skills gap did not trigger the change, although there may be a skills gap on the team that now has to implement alerting.

6. C. The correct option is C. The program manager should use a change management methodology to control and better understand changes. Option A is incorrect. A program manager may not be able to stop some changes, such as changes due to regulatory changes, without adverse consequences. Option B is incorrect because it does not solve the problem presented but may be part of a solution that includes using a change management strategy. Option D is incorrect, as cost controls will not help the program manager understand the impact of changes.

7. B. The correct answer is B. This is an example of a digital transformation initiative that is attempting fundamental changes in the way that the company delivers value to its customers. Option A is incorrect. This is not a typical change management issue because it involves the entire enterprise introducing multiple new technologies. Option C is incorrect. The scope of this initiative is in response to more than a single competitor. Option D is incorrect. This is not a cost management initiative.

8. B. The correct answer is B. This exercise is an attempt to identify a skills gap—in this case mobile development skills. Option A is incorrect. This is not about defining skills needed,

as that has already been done. Option C is incorrect because it is premature to develop a plan until the gaps are understood. Option D is incorrect because there is no mention of hiring additional engineers.

9. C. The correct answer is C. This is an example of developing the skills of individual contributors. Option A is incorrect. This is not about defining skills needed. Option B is incorrect. This is not about identifying skills gaps, as that has already been done. Option D is incorrect because it does not entail recruiting.

10. D. The correct answer is D. This is an example of recruiting. Option A is incorrect, as this is not about defining skills needed. Option B is incorrect. This is not about identifying skills gaps, as that has already been done. Option C is incorrect because it does not entail planning training and skill development.

11. C. The correct answer is C. This is an example of professional services because it involves custom support and development for customers. Option A is incorrect because the customer is already acquired. Option B is incorrect because there is no marketing or sales involved. Option D is incorrect because this is a consulting engagement and not a training activity.

12. D. The correct answer is D. This is an example of training and support because those are support activities. Option A is incorrect because the customer is already acquired. Option B is incorrect because there is no marketing or sales involved. Option C is incorrect because this is not a consulting engagement.

13. A. The correct answer is A. This is an example of acquiring customers. Option B is incorrect because there is no marketing or sales involved. Option C is incorrect because this is not a consulting engagement. Option D is incorrect because this does not involve training and support activities.

14. A. The correct answer is A. This is an example of resource planning because it involves prioritizing projects and programs. Options B and C are incorrect because there is no cost estimating or budgeting done in the meeting. Option D is incorrect because it does not involve expenditure approvals or reporting.

15. D. The correct answer is D. This effort involves reporting on expenditures. Option A is incorrect because there is no review of proposed projects or discussion of priorities. Options B and C are incorrect because there is no cost estimating or budgeting done in the meeting.

Chapter 11: Development and Operations

1. C. The correct answer is C. This is an example of waterfall methodology because each stage of the software development lifecycle is performed once and never revisited. Option A is incorrect. Extreme programming is a type of agile methodology. Option B is incorrect because there is no tight collaboration, rapid development and deployment, and frequent testing. Option D is incorrect because the steps of the software development lifecycle are

not repeated with each iteration focused on defining a subset of work and identifying risks.

2. D. The correct answer is D. This is an example of spiral methodology because each stage of the software development lifecycle is repeated in a cyclical manner, and each iteration begins with scoping work and identifying risks. Option A is incorrect. Extreme programming is a type of agile methodology. Option B is incorrect because there is no tight collaboration, rapid development and deployment, and frequent testing. Option C is incorrect because the steps of the software development lifecycle are repeated.

3. B. The correct answer is B. This is an example of an agile methodology because developers and stakeholders work closely together, development is done in small units of work that include frequent testing and release, and the team is able to adapt to changes in requirements without following a rigid linear or cyclical process. Option A is incorrect. Continuous integration is not an application development methodology. Option D is incorrect because the steps of the software development lifecycle are not repeated with each iteration focused on defining a subset of work and identifying risks.

4. A. The correct answer is A. You are incurring technical debt by making a suboptimal design and coding choice in order to meet other requirements or constraints. The code will need to be refactored in the future. Option B is incorrect. This is not an example of refactoring suboptimal code. Option C is incorrect, as there is no shifting or transferring of risk. Option D is incorrect. There is no mention that this change would improve the confidentiality, integrity, or availability of the service.

5. B. The correct answer is B. You are paying down technical debt by changing suboptimal code that was intentionally used to mitigate but not correct a bug. Option A is incorrect. This is not an example of incurring technical debt because you are not introducing suboptimal code in order to meet other requirements or constraints. Option C is incorrect. There is no shifting or transferring of risk. Option D is incorrect. There is no mention that this change would improve the confidentiality, integrity, or availability of the service.

6. B. The correct answer is B. The standard API operations are list, get, create, update, and delete. Options A, C, and D are incorrect because they are all missing at least one of the standard functions.

7. B. The correct answer is B. The API should return a standard status code used for errors, in other words, from the 400s or 500s, and include additional details in the payload. Option A is incorrect. 200 is the standard HTTP success code. Option C is incorrect because it does not return a standard error code. Option D is incorrect because HTTP APIs should follow broadly accepted conventions so that users of the API can process standard error messages and not have to learn application-specific error messages.

8. A. The correct answer is A. JWTs are a standard way to make authentication assertions securely. Option B is incorrect. API keys can be used for authentication, but they do not carry authentication assertions. Option C is incorrect. Encryption does not specify authentication information. Option D is incorrect. HTTPS does not provide authentication assertions.

9. D. The correct answer is D. This is an example of rate limiting because it is putting a cap on the number of function calls allowed by a user during a specified period of time. Option

A is incorrect. This is not encryption. Option B is incorrect because defense in depth requires at least two distinct security controls. Option C is incorrect. The solution does not limit privileges based on a user's role. In this case, most users are players. They continue to have the same privileges that they had before resource limiting was put in place.

10. A. The correct answer is A. This is an example of data-driven testing because the input data and expected output data are stated as part of the test. Option B is incorrect because this testing approach does not include two or more frameworks. Option C is incorrect because it does not include a set of detailed instructions for executing the test. Option D is incorrect. No simulator is used to generate inputs and expected outputs.

11. A. The correct answer is A. This is a lift-and-shift migration because only required changes are made to move the application to the cloud. Option B and Option C are incorrect because there is no new development in this migration. Option D is not a valid type of migration strategy.

12. A. The correct answer is the Google Transfer Service, which executes jobs that specify source and target locations. It is the recommended method for transferring data from other clouds. Option B could be used, but it is not the recommended practice, so it should not be the first option considered. Option C is incorrect. The Google Transfer Service has to be installed in your data center, so it is not an option for migrating data from a public cloud. Option D is incorrect. Cloud Dataproc is a managed Hadoop and Spark service. It is not used for data migrations.

13. C. The correct answer is C. The Cloud Transfer Appliance should be used. Sending 5 PB over a 10 GB network would take approximately two months to transfer. Option A and Option D are not correct because they would use the 10 GB network, and that would take too long to transfer and consume network resources. Option B is incorrect. gcloud is used to manage many GCP services; it is not used to transfer data from on-premises data centers to Cloud Storage.

14. B. The correct answer is B. bq is the GCP SDK component used to manage BigQuery. Option A is incorrect. cbt is used to manage Bigtable. Option C is incorrect. gsutil is used to work with Cloud Storage. Option D is incorrect. kubect is used to work with Kubernetes.

15. C. The correct answer is C. gcloud is the utility that manages SDK components. Option A is incorrect. gsutil is for working with Cloud Storage. Option B is incorrect. cbt is for working with Bigtable. Option D is incorrect. bq is used for working with BigQuery.

Chapter 12: Migration Planning

1. A. The correct answer is A. Before migrating to the cloud, one of the first steps is understanding your own infrastructure, dependencies, compliance issues, and licensing structure. Option B is incorrect. Without an understanding of what you want from a cloud vendor, it is not possible to create a request for proposal. Option C is incorrect. It is too early to discuss licensing if you don't understand your current licensing situation and what licensing you want to have in the cloud. Option D is incorrect. It is a reasonable thing to do as a

CTO, but it is too broad of a topic, and instead discussions should be focused on IT-related pain points.

2. B. The correct answer is B. Conducting a pilot project will provide an opportunity to learn about the cloud environment. Option A is incorrect, as applications should be migrated after data. Option C is incorrect. There is no need to migrate all identities and access controls until you understand which identities will need particular roles in the cloud. Option D is incorrect. There is no reason given that would warrant redesigning a relational database as part of the migration.

3. C. The correct answer is C. You should be looking for a recognition that data classification and regulation needs to be considered and addressed. Option A is incorrect. Database and network administrators will manage database configuration details when additional information on database implementations are known. Option B is incorrect. It is not necessary to specify firewall rules at this stage, since the plan has not been approved. Option D is incorrect. Current backup operations are not relevant to the migration plan any more than any other routine operational procedures.

4. A. The correct answer is A. Java is a widely used, widely supported language for developing a range of applications, including enterprise applications. There is little risk moving a Java application from an on-premises platform to the cloud. All other options are considerable factors in assessing the risk of moving the application.

5. C. The correct answer is C. Because of the strict SLAs, the database should not be down as long as would be required if a MySQL export were used. Option A and Option B would leave the database unavailable longer than allowed or needed. Option D is not needed because of the small data volume, and it would require the database to be down longer than allowed by the SLA.

6. B. The correct answer is B. This is an example of bring your own license. Option A is a fictitious term. Options C and D both refer to pay based on usage in the cloud.

7. C. The correct answer is C. This is an example of pay-as-you-go licensing. Options A and D are fictitious terms. Option B is incorrect. You are not using a license that you own in this scenario.

8. C. The correct answer is C. VPCs are the highest networking abstraction and constitute a collection of network components. Options A, B, and C are wrong because they are lower-level components within a VPC.

9. D. The correct answer is D. It is not an RFC 1918 private address, which is within the address ranges used with subnets. Options A, B, and C are all incorrect because they are private address ranges and may be used with subnets.

10. B. The correct answer is B because each VPN endpoint supports up to 3 Gbps, so two will be sufficient. Option A is incorrect. That would provide only half of the needed bandwidth. Options C and D are incorrect because, although they would have sufficient bandwidth, they would cost more and there is no business justification for the additional cost.

11. B. The correct answer is B. Firewall rules are used to control the flow of traffic. Option A is incorrect because IAM roles are used to assign permissions to identities, such as users or

service accounts. Option C is incorrect. A VPN is a network link between Google Cloud and on-premises networks. Option D is incorrect. VPCs are high-level abstractions grouping lower-level network components.

12. A. The correct answer is A. IAM roles are used to assign permissions to identities, such as users or service accounts. These permissions are assigned to roles which are assigned to users. Option B is incorrect. Firewall rules are used to control the flow of traffic between subnets. Option C is incorrect. A VPN is a network link between the Google Cloud and on-premises networks. Option D is incorrect. VPCs are high-level abstractions grouping lower-level network components.

13. A. The correct answer is A. Global load balancing is the service that would route traffic to the nearest healthy instance using Premium Network Tier. Option B is incorrect. SNMP is a management protocol, and it does not enable global routing. Options C and D are wrong because they are network services but do not enable global routing.

14. A. The correct answer is A, global load balancing will route traffic to the nearest healthy instance. Option B is incorrect, Cloud Interconnect is a way to implement hybrid computing. Option C is incorrect. Content delivery networks are used to distribute content in order to reduce latency when delivering that content. Option D is incorrect. VPNs link on-premises data centers to the Google Cloud.

15. C. The correct answer is C. A content delivery network would be used to distribute video content globally to reduce network latency. Option A is incorrect. Routes are used to control traffic flow and are not directly related to reducing latency of content delivery, although a poorly configured set of routes could cause unnecessarily long latencies. Option B is incorrect. Firewalls will not reduce latency. Option D is incorrect because VPNs are used to link on-premises data centers to the Google Cloud.

Index

T

Online Test Bank

Register to gain one year of FREE access to the online interactive test bank to help you study for your Google Professional Cloud Architect certification exam—included with your purchase of this book! All of the chapter review questions, the practice tests in this book are included in the online test bank so you can practice in a timed and graded setting.

Register and Access the Online Test Bank

To register your book and get access to the online test bank, follow these steps:

1. Go to bit.ly/SybexTest (this address is case sensitive)!
2. Select your book from the list.
3. Complete the required registration information, including answering the security verification to prove book ownership. You will be emailed a pin code.
4. Follow the directions in the email or go to www.wiley.com/go/sybextestprep.
5. Find your book in the list in that page and click the "Register or Login" link with it. Then enter the pin code you received and click the "Activate PIN" button.
6. On the Create an Account or Login page, enter your username and password, and click Login or if you don't have an account already, create a new account.
7. At this point, you should be in the testbank site with your new testbank listed at the top of the page. If you do not see it there, please refresh the page or log out and log back in.